W0008087

Franklin Steak

FRANKLIN STEAK

DRY-AGED • LIVE-FIRED • PURE BEEF

AARON FRANKLIN
and
JORDAN MACKAY

Photographs by Wyatt McSpadden
Illustrations by Bryan B. Butler

TEN SPEED PRESS
California | New York

Part III
STEAK PERFECTION

Preface

Boy, do I ever love a good steak! And I eat a lot of it, which, along with beer, is how I managed to achieve this awesome bod. Nevertheless, since I'm known for Central Texas barbecue, many people will ask, why a book about steak? Well, I'm glad you asked. . . .

My love of steak goes back a long way. When I was a kid, it was a huge, really big deal if we ate steaks for dinner. My folks cooked and stuff, but not like we cook today. It was the 1970s and 1980s, you know, and Tuna Helper was standard pantry fare and pretty darn good. But steak night was an event. In Bryan, Texas, where I was born, my dad was actually a restaurant manager at a steak house. I'd guess my dad used a few tricks from that stint when he cooked for us.

In hindsight, my dad probably just put a bunch of Lawry's on steak. (That's all right by me, as I still put Lawry's on tons of stuff!) He'd always cook a T-bone, about an inch thick or something like that, on a grill with charcoal—nothing special or specific about it. His grill was likely just a shallow hotel pan with a grate on top of it. But those flavors—really salty and beefy—have always stuck with me.

I never really started cooking until I left home when I was eighteen. I moved to Austin to an area called West Campus, adjacent to the University of Texas, which was known for its ample frat and sorority houses and dozens and dozens of apartment buildings for student housing. Now, I wasn't a student, but I lived there anyway because it was cheap. I had an apartment with a small patio, and on that patio, a little Weber grill. Not really being a

very good cook—never having cooked in a restaurant kitchen—I remember getting super-cheap grocery-store steaks and, at like four o'clock in the morning, firing up the grill and eating steaks with my roommate while watching the sun come up. We'd get the cheapest charcoal, the cheapest meat, and iodized salt packets from the taco stand for seasoning. It was absolutely the least expensive, foulest way to eat steak, but we still felt like kings. Nineteen years old, living on, like, twelve dollars a month, and drinking beer at six in the morning—that was a straight line from the way my dad cooked steaks, but I didn't know anything about charcoal or wood or grilling. Or meat, for that matter, especially the quality kind.

It was that same nostalgia that got me into barbecue. When I *really* got into barbecue, a bunch of lightbulbs started going off: what do I do with all these coals? I was around fire all the time and my relationship with fire and the nighttime is what got me into steak. If I have to sit there watching the fire for twelve hours, why not use the fire to feed myself something that would sustain me? I wasn't going to be eating barbecue because that's what I had to sell. But a steak was the quick, easy way to taste that beautiful union of beef and fire.

One of the most memorable steaks I ever ate was from Tom Perini of Perini Ranch in West Texas. While I was working on the PBS show *BBQ with Franklin*, we did a shoot at the ranch. Tom is a heck of a guy and a really talented chuck-wagon cook, which he started doing on the ranch in the 1970s, eventually going on to open a steak house in 1983. Later, at a live-fire event, our dish was loosely inspired by Perini: fifty tri-tips dipped in Cognac. We grilled the steaks over mesquite and let them cool down. Finally, we set up two PK Grills and got them raging hot (it felt like we were going to melt the bottoms out of them) and poured Cognac into a bucket. Yes, you read that right: a *bucket* of Cognac. We dipped the tri-tips in the Cognac and flambéed them on the grill—that's how we brought everything back up to temp. Man, what a great memory.

A person can eat only so much barbecue. I'm sure you understand: if, for your day job, you worked in a place that smelled powerfully of meat, fat, and smoke and then, when you went home, *you* smelled powerfully of meat, fat, and smoke, too! The smell of a grilled steak is always refreshing, bright, and less rich. While that fact might impact my hunger for barbecue, nothing ever seems to get in the way of my appetite for a good steak. I never get tired of it.

And that's part of the way this book happened. When Jordan and I were working on our first book, *Franklin Barbecue*, he noticed that dinner at my house very often ended up being steak. And over the course of many long nights out-side on cooks, we spent a lot of time gazing at flames and hot coals and talking about grilling and meat. Without knowing it, we had started to plan a second book.

And what's more deserving of a book-length tribute than steak? It's as common in America (well, almost) as hamburgers and hot dogs, yet because it's so precious, cooking it is loaded with pressure not to screw it up. So we figured we might be able to lend folks a hand by helping them sharpen their steak skills and knowledge.

And that's all this book is meant to do. But along the way, we realized that most people don't have a great understanding of the modern beef industry, and I think it's important to know, as best as you can, where your beef comes from, be it the actual farm or at least a trusted supplier. Every year, I fire up the old truck and head up I-35 to Kansas to visit Creekstone Farms, which supplies our barbecue restaurant with excellent, all-natural briskets, and Loro, a new Austin restaurant I'm involved in, with bavettes and brisket. This is because I like to check in on where the beef is coming from and the people who manage it. It's a long drive every year but well worth it.

Then, it turns out, I have a lot of thoughts about wood, charcoal, and grills, too. People might think I just smoke meat all the time, but in fact, I grill just as much—for events, for parties, or just on a weeknight for me, my wife, Stacy, and my daughter, Vivian. Over time, I've developed some ideas about cooking steaks—different methods for different cuts and so on—that I thought might be useful to those of you out there who are as geeky as I am about live-fire cooking. And since Jordan travels around a lot writing about wine, he got some inspiration from other countries, especially Spain but Japan, France, and Sweden, too. All together, we thought we would make this book our so-called love letter to steak.

I hope you enjoy the book as much as I loved making it.

• **Aaron Franklin**

Introduction

In the past year, whenever we mentioned to some- one that we were working on a book about steak, the unfailing response would be, "Steak? How can anyone write a whole book about steak?"

That's funny, as our sense has always been the opposite: "How can we ever meaningfully cover steak in just one book?"

But those two differing responses basically sum up the current state of steak in America and make a good case for why this book needs to exist. On the one hand, steak is among the simplest, most convenient, and most elemental of all foods. It is beef plus fire. Preparing steak requires very little in terms of money, thought, time, and equipment. But a *sublime* steak? That requires a fair bit of moola, consideration, patience, and accessories.

Clearly, then, this book is meant as a compan- ion in the pursuit of sublime steak. And to get there, we believe you have to think through the meat from its source until it comes off the grill.

The first section of this book is all about beef. It will help you to know a little bit more about its history, the industry in general, breeds and feeds, and some of the core issues surrounding steak consumption today. We tell you how to find the best possible raw materials from the best purveyors—ranchers, butchers, and more. We talk about the wide and wonderful world of steak cuts, from the usual suspects, like porter- house and T-bone, to the new wave of "butcher's cuts," like hanger and bavette. In the second section, we share some tips and tricks for taking your steaks to the next level, dry aging being the big one. (Spoiler alert: It's not that hard and,

in fact, it's really fun to dry age at home.) Finally, we get into cooking steak—how to prep the meat, build an effective and flavor-delivering coal bed, and cook the steak to perfection. And to finish up, we offer a handful of ridiculously uncomplicated sides (because simple is best, in our opinion) and a few suggestions on what to drink. Along the way, we try to offer a limited global appreciation of delicious steak and some personal anecdotes of steaks past. Easy!

Hopefully, this information will help when you're trying to make choices about what kind of steak to buy and how to cook it. Of course, humbly, we answer the question above—How can you cover steak in just one volume?—with the admis- sion that we can't. There are, inevitably, gaps here. For one, we would have loved to delve far deeper into the timely questions of cattle and environment, and the debate among those who think cattle are heavily responsible for destroy- ing the environment and those who think cattle will be the ones to save it. So many fascinating issues surround the science behind grass and grain feeding, and we've barely scratched the surface. But just because we didn't include that topic here doesn't mean we're not interested.

Finally, a note to those savvy about cattle: Yes, we know that technically much of the steak we eat comes from steers. And we know the techni- cal differences among heifers, steers, cows, bulls, and the like. For convenience and flow, though, we chose to use the familiar and eternal word *cow* when describing the sacred and venerable animal whose sacrifice graces us with steak. With that, happy cooking and may you never overcook your beef!

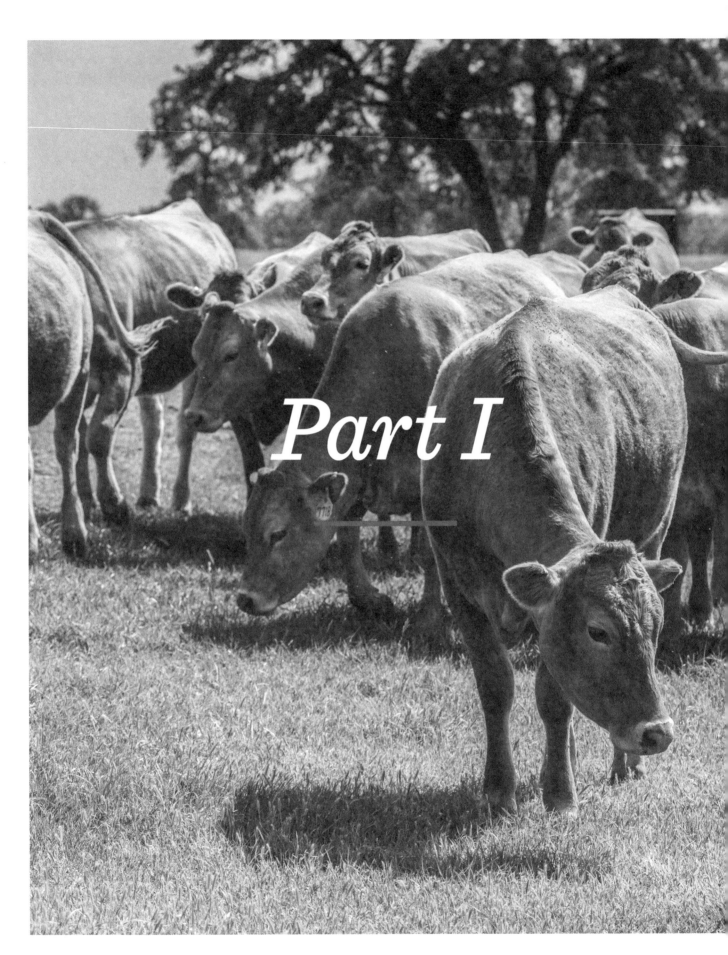

Part I

KNOW
THY
BEEF

CHAPTER 1

The Story of Beef

It happens occasionally—to most of us. You're walking down the street, having a conversation, minding your own business, whatever. Suddenly you stop and lift your head. Nose to the air, you take a couple of quick inhalations. You can't help but twitch in the direction of an aroma so unmistakable and irresistible: a whiff of smoke, of gently burning oak, then that mixture of scents—savory, salty, smoky, and a bit sweet. It triggers something deep in your bones, flowing in your blood. Powerless to control your reaction, you stop in your tracks and spin your head, like a wolf on the prairie, to try and determine from which house that inimitable scent is coming. Someone is grilling steaks.

The fact that we completely freeze because of a primal, involuntary attraction to the smell of beef cooking over fire is understandable. People have been stopped dead in their tracks by the smell of beef for tens of thousands of years. Indeed, they've also likely been singing songs and telling stories about it. We know they painted pictures of beef. At least that's what the cave paintings at Lascaux in southwestern France (ca. 17,000 BCE), tell us. As do the cave paintings at Chauvet-Pont-d'Arc in France (ca. 30,000 BCE) and El Castillo in Spain (ca. 39,000 BCE) and the engraving at Abri Blanchard (ca. 38,000 BCE), not far from Lascaux. These are not line drawings of New York strips or ribeyes, of course, but images of wild cattle.

Cattle—wild and domestic—have been an essential part of human culture for thousands, probably hundreds of thousands and even a million, years. These animals have provided milk, meat, leather, labor, strength, transport. They've exponentially expanded—for better and worse—the capacity of what humans have been able to accomplish. We must marvel at them but also recognize that our love of and instinctive response to the smell of cooking beef is not some sort of quirk. It's hardly even a choice for most people. It's hardwired—something we're not powerless to refuse but certainly programmed to savor.

The enjoyment of steak, therefore, goes back a long way, intertwined inseparably into the early moments of human evolution. In a way, you could say steak (and beef in general) is part of what makes people *people*.

Early Steak

It's not necessary to know about the history of cattle when driving to the grocery store to pick up a couple of steaks to grill out back on a Saturday night. Yet it is interesting and somewhat profound to consider the earliest origins of beef. To know that, while on this errand, you are walking stride for stride with Grog and Thak as they stalked a wandering bull is a powerful notion (or at least an amusing one). Along with salt and pepper, sprinkle your steaks with meaning in a vast natural and historical context; it's good seasoning. Consider, friends, the aurochs.

Our ancient ancestors did more than merely consider the primogenitors of all modern cattle. They revered them. We know this because in those ancient cave paintings we see beautiful, skilled, sometimes full-size line drawings of these animals, which were about a third larger than modern cattle. One painting depicts a beast seventeen feet long, standing six feet tall at the shoulders, with fearsome curved horns. Aurochs were creatures to be reckoned with.

Tens of thousands of years later than the cave art, Julius Caesar, writing in his *Commentaries on the Gallic War* (when he headed into the wild lands north of Rome to make his fortune expanding the empire up into modern France, Germany, and Britain by conquering and pillaging the native tribes), would describe much of the exotic fauna he encountered. This included the wild aurochs—cattle had long been domesticated—which he described as "a little below the elephant in size, and of the appearance, color, and shape of a bull. Their strength and speed are extraordinary; they spare neither man nor wild beast that they have espied." He noted that the local tribes "take with much pains in pits and kill them. . . . But not even when taken very young can they be rendered familiar to men and tamed. The size, shape, and appearance of their horns differ much from the horns of our oxen. These they anxiously seek after, and bind at the tips with silver, and use as cups at their most sumptuous entertainments."

Julius Caesar's description is considered pretty accurate, especially if you consider he was likely comparing the aurochs's size to the relatively diminutive North African elephant (now extinct). The horns of an aurochs could reach three feet in length. You can imagine the difficulty Paleolithic humans would have had in bringing down one of these massive, dangerous animals, which likely weighed around two thousand pounds (compared to the one thousand pounds of beef cattle today). But you can also imagine how much those early people on their actual paleo diets must have savored the flavor of the steak dinners that came after.

Known as *Bos primigenius*, the aurochs evolved earlier than *Homo sapiens* did, with a history going back about 2 million years in India. Leading up to this in the Pliocene epoch (5.3 to 2.6 million years ago), global cooling (how refreshing) and drying from the warmer, wetter Miocene caused a retreat of forests and jungles and a vast expansion of grasslands and savannas. The shift in vegetation sparked the evolution of grazing animals, which came to the fore in this period. Following the Pliocene, the Pleistocene (at the tail end of which modern humans evolved) saw aurochs spread throughout much of the world, reaching Asia, the Middle East, and Africa. Popularly known as the Ice Age, the Pleistocene arrived in what is now Europe sometime around 270,000 years ago, not (relatively) long before the appearance of modern *Homo sapiens*, which

occurred about 200,000 years ago. *Homo erectus*, however, dates to at least 1.8 million years ago, and scientists have theorized that hunting and meat eating go back at least that far. That means human ancestors may have been eating steak for well over a million years, probably closer to two. Indeed, scientists now estimate that the earliest evidence of human ancestors cooking occurred around 1.9 million years ago, so perhaps steaks were some of the first things ever cooked. Perhaps cooking was invented for steaks!

Hunting giant, angry aurochs would have been unpleasant. It is much easier to select from a bunch of smaller, dumber, and tamer versions of the animals. Enter the domestication of cattle, which dates to as recently as 8500 BCE. Study of DNA suggests that all cattle today are descended from only about eighty animals, perhaps one small herd. No one knows exactly how an animal as fierce and enormous as the aurochs was domesticated, but the easiest scenario to imagine is that some babies were captured and raised away from the parents.

Domestication brings many changes. Both physical size and brain size diminish. With their movement, feeding, and reproduction now controlled by humans, animals become more docile and, well, not smart. They also generally change in physical appearance, developing colorations and marks that distinguish them from their wild relatives (think of the black and white blotches of Holstein cows—that did not occur in nature). Domesticated species lose some of their original strength, health, hardiness, and ability to cope with adversity.

All of this sounds sort of insidious when described so clinically. But it is true that the domestication of cattle has changed us even

History's first recorded extinction was sadly the aurochs, in 1627, when the last one, a female, was killed in a forest in Poland by a nobleman. (They had survived that long because only the nobility were allowed to hunt in Poland at the time.) But on several occasions in the last hundred years, a surprising project has arisen: to revive the aurochs. We're not talking DNA suspended in a prehistoric drop of amber here (the DNA of the aurochs has already been sequenced), but resurrecting the animals themselves using the process of back breeding. This requires finding surviving cattle that retain some of the characteristics of the aurochs—size, shape and breadth of horns, color and markings, and the like—and breeding them together in a way to cause these genes to recombine and remain expressive. Scientists have even used cave paintings as one of their anatomical guides in this endeavor. The first attempt was made by two German zookeeper brothers in the 1920s. For them, success in restoring the aurochs would have been a potent example of a past of racial purity—of the power of Aryan eugenics. Fortunately, the cattle they produced bore some aurochs-like characteristics but were never taken too seriously.

In the last twenty years, however, new efforts have begun again with the far more noble purposes of "Rewilding Europe," as one of the several nongovernmental organizations working toward the goal is called. The reasons for restoring the aurochs are ecological. By some estimates, European farmers are abandoning their small farms at the rate of thousands of acres of agricultural land lost every year. Without the activity of large herbivores, unused land either reverts to forest or becomes barren because the soils have been ravaged by modern agriculture. The action of ruminants restores and protects grasslands, which become diverse natural habitats for numerous native animal and insect populations. Wolves have destroyed other herds of herbivores, but the aurochs-like cattle have been strong enough to suffer few losses.

Aurochs in Nature, 1889

as it has changed them. For instance, at one time, humans became lactose intolerant at the onset of adulthood. But over the millennia, this changed, as being able to digest milk protein and fat conferred some sort of evolutionary advantage on the people who could do that. Of course, domesticated cattle sped change in human culture in obvious ways, as well. The availability of strong oxen to help with work in the fields allowed the expansion of farming. Leather from cowhides became a hugely important substance with all sorts of applications, from shoes and clothes to shelter. Having a convenient source of nutrient-dense food available in the form of beef furthered almost all human endeavors. Cattle were the powerful engines of progress.

As the project of domestication itself evolved through controlled reproduction—a sort of fast-tracked evolution—people began shaping cattle to suit their specific needs. These take many familiar forms, such as physical strength, dairy, meat, or even an ornery temperament (which is bred into Spanish bullfighting bulls). Cattle have also been bred to exist in environments with different terrains, climates, and food sources. Over the centuries, this constant and selective breeding has given rise to a tremendous expanse of genetic diversity. These are the distinct breeds of cattle, which number somewhere around eight hundred.

However, in recent decades, globalization and technology have compelled people to focus on only certain breeds deemed more desirable than others, resulting in a winnowing that many expert observers consider dangerous. Hundreds of recognized cattle breeds, representing a valuable genetic resource of various types bred for specific environments, are threatened with extinction. As Valerie Porter points out in

her book, *Cattle: A Handbook to the Breeds of the World*, "It is much easier to destroy such resources than to create them." The ability to produce great steaks is certainly considered a valuable genetic resource. After all, these cattle breeds have proliferated more than any other— all thanks to their superior ability to deliver that irresistible taste of beef.

The Taste of Beef

The flavor of beef is sui generis, prompting even the modestly curious to ask, what makes beef taste so beefy? When Jordan posed that question to Jerrad Legako, an assistant professor specializing in beef in the Department of Animal and Food Sciences at Texas Tech, the answer was surprising. "We don't have the full picture yet," says Legako.

We do know that even though raw meat is bland, it contains a vast pool of precursor compounds such as amino acids, reducing sugars, and fats. Cooking converts these into the aroma and flavor of beef, thanks to processes such as the Maillard reaction and lipid oxidation and the cascading series of interactions between them.

Legako notes that what we perceive on the tongue when eating cooked beef is related to umami— amino acids and small peptides. "And then in the aroma fraction, you find more of the sulfur-containing compounds," he says. "Lipids [fats] also play a big role, but they're tricky because a little lipid oxidation is attractive, but too much lipid breakdown becomes rancid tasting."

Most of beef's flavor emerges during cooking, when heat allows the amino acids to break down over time, layering their flavors. Sulfurous compounds come from the lean muscle.

At low levels, they're meaty, he notes, but at higher levels they can be revolting, like rotten eggs. Fat, too, plays a huge role. While the fat in marbling doesn't have a lot of flavor itself (for more on this, see page 41), Legako says, "it acts as a reservoir for the flavor compounds during cooking and delivers them across the mouth. We refer to some of these flavor compounds as lipophilic, meaning they have an affinity to fats and will more or less absorb into the fat and become available for taste."

If beef flavor can't be reduced to a single or even discrete set of compounds, where does it come from? What are the important influences on beef flavor? Basically the question is this: how do we find the tastiest steaks?

One beef expert we talked to said that the conventional wisdom in the beef industry is that three all-important elements contribute to the taste and culinary experience of beef: genetics, environment (feeding and lifestyle), and age. With a reasonable understanding of these, you can obtain an inkling of how a particular steak will taste.

Genetics

It didn't take long for the domesticated aurochs, accompanying migrating peoples, to start making its way from the site of its domestication in the Fertile Crescent to parts throughout the Old World. As the aurochs found its way into climates ranging from subtropical to subarctic, from desert to forest, from plains to mountains, it changed. In each place, people developed their own types of cattle, bred for environmental suitability. As those traits stabilized, breeding became even more specific.

The first types of cattle were bred for strength, to pull plows or timber or rocks. Later, cattle evolved traits beneficial for meat or milk production, but modern meat and dairy cattle are fairly recent developments, coming after horses and then tractors took over the heavy lifting of labor. Improvements in farming allowed the production of silage (wet hay or other feed compacted and stored anaerobically, whether in a silo or just a massive pile) for fattening cattle over winter. In time, cattle became a bankable food source, and the density of the calories and nutrition in meat drove the expansion of cities and other centers not based around farming.

When you visit meat producers today, you still hear a lot about genetics, as they are constantly looking to refine the gene pools of their herds, favoring some traits while discouraging others. Most of the traits they track meticulously are much more important to them than to the end consumer. These can be measurable, like yearling weight (how much the animal can be made to weigh after one year), calmness, or how easily and safely they give birth. Some traits, however, such as ribeye area, may very well matter to the end consumer.

These qualities beg the question, do different breeds produce different flavors? Are they like wine grapes, where Cabernet Sauvignon offers a completely different taste than Pinot Noir? Some steak houses and butcheries in Europe suggest the answer is yes, offering for sale, similar to a wine list, a variety of steaks with breed and place of origin listed on the menu.

In general, however, beef experts say no: beef flavor is largely beef flavor regardless of breed. What the animal ate and where it was raised are of much greater importance in determining flavor. Furthermore, almost all of the cattle we see—and eat—today are mixed breed. Just as mixed breed (mutt) dogs tend to be healthier and more resilient than purebred ones, so with cattle. DNA samples of most cattle will reveal a heritage of a number of different kinds of animals (even if some brands advertise a piece of steak as 100 percent one breed).

Nevertheless, breeds do remain important, as the breed itself may be inseparably intertwined with where the cattle are raised. For instance, in the southern United States, you find many cattle with strains of Brahman in them, which is a breed based on *Bos indicus*, the subspecies of cattle from India. Notable for the signature hump on its back, the Brahman was developed for its ability to tolerate heat and resistance to insects (and are not considered great eating).

Even if the specific breed of cattle is generally not crucial to the meat quality, there are exceptions, and we're going to be hearing more about breed in regard to steak in the United States in coming years. So here's a brief rundown of the major cattle breeds you'll find here and in other countries as they pertain to producing steaks.

ANGUS

The most prolific beef producer in the United States, Angus is described in *Cattle: A Handbook to the Breeds of the World* as "the mild-eyed breed which produces possibly the best beef in the world—lightly marbled, succulent, and tender . . . it remains a most economical breed to rear, able to thrive on rough grazing and to fatten on low cost rations." You can understand the popularity: it's a win-win for consumers and ranchers. A Scottish breed with roots going back to the mid-eighteenth century, the Aberdeen Angus was officially described in 1862. The first bulls came to the United States in 1873.

Despite the popularity and use of the name, what we eat today is not purebred Angus, as from the beginning and over the following generations, the breed has been intermixed countless times. To be certified Angus, either one parent or both grandparents have to have been Angus (but that doesn't mean purebred Aberdeen Angus). For instance, for a cow to be eligible for the Certified Angus Beef brand, the United States Department of Agriculture (USDA) definition states only that the live animal has to be "predominantly solid black." A litany of further carcass specifications define the quality necessary to make the grade— "modest or higher marbling, 10- to 16-inch ribeye area, no neck hump exceeding 2 inches (reduces *Bos indicus* influence)."

So really what's talked about with regard to Angus beef is Angus-type cattle. These are mostly black, stocky animals, though some white areas may be present. Red Angus can also be included, and the consensus is that the red color doesn't make a difference. Indeed, most high-quality brands, such as Creekstone Farms or 44 Farms, trumpet not just the fact that they sell Angus beef but also the quality of their own proprietary genetics.

WAGYU

The famous Wagyu from Japan seems destined to be the newest It breed, the Next Big Thing. Why? Because of its ability to marble. Wagyu can be a source of outstanding, high-end steaks. Travel around the United States and you'll find new Wagyu-focused cattle herds popping up all over.

In Japan, these are the cattle that produce those incredible, bizarre-looking steaks—steaks so marbled that they appear more white than pink. This kind of meat is a delicacy, is very expensive, and comes from purebred animals that are confined for their entire lives and fed only grain. Contrary to popular myth, they are not fed beer or massaged. We see very little of this high-level Japanese Wagyu beef in the States, as only tiny amounts are imported. American Wagyu cattle are neither bred nor raised to produce such extreme meat.

Wagyu, which simply means Japanese (*Wa*) beef (*gyu*), has a long and somewhat convoluted history. Some DNA evidence suggests genetic separation of the strain as far back as thirty-five thousand years ago. The animals were originally bred as pack animals, which is an important detail. Marbling—the ability to grow that intramuscular fat—is a trait that provides slow-twitch energy to the animal. Over the centuries, the Japanese emphasis on strength and endurance has led to beef of hedonistic juiciness. Wagyu cattle got an infusion of European genetics (Brown Swiss, Devon, Shorthorn, Simmental, Ayrshire) in the 1800s due to some imported cattle, but that was shut down again in 1910. Four distinct types of Wagyu exist in Japan: black, red (also known as brown), polled (hornless), and shorthorn. The latter two are found only in Japan. The first two, black and red, have been exported to other countries in extremely limited amounts.

The Japanese subtypes of Wagyu are distinct, as the rugged, mountainous nature of a country composed of islands has kept herds isolated from one another in separate pockets. While beef from Kobe is the most famous, the northern island of Hokkaido is also known for superior quality. And recent national competitions have been won by the Miyazaki region in the south, which today is regarded by many as home to Japan's best beef. Breeding is strictly regulated and registered, with every animal having papers and a lineage that can be traced over many generations.

Only a handful of Wagyu cattle have ever been imported to the United States, first in 1976 (two black and two red bulls) and not again until 1993 (two male and three female black) and 1994 (thirty-five animals, mixed black and red). Since then, Japan, zealously guarding the preciousness of its genetic resource, has not allowed any more out of the country. Significant numbers of Wagyu also exist in Australia, New Zealand, and Canada.

In the United States, Wagyu beef looks different for a number of reasons. One, the meat here predominantly comes from crossed animals—Wagyu that has been mixed with any number of other breeds, but mostly Angus type. These cattle simply don't have the genes to marble like the full-bred Japanese Wagyu, even if they are raised as the Japanese do. All consumers should be aware that when they buy a Wagyu steak in the United States, it has very little to do with Japan—just some traces in the cow's genetics.

Furthermore, the Japanese eat their beef only in tiny amounts, rarely if ever indulging in the comparatively enormous steaks we Americans like to eat. An American-style ribeye steak of A-5 marbling (the top-level grade in Japan) would be simply too rich to consume entirely.

Nevertheless, even mixed American Wagyu is usually good meat. The most prominent brands are Snake River Farms from Idaho, which produces from black Wagyu crosses, and HeartBrand Beef from Texas, which specializes in Akaushi crosses, a red Wagyu. Japanese beef experts agree that black Wagyu types marble better than red, but the Akaushi still produces

Angus

Wagyu

Holstein

Highland

Hereford

great steaks. Other outfits are also producing serious stuff. For instance, Fresh From OK, a local brand in Oklahoma, provides incredible pasture-raised Wagyu. First Light, based in New Zealand, is a farm cooperative with likewise superior meat, entirely grass fed on New Zealand's famously lush pasture. At the moment, First Light is imported only to the western United States.

The other notable trait of Wagyu is the high percentage of oleic acid in its fat, the kind of "healthy" fatty acid found in olive oil. Wagyu is also touted for having higher percentages of omega-3 fatty acids than standard breeds do. This is true, says Steve Smith, a professor at Texas A&M who specializes in beef fat. But while the concentration of omega-3 acids in Wagyu is higher than in conventional beef, it is still far lower than in fatty fish from cold waters. And despite the hype, omega-3 fatty acids have yet to be scientifically proven to be more important than other nutrients.

HOLSTEIN

Another "new" trend is meat from Holstein cattle, a breed primarily known as a dairy cow. It's not common knowledge, says Legako of Texas Tech, "but about 20 percent of our beef supply is Holstein. We've reduced our beef herd in the US significantly in the last few years due to drought and other factors, and that's allowed the dairy industry to sell Holstein steers at a profit." Typically, Holstein steers wouldn't have had much value, as the females are the dairy engines. But Holsteins are predisposed to marble, he says, and have "a different muscle structure and fiber than traditional beef breeds, making them a positive in palatability." (This is how meat scientists talk about steak.)

There are some important fans of Holstein out there, notably Bryan and Katie Flannery of Flannery Beef (see page 33), who are aging and selling Prime-graded Holstein.

HIGHLAND

A great Scottish breed, Highland cattle are the shaggy, horned cattle you might occasionally see, especially in northern climates. Famous for being aloof and hardy, these cattle are from the rugged highlands of Scotland, where they could be left to wander and graze and largely take care of themselves. One of the oldest, purest breeds in Britain, Highlands can survive on sparse grazing and be productive in places other cattle could never endure.

"Temperament's a key thing for Highlands," says John McLaughlin, who raises excellent grass-fed Highland cattle at his family's eponymous farm in Michigan. "When they originated, the cattle were raised in close proximity to the children of their owners. You couldn't have an animal with these big horns killing your kids! So they were selected for temperament."

The other thing McLaughlin notes about Highlands is that they're slower-maturing animals. "It's more costly to raise them than other breeds, especially on grass," he says. "The typical Highland on a more grain-based diet

will take at least twenty-four months, whereas the beef you're getting in the grocery store is probably thirteen or fourteen months old." But because of the age, the Highlands can have a lot of flavor, particularly those aged on grass, like McLaughlin's herd.

HEREFORD

The origin of this British breed can be traced back to draught animals used in Roman times. Over the millennia, the breed—notable for its red or orange coat and white head and belly—was converted into efficient beef cattle. Popular meat animals for centuries, Herefords today are prized for being muscular and quite enormous—males can get up to eighteen hundred pounds—and for their propensity to fill out admirably in the more valuable cut areas. Furthermore, they're considered vigorous and with good foraging ability, and they gain weight quickly.

Environment

As already noted, what a cow eats and how it was raised are considered far more important to its flavor than breed. "Temperament is tenderness," John McLaughlin is fond of saying. He's looking for and breeds well-tempered cattle, but their temperament also depends on how they're treated. Indeed, gentle and compassionate treatment of animals is vitally important across the board, but in the case of beef, it also has a crucial role to play in the meat's flavor and tenderness. An animal that is stressed or fearful releases hormones into its system that affect the flavor of its meat. Good farmers and ranchers know this and strive to see their animals treated well, as it's a moral issue that also directly affects their pocketbooks.

AG

Kronobergsgatan 37
Stockholm, Sweden
tel: (+46) 8-410-61-00 • restaurangag.se

One of the inspirations for this book, the remarkable Swedish steak house AG has taken steak to a new level of fetishization. It is housed on the second floor of an old industrial building—it used to be a silver factory, hence the name AG, the chemical symbol of silver—and the entrance brings you immediately face-to-face with the glass-walled dry-aging room in which numerous sides of beef are hanging.

AG was one of the first places to look at steak not just as beef, but as a vehicle for expressing characteristics of breed, place, and farmer. It typically carries dry-aged steaks from Sweden, Highland steaks from Scotland, and selected beef from Poland, which owners Johan Jureskog and Klas Ljungquist say is tragically overlooked as a beef-producing country. Its industry has yet to industrialize, they say, and thus the cattle live long, calm, pastoral lives on grass. The deep, beefy steaks those Polish cattle provide are worth traveling to Sweden for.

How cattle are fed is another huge discussion in the beef world these days. *Grass fed* and *grain fed* have become loaded terms that generate discussion and sometimes heated reactions. And while the focus of this book is on the flavor of beef, the issues surrounding how cattle are fed have implications far beyond the kitchen, into the realms of animal welfare, public safety, the environment, climate change, and more. It would be improper to pretend they don't exist and ignore them here. Yet hundreds of articles and books and a number of films have been made that look into the beef cattle industry in this country, so this section will simply summarize the main points of discussion in the hope that you will be inspired to look more deeply into these heady questions.

But before that, let's answer the big, simple question about flavor: which steak should you seek out, grass fed or grain fed?

Of course, everyone's taste is different. But in terms of flavor potential, the answer is grass fed. If you like beef with lots of complex, beefy savor, and flavor matters to you over tenderness, then there's no question that you should seek out the best grass-fed beef available. And it makes sense: A diet of forage—including grass, herbs, legumes, and forbs—simply incorporates a far greater diversity of nutrients than a diet of corn. The nutrients from forage make their way into the meat and fat of the animal and eventually express themselves as flavor.

Occasionally this flavor is even visible. You can see it in the yellow tint of the fat of a grass-fed cow that has lived long enough to bank the nutrients. The color comes from beta-carotene, a natural form of vitamin A and an antioxidant. Beta-carotene gives produce

such as squashes, pumpkins, and carrots their signature yellow-orange colors but also occurs in the grasses and legumes that comprise a lot of pastureland. Fat soluble, it gets stored in the fat of grass-fed beef and is transferred to people who eat the meat.

Grain-fed beef, on the other hand, will have less flavor. This is preferable to those who shy away from strong flavors in their food. And for those who demand more flavor, dry aging of the meat can augment that to a degree. But grain-fed beef is also likely to be more tender, especially on the high end of Prime and in high-graded Japanese Wagyu. After all, cattle fattened on grain will move less than cattle that graze openly in a field. Reduced movement equates to less developed muscles and more tenderness. Furthermore, the kind of fat that creates marbling, which is deposited during the months the animals are on high rations of corn, is the kind of fat that melts at low temperatures, providing in the mouth the sensation of juiciness and silkiness.

But these days it's difficult to make beef choices in a vacuum, ignoring the social, ethical, economic, and environmental questions at the heart of this divide.

THE CASE FOR GRASS FED

"What I can tell you is this," says Dr. Allen Williams, "well-produced grass-fed beef far surpasses grain in flavor and quality. If you can seek out and find the right grass fed, it's far more memorable." That Williams says this is not surprising, considering he's one of the leading consultants on grass-fed beef on the continent, traveling all over North America to help ranchers get their soils and grasses to optimum condition

for grazing their animals. Grass is his life. But he also worked for a long time with grain-fed beef on his family's own ranch and once considered himself a proponent of it.

One of the challenges facing grass-fed beef as a category, however, is that not all of it is good. Indeed, it's depressingly easy to get a disappointing grass-fed steak these days, and grass-fed beef has gotten a bad rap because of that. And the stakes are high for the grass-fed movement (no cheap pun intended): one unsatisfactory experience of grass-fed beef apparently has the ability to turn people off it for life.

That drives Williams crazy. "Not all grain-fed beef is good," he says. "A lot of it is really bad, and people seem to forget that. No one ever says, 'I'm swearing off beef because that one steak I had was tough [or flavorless or off].' They keep buying it. So why do people put that onus on grass fed? They should be fair and judge their grain-fed beef just as honestly."

People aren't as tough on grain fed as they are on grass fed probably because the former fails less spectacularly. A bad piece of grain fed is likely to be . . . disappointing, forgettable. It may be flavorless or tough, and it may piss you off because you got ripped off, but it doesn't turn you off beef in general. A bad piece of grass-fed beef, however, may be pungently gamy or taste like liver *and* be as tough as nails. Being viscerally off-putting is what makes people say, "Ick, I never want to experience this again." That one individual steak shouldn't be an indictment of grass-fed beef, but, alas, it often is, for a number of reasons.

One, we've been trained to prefer bland grain-fed beef, which has set the palate for steak in America—tender and sweet. It tastes that way

because the cow probably ate more than three thousand pounds of corn in five months. It takes just over two pounds of corn to make one pound of beef. And that's the same, familiar corn that sweetens most American processed foods.

Also, not all grass fed is the same. Good grass-fed beef requires a real program and real intention. Ranchers need to know how to graze their cattle, to pay attention to what they are eating. They need to harvest them at the right time. A lot of what passes as grass-fed beef in farmers' markets or roadside stands may simply be from scrawny old dairy cows that were never intended to be great beef. Or perhaps it is cheater grass-fed beef, in which the cattle are confined on a feedlot and just fed concentrated grass pellets, which are legal under the term.

Along the way from birth to slaughter are lots of places for grass-fed beef to go south. Jordan got clued in to this by observing the evolution of Long Meadow Ranch, a farm-to-table operation and wine producer in Napa Valley.

Jordan was excited when he learned the owners had the ambitious program of raising their own herd of Highland cattle for beef to serve at their restaurant in St. Helena and to sell at the farmers' market. But the first time he tried it, the flavor wasn't great and the steak was tough. Apparently they recognized this too and were already working to change the program. They started by interbreeding Angus with their pure Highland cattle to try for better-marbled beef. And they put the cattle on richer pastures and also upgraded their selection process for slaughter. Before that, their guy had sort of indiscriminately been choosing animals when the restaurant was running out of beef, paying little attention to the state of the cattle. Now, they've learned that they need to be harvesting seasonally in late spring or late fall, when the grass is green and the cattle are on richer forage. They needed a better eye for selecting individual animals who were at their peak. When the grass dries out in the summer, the cattle actually lose fat because they need as much or more energy to digest the dried grass as they get from eating it. The Long Meadow beef sold at the market and at its restaurant Farmstead is now delicious and getting even better. (They're even opening a butcher shop adjacent to the restaurant.)

Mainstream grass-fed beef has to improve across the board. And another reason to support grass-fed beef and help drive its improvement is that it's beef in accordance with nature. Pastures are where cattle are supposed to be— and this lifestyle is better for them and better for the world. Indeed, there's a great pleasure in marveling at the coevolutionary miracle of nature that is the relationship between cows and grass. It's one of those beautiful examples of symbiosis from which all beings profit.

Ruminants—be they cattle, buffalo, sheep, or elk—both support and feed off the grasses. They protect grasslands by keeping trees and brambles from encroaching, and they fertilize the ground with their manure and urine, spread grass seed, and plant the seed in the soil with their hooves. Grasses grow back stronger than before after being munched on; they evolved to resist the grazing of ruminants. In turn, the cattle get an endless lunch, for they evolved to do something most mammals can't: digest cellulose. The most abundant organic molecule on the planet, cellulose—an organic structural component of wood, grass, leaves, and the like— is created by plants using the sun's energy.

Other organisms win in this relationship, too. Grasslands regenerate themselves after grazing (if they are not overgrazed). As they grow, grasses shed their roots, depositing carbon into the soil, and then regrow even more and deeper roots. In turn, this subterranean environment provides home to the thriving community of bacteria and fungi that support countless other organisms by breaking down the organic matter of plants into humus while simultaneously feeding essential minerals from the ground to the roots of the plants. As this soil becomes deeper and more alive, it pulls more carbon out of the air and sequesters it, creating new pathways to store water in the process.

A growing movement of farmers and scientists see cattle and other ruminants as crucial to rebuilding soils worldwide that are being lost to erosion and desertification thanks to deforestation and industrial agriculture. Although some critics say that ruminants are a major cause of climate change, others posit the problem as being that too few of them feed on grass anymore, promoting carbon sequestration.

Humans thrive from the cow-grass relationship, too. We need the sun's energy to live but can't get it directly from light. Eating meat is one way to harvest that energy. Basically, when we dine on beef, we are consuming grass and other plants, some of the most plentiful substances on Earth. Raising meat on grass can be sensible ecologically as well. Yes, vegetable and grain crops can also provide energy, but they don't grow well everywhere. Much of the land on which cattle graze is too stony, arid, and hilly to grow crops profitably without major inputs such as irrigation and fertilizer. But grasses grow in much thinner soils than crops, and the action of ruminants helps soils store water (requiring no irrigation) and fix nitrogen (obviating fertilizer). When it all works as it's supposed to, it's a virtuous circle.

Betsy Ross on her ranch outside of Austin, Texas

Indeed, the great deep soils that turned the American Midwest into an agricultural powerhouse were achieved thanks to passage of the bison over grasslands for thousands of years.

To get a sense of how right this feels, go out and visit an enlightened grass-fed operation like Betsy Ross's, just outside of Austin, Texas. There, her herd of Devon cattle graze on a brilliant spread of pastureland—flowering plants, wild herbs, grasses, weeds, and thistles. Ross practices what's called holistic management. Like most people who observe this, she'd consider herself more a grass farmer than a cattle rancher. Scratch that, they consider themselves soil farmers, as grass and cattle are really just parts of an ecosystem that builds soil. And that soil is what keeps the ecology in balance, supplies water when it's scarce, and keeps

the climate stable. The cattle, busy munching away and not at all afraid of the humans standing amid them, seem happy. The meadow is robust and full of life. It just seems good.

"When we started this in 1992, the prevailing wisdom was that we couldn't do this," says Ross, a spry woman of seventy-eight. "The prevailing wisdom said you couldn't raise them for their lifetime on grass without supplementing. At that time, the cost of carrying a cow through the winter was $513, so you had to sell for more than that to break even. Now it's up to about $750. We don't spend nearly that because we're powered by the sun, not chemicals. We spend that money on people here."

Ross looks at herself as a steward of a system that can manage itself. "We don't feed minerals, we let the weeds bring the minerals up. It's a harmony. It's a symphony. Sometimes the animal itself is the dominating figure, other times the grass is, other times the insects, other times the water. Grass-fed beef is an experience not just about raising beef. Hopefully you feel good; there's a different energy here."

She's right. And when you eat her beef, you get a different feeling. It tastes different from conventional beef. She gave some to Jordan, and he served it to a bunch of friends along with some steaks from other producers. It was one of the favorites of the group and elicited an unusual comment. One diner said, "It's so mineral—like eating an oyster. It doesn't taste like an oyster," she added, but noted that you get a rush from a sensation of minerals surging into your body.

That wasn't an overstatement. Grass-fed beef is significantly higher than grain fed in beta-carotene, selenium, potassium, magnesium, zinc, and more. And there's that fatty acid profile: grass fed is higher in healthy conjugated linoleic acid.

So, grass-fed beef is better for humans, cattle, microbes, and the health of the entire planet. What's not to like? Ah, yes, the flavor of that beef. That's where it becomes incumbent on the ranchers themselves to make this work. They must be aware of the necessity of having truly delicious grass-fed beef to offer. It means making sure the cattle's diet of grass and silage is rich and diverse. This requires only harvesting it when the beef is full and marbled, which generally means an older animal. But we diners should also open our minds to a product with a slightly different flavor than what we're used to. Also, we must remember that grass-fed beef is an agricultural, not an industrial, product, and is therefore as prone to variation as the

produce we find in the store. But the more we support the good grass-fed producers with our dollars, the greater the incentive for others to join the cause and up their game.

THE TRUTH ABOUT GRAIN FED

Arguments supporting grain feeding of cattle are far slimmer than the very brief summary of the benefits of grass feeding just offered. Grain feeding might produce some qualities of beef that we like, but quite simply its existence represents the opposite of a harmonious natural system. After all, feeding cattle massive amounts of corn perverts what Mother Nature intended for ruminants. Instead, it represents a solution to the man-made political, economic, and industrial problems of overproduction of corn. As Michael Pollan lays out in *The Omnivore's Dilemma*, the roots of this problem, which are deep and convoluted, involve the shift to producing industrially made, petroleum-based chemical fertilizers in order to use up the vast surplus of ammonium nitrate, a key ingredient in explosives, left over after World War II. New hybrid strains of corn (which grow faster and with higher yields than heritage breeds) required the huge amounts of soil nitrogen only these fertilizers could supply. Suddenly, corn farmers could produce exponentially more corn per acre than had ever been possible in history.

Starting in the 1950s and surging in the 1970s, issues relating to politics, economics, and food security pushed farmers to overproduce corn. Despite the resolution of these issues, production has remained ridiculously high, which theoretically should drive down the price and cause farmers to cut production. But because, for political reasons, politicians have continually supported farmers with direct payments, there has been no incentive to slow cultivation. In short, the corn market is artificially supported by tax dollars.

Something had to be done with all that corn, and the idea was hit upon to use its calories systematically to fatten the country's cattle, fundamentally changing the traditional life cycle of the cow. It's not new to supplement a cow's diet with grain, but it is new to only or primarily feed cattle grain for a good chunk of their lives.

Whereas in the past a beef cow's life would have been largely spent on pasture, now they spend only the first five or six months on pasture before heading to feedlots. Here's where the race to fatten them as quickly and as cheaply as possible begins until they make a decent weight and head off to slaughter. This whole system has been much documented, so it won't be belabored here. But you should probably know that much of the cattle raised to produce industrial beef have been given antibiotics to stave off infections caused by confinement in overcrowded living quarters and by problems associated with a corn diet. Cows can tolerate eating corn as long as it is accompanied with the right percentage of roughage. Too much corn causes fatal bloating and painful acidosis. Hormones and other chemicals are also given to speed growth. Today, cattle are being specifically bred to better tolerate a corn diet (salmon are too). A balance of grass in the diet can alleviate these issues, but it will also slow down the fattening.

Corn feeding does fatten the animals quickly and causes them to marble well. That greater marbling (see page 41) is the driving force of the government's beef-grading system is simply a reinforcement of this perverse economy. Cementing the system, in just seventy years, the

American taste for beef has become the sweet, tender meat produced by feeding cattle corn.

The typical American beef cow will spend its first five or six months on grass with its mother in what are known as cow-calf operations. These are mostly small, family-run farms, and there are hundreds of thousands of such operations across the country. They are the idyllic places where young cattle do what they're supposed to do. Indeed, cattle are routinely trucked all over the country to places grasses grow best to complete this stage of life and then shipped back for the next. When they reach five or six hundred pounds, they're transitioned for life in the feedlot.

Not all feedlots are the wretched, filth-strewn cow megacities that have been (rightfully) demonized. Some are much more humane, clean, well-kept places. Pollution from decomposing manure and runoff are serious environmental problems, however. Nevertheless, the feedlot is where the cattle put on their next five hundred to seven hundred pounds as quickly as possible. When they reach the correct weight and form, they are sold back to the beef processors. Most beef cattle are slaughtered between thirteen and eighteen months. It could take a grass-fed animal another year to make it to the twelve-hundred-pound weight preferred at slaughter. That's another year or more of not profiting on the animal. And 85 percent of all beef comes from the big four processors: Cargill, National, JBS, and Tyson.

The arguments in favor of this system basically amount to this: If we didn't have the ability to grow these massive amounts of corn (and soybeans) we wouldn't be able to feed all of the people on the planet. Technically, concentrating beef cattle on feedlots could preserve the land needed to graze them for better uses. Raising cattle does require considerable land and time. As a food source, the current system may be faster and cheaper. What those costs would be without subsidized corn, however, are up for debate. Some estimates suggest a 33 percent increase in price, but it would probably be a lot more.

The best argument for grain-fed beef is that people really like it. And, no question, there is some exceptional grain-fed beef out there, brands such as Creekstone and HeartBrand. But at what cost do we maintain this system?

GRAIN FINISHING

Not all grain finishing is the same. It's not hard to find beef marketed as grass fed but grain finished. In basic terms, that means very little. It could describe cattle that spent six months on a corn diet in a concentrated feedlot. Or it could be used for pastured animals that spent their last month on a diet supplemented with a mixture of non-corn grains—millet, rye, oats—grown organically on the very farm where they were raised. Many ranchers believe such a way of finishing the cattle gives them a little extra marbling and perhaps tones down any edgy flavors the beef might have gained from time on grass. Grain finishing of this type may sweeten and soften the meat, making it more palatable, but the longer the time off grass, the greater the reduction of healthy compounds and fatty acids.

Age

The one piece of the beef flavor puzzle that goes missing in this country is the factor of age. Meat from older animals has more flavor. If you want

proof, go to Spain. Here in the United States, producers pride themselves on the quickness they can get a cow to slaughter, the younger the better. If they can be harvesting cattle at twelve months, they are really making money. In Spain, people celebrate how old the cow is.

Jordan experienced this firsthand on a trip to Spain. He was in the town of Ávila, just randomly at a meat restaurant on the outskirts of town. This place specialized in beef, so he ordered a ribeye. It was lunch. When the beef came out and was set in front of him, his saliva glands instantly started firing. No steak he'd ever had smelled so beefy. First bite, he couldn't believe what he was tasting. It was a deep, rich, savory sensation of beef he'd never experienced before. He found himself thinking, "Maybe Spain has the best-tasting beef in the world." That steak became one of the inspirations for this book. It came from a steer about six years old. Was it tender? He can't remember. That didn't even matter because it tasted so damn good.

Older animals always have more intense flavor than younger ones. It's true in chickens and it's true in cattle. Sadly, for reasons of economics, in the United States our industries are incentivized to harvest animals as young as possible, meaning that flavor is greatly diminished. We eat a lot of incredibly bland meat, hardly ever experiencing what true chicken flavor or real beef flavor is all about.

True flavor comes from animals that have lived life. A steer's work, its movement, and its diet are what create flavor. The longer it's had to live, to move, and to eat a variety of foods, the more savory and beefy it's going to become. Wagyu cattle, for instance, are slower maturing. This means that it takes them longer to get to slaughter weight. It makes the meat more expensive but also explains some of its enhanced flavor. Age also accounts for some of the flavor advantages of good grass-fed beef. Because grass-fed cattle take longer to reach a decent slaughtering weight, they not only move more in their lives, building more flavorful muscles, but also spend more time putting on weight. Consequently, grass-fed beef usually has more flavor.

The gastronomic argument against older cattle usually has to do with tenderness. In some studies, many Americans have stated a preference for tenderness over flavor. So long as the steak is juicy and melts in your mouth, people don't seem to care that it's bland. When a cow lives only fourteen months and is fed corn for almost half that time, it's had little chance to develop flavor but it will likely be tender. But for those who love flavor and don't mind a little chewiness, there are few choices.

The limiting factor for raising older animals, of course, is cost. No rancher wants to pay to feed a cow an extra six months or a year or four. It's expensive and risky (more opportunities for the cow to get sick or injured), and at this point, there's not a market where the cost of the steak can be high enough to recoup that investment.

But in other countries that market exists. In Spain, farmers will take dairy cows who have retired from producing milk after four or five years and put them back on the pasture for another few years. Now, you're getting a cow that is eight years old. Or there's the madness of chef José Gordón of El Capricho (see page 62), who buys oxen at three years old and pastures them on his ranch (at great expense) in León Province until they're ready, usually between eight and twelve years of age. This might be the most flavorful steak in the world.

Of course, we have older cattle in the United States, and they do get slaughtered—just not for steaks. Indeed, one of the little-known facts about hamburgers is that one reason they're so beefy and delicious is because much of their meat comes from older cows whose steaks would be too old to get a grade of Prime or even Choice. This instantly downgrades them into the category of cheap meat, so—no matter how flavorful—they usually go into hamburger. This is great for the nation's hamburgers, but, if handled with more care and intention, older beef could be used more profitably and perhaps satisfy people in other ways.

While Spain is the king of old cows, things may be changing in favor of older beef in other countries. High-end food scenes in Europe are catching on to the deliciousness of steaks from older cattle, and Spain can provide only so many (older cattle are a diminishing resource). However, the new taste for highly flavored meat from old cows may spark other countries to convert part of their industries to conserving and reconditioning older cattle.

Will Americans ever develop such a taste? Glenn Elzinga, of Alderspring Ranch in Idaho, is doubtful. "In Spain or France, those people can tolerate an incredible amount of flavor, but Americans are on Nebraska corn-fed beef since 1950," he says. "Even people who are food people are not ready for the intensity of flavor development after thirty-six months. I can eat that intense steak off our grass. That is an intense steak. But I serve up this incredible steak to people, and they can't handle it. They'll say it's too beefy. We have an American clientele who are steak lovers but have never really experienced flavor of that intensity, and as a result, it's a no sale."

But perhaps a high-end market could be developed for a small number of people who love the taste of beef and are willing to pay extra to support older cattle. In California, a top-end meat supplier called Cream Co. is experimenting with just this—putting retired dairy cattle onto pasture for a time to recover and develop more fat. At a tasting in Austin with Cliff Pollard, Cream Co.'s founder, we tried some of this steak, and it was outstandingly flavorful and not at all tough. Not quite at the level of Spanish beef, but highly encouraging. It doesn't seem ridiculous to think that such a market could develop in the United States.

The Upshot

In the interest of flavor and eating experience, what is the hypothetical best steak you could buy? It would be from a grass-fed, grass-finished animal at least five years of age. Right now, that steak doesn't exist in the United States. So beyond that, in the realm of choice, what should you look for?

Some good-tasting corn-fed beef is out there, but it's few and far between. Most of it—and the vast majority of beef in this country—comes out of a system that does not produce much good meat and is also negative in terms of animal welfare, public health, and the global environment.

Grass fed is the right way to go for reasons of health, social responsibility, and—at its best—taste. But finding great grass-fed beef isn't always easy. The best thing to do is locate a great source and support that producer. It will likely be more expensive and harder to source. If that's worth it to you, then consider the idea of eating less but higher-quality steak.

They call it "grass-fed gold." Just as we were finishing the book, we made a steak discovery that could be a game changer in the United States—at least for those of us who want fuller-flavored, well-marbled grass-fed beef. Most people think that's impossible, but it's not. It simply requires older cattle—cattle that no one was committed to keeping around and feeding until now. Enter Carter Country Meats, a family-owned ranch and beef business in Wyoming. For the first time, they are marketing dry-aged beef from five- to ten-year-old cattle that have grazed on nothing but mountain pasture their entire lives (save the winters, when they are fed home-grown and fermented silage). The beef is exquisite, with a deep, beefy savor, long-lingering flavor, and a remarkable degree of tenderness. And it came about mostly by accident.

RC Carter and family manage a cow-calf operation on forty-five thousand acres of mountain pasture in the Bighorn Range and an additional four hundred square miles of rangeland in southern Wyoming. They maintain a large herd of cattle throughout the year, including cows from five to ten years of age that have gone dry and stopped becoming pregnant. The typical fate of these animals is to be sold on the commodity market, where they fetch sixty cents a pound (or about nine hundred dollars an animal). "That's not a lucrative profession," says RC. "The commodity guys have convinced everybody that these cows aren't worth anything. They usually try to discount you because they're so old." RC wouldn't have known any better himself, but he happened to see *Steak Revolution*, a 2014 French documentary that included José Gordón of Spain's El Capricho (see page 62) talking about turning his older oxen into some of the best steaks in the world.

RC got an idea. He gathered his dad and brother and they drove down to southern Wyoming to check out their cattle. "There are wild horses roaming and antelope and our cows, just purely on open grassy range. We spent a week gathering up all of these cows [as they now do annually], and some of them were superfat. Having eaten grass all summer long, they looked like finished beef." The Carters took nine of them. Shockingly (to them), 30 percent graded Prime. "They were considered throwaway cows," says RC, "but it turns out they're better than the younger animals anyway—hands-down. If I sold them commodity, I might get nine hundred dollars a cow, but that same animal I can sell to Nate for four thousand dollars."

Nate is Nate Singer, a talented butcher who runs Black Belly, a great shop in Boulder, Colorado. Having grown up in Wyoming, Nate knew the Carters and he also knew good beef (his dad is a butcher with a restaurant in Cody). Now, in addition to holding down his job at Black Belly, he serves as an ambassador and agent for Carter Country's beef program. "I'll never forget those first animals we harvested," says Nate. "Their meat was gorgeous, their fat a deep yellow color. They were the most beautiful animals. 'Grass-fed gold' is what we called it."

Nate says that the biggest problem with selling older cows is dry aging. Older grass-fed animals (and there aren't older grain-fed ones because no one will pay to feed them corn for more than a few months) will have more developed muscles, so they need some dry aging for tenderness. But dry aging has been next to impossible to come by for older cattle because of the thirty-month rule.

What's the thirty-month rule? That's the rule the USDA imposed that says cattle slaughtered over the (rather arbitrary) age of thirty months need to have their spinal column (and certain other parts) separated from the carcass before the meat leaves the slaughterhouse, to prevent mad cow disease. Whether that's reasonable or even necessary is a whole other argument, but it's the law. Because of this rule, slaughterhouses are loathe to process older animals because they require a special run, with thorough cleaning of equipment before going back to conventional younger cattle, which make up almost all their business. Furthermore, beef wholesalers don't want to age the meat, because in losing the spine bones a valuable form of protection from dehydration is gone. And finally, there's a bias against older animals in the USDA grading protocol, meaning they can't grade high on the commercial scale no matter how marbled the meat. Basically, the entire system is rigged against older cattle.

"When you think about raising grass-fed beef," Nate says, "well at thirty months of age, the animal is like a fifteen-year-old kid—they're skinny, hyper, and nuts. But when they get older, they start to marble and hold fat on their carcasses. By the time they're five to six years old, they're starting to pack it on, this beautiful golden-tinged fat." As for the expense most ranchers face when keeping animals

past the typical twenty-four to thirty months, well that's where the Carter family's access to forty thousand acres and twenty-seven natural springs comes in. "It's why we've got to conserve these old ranches and land," continues RC. "This is beautiful cattle country that grows its own resources in grass and water. It's the opposite of a feedlot that's a drain on resources."

Nate and RC were able to work a deal with a local slaughterhouse to harvest their older cows once every two weeks and then hang the whole carcasses anywhere from fourteen to forty days, depending on space. The spines are removed just before the meat is shipped. Nate may age some other cuts longer in his shop, but there are no porterhouses or T-bones (because the spine has been removed). They hope to create some greater slaughterhouse flexibility in the future to expand their offerings.

Eating older cattle is an answer to many of the beef industry's annoying problems. The meat tastes exponentially better. It's from untreated, 100 percent grass-fed cattle that live a bountiful life as they were meant to live, while regenerating open rangeland and consuming only naturally occurring resources. Ranchers make more money and carnivores can have a better experience. Much like California's Cream Co. (see page 25), which is revitalizing older dairy cows on grass before sale, it's a win-win-win for all involved. Now if only the entire industry would get involved, we would have a real steak revolution.

The iconic Prause Meat Market
in La Grange, Texas

CHAPTER 2

Buying Steaks

Figuring out how and where to get the best steaks can be a dizzying experience. Well, it can also be a darn simple experience. One thing's for sure: finding the best steaks becomes more and more complicated and more confusing the farther away from the actual producer you get. In Texas, Aaron is lucky to have access to Dai Due, Lee's, and Salt & Time (more on Salt & Time in the next chapter). In California, Jordan has Olivier's, 4505 Meats, Clove and Hoof, and the Fatted Calf. The most common ways we Americans find steaks these days are via three main methods: straight from the rancher or farmer, from a butcher or other curator, and through some sort of branded program (or just from your local grocery store). Each has its pros and cons, always involving that all-important connection to the source.

The farther you get from the ranch, the more the quality of the beef declines. And when there's no way of determining the source or even who's selling the meat or where it's from, it's hard to make any guarantees about quality or provenance. It's hard to find guarantees no matter what, but the best bets always rely on some degree of trust.

Straight from the Farm

If you've read chapter 1, you know the care and work that goes into raising high-quality beef cows. One way to guarantee your beef is the best it can be is to get it directly from the source, that is, the rancher who raised the cow. This could be someone in your area from whom you can buy locally at the farmers' market or even at his or her own farmstead, or this could be done from across the country thanks to the miracle of interstate shipping.

Despite the dominance of national grocers like Whole Foods, Costco, and Kroger, buying locally from the person who actually raised the animals is increasingly easy, as many farmers and ranchers have developed casual direct-to-consumer programs and achieved loyal followings. Every state has ample opportunities to buy meat this way. And it's fun to shop locally, too. If you're on a road trip, buying a steak is a pleasant way to start a conversation with a native and sample the local beef *terroir*. It's hard to resist getting a piece of grass-fed beef when driving through the lush, emerald valleys of Vermont, The Green Mountain State. That's equally true if you're cruising through Central Texas and see groups of mighty longhorns glaring at you from a pasture or if you are traveling past a wildflower-strewn meadow in Wisconsin where plump cattle are grazing.

Of course, local beef isn't always a hit. When you're a tourist, you never really know what you're going to get. For instance, Jordan actually was that tourist, and after seeing all those lush Vermont pastures, he just *had* to find some delicious local grass-fed steaks. Unfortunately, what he located was an example of "bad" grass-fed beef, meaning that it was lean, tough, and tasted more like liver than loin. It spoke of a farmer who probably raised cattle primarily for dairy and not meat and didn't really know how to or care to finish his beef properly. Disappointing!

But when you find a tried-and-true local producer of good quality, there's almost nothing better. If you've got freezer space, you can buy a quarter of a cow (about one hundred pounds) or more at one time, saving money on a per-pound basis while making the life of the farmer easier. Many folks go in on such a deal as a group, sharing an entire animal. Of course, you're going to get more than just steaks if you go this route. But even though this is a steak book, we highly encourage you to learn what to do with all the rest of the animal!

But given that steaks are a luxury item, the idea of buying the best you can find from a producer in another state and spending a bit on shipping isn't so far-fetched. After all, without a second thought, we purchase everything from Nerf Official N-Strike Elite Strongarm Blasters to high-waist yoga pants (both recent best sellers on Amazon) through the mail these days. Why not meat? In fact, there's a long tradition of sending frozen meat by mail, just as there is boxes of grapefruits or pears. Omaha Steaks started shipping to front doors in 1952.

One concern with mail-order meat, besides the sometimes extravagant cost of shipping, is the environmental costs of packaging materials, which even in our more eco-conscious age are still often Styrofoam and gel packs. Some outfits are counteracting this standard, however, like Alderspring Ranch of Idaho, whose packaging is recyclable and also returnable. Alderspring includes a prepaid return label in every shipment and offers a five-dollar rebate on your next order if you send the box back.

Beyond that generous and responsible recycling program (and the fact that the company eats the estimated ten-dollar cost of returns), Alderspring is a prime example of what you can get by ordering directly from a farm. If you're interested in grass-fed beef of the highest quality, this is the place. Alderspring is a family-run ranch located in remote May, Idaho, in the Pahsimeroi Valley. They have about eight hundred acres of grassland in the valley, but more important, in the summer, they saddle up their horses and take the cattle into the mountains the old-fashioned way, leaving them on seventy square miles of mountain meadow and pasture. "We basically follow the snow line up the mountain," says founder Glenn Elzinga. In the summer, the cattle eat a rich and diverse diet based on hundreds of native plant species growing on untouched, virgin soils. During this time, the cattle walk around and get to choose what they want to munch on. The beef is dry aged for tenderization for a couple of weeks and is then shipped out.

It's American Angus beef like no other, and you can get it delivered to your door—one of the amazing aspects of being alive today.

Butchers and Curators

The very best butchers are just a half step further from the source. Old-fashioned whole-animal butchery is being revived as a craft and a business, a stark contrast from industrial butchers who get their beef parts in boxes and are merely responsible for separating them into steaks (if even that). In contrast, the new crop of throwback butchers buy entire carcasses and use their ingenuity and the superior sharpness of their knives not only to create great steaks but also all manner of other beef products, too.

In the case of a superior butchery like Austin's Salt & Time (see page 50), a lot of the steaks (and other meats) come directly from single farms and ranches. The butchers have visited these producers, or at least had long, probing conversations, and are fluent in the nature of the beef, the breed, and the conditions in which the cattle are raised.

SOME OF OUR FAVORITE REGIONAL PURVEYORS

In the next chapter, we talk with Ben Runkle and Bryan Butler, our friends and the owner-operators of Salt & Time in Austin, Texas. But if you're not lucky enough to live in Austin, fear not; there are great artisanal butcher shops and meat purveyors across the country. Some ship by mail and some you've just got to be there for. Here are a few of our favorites.

Olivier's, San Francisco, California

All butchers have their own unique approaches and specialties. Olivier Cordier is a passionate and voluble Frenchman who offers high-quality beef sold in the classic French cuts: *côte de boeuf, entrecôte, faux-filet, onglet,* and more. He dry ages his beef in the American style, sometimes for very long periods of time, inviting customers to reserve cuts of 60-, 120-, and 200-day dry-aged beef months in advance.

MEAT
IS
YUMMY

When it comes to sourcing, however, Olivier won't divulge where his beef comes from. In the Bay Area, where diners cynically joke about how restaurant menus tout the farms on which each morsel of food was grown, such a response is at first a bit shocking. But in such a competitive marketplace, Olivier figures if he literally gives away the farm, someone will try to horn in on his source or that source will cut him out, using his patronage as a stepping-stone to becoming a stand-alone brand. In this case, you just have to trust him . . . an easy thing to do after you cook up one of his steaks.

Flannery Beef, San Rafael, California

In a large space whirring with refrigeration and perpetual fans, in an anonymous industrial park, operates a butchery that has become internationally renowned for the quality of its beef. Bryan Flannery used to run a retail butcher shop but gave it up as his mail-order business took off. The spread of Flannery's fame predates social media and has largely been due to word of mouth. His steaks have been buoyed by landing on the tables of some truly influential diners. For years, one of Flannery's most high-profile clients has been Robert Parker, the world's most prominent wine critic. In his newsletter, Parker often chronicles his always epic meals, occasionally writing things like, "The 55-day dry-aged Private Reserve Sirloin Strips from Bryan Flannery were, as usual, unreal. If this guy is not the best and most consistent purveyor of high-quality American beef, I would be interested in knowing who is."

Like Olivier Cordier, Flannery doesn't detail the sources of his beef, just listing California, Midwestern, and Montana (for Wagyu). The point is that Flannery Beef is the trusted source,

and to that end, all of the meat they buy is chosen and regraded by Bryan and his daughter, Katie, his business partner and successor. "We buy Prime beef," says Katie, "but it happens all the time that we get meat delivered [on which] we have to downgrade the rating. Our standards are more exacting." The Flannerys also age their beef, usually a minimum of thirty days, but work with individual customers and will age to specified lengths of time.

Crowd Cow, Seattle, Washington

Joe Heitzeberg and his cofounder, Ethan Lowry, came at their business thinking like consumers. A lifelong steak lover, Joe notes how steak has been regarded—and still is—as a commodity; you never know where it's from or who raised it. But, he points out, coffee and chocolate were like that too, yet those products have become decommoditized. Today, you can buy single-origin, fair-trade, farm-specific versions of both from a dizzying number of global places. Joe and Ethan wondered why steak, such a special food, couldn't be seen in the same light. At some point, a friend happened to mention to Joe that he was buying mind-blowing beef directly from a farm. The purchasing required a fair bit of coordination (arranging multiple people to contribute toward the cost of shares in a whole cow) as well as freezer space for maybe a hundred or more pounds of beef.

So, in the digital spirit of the times, Ethan and Joe hit on the idea of crowdfunding a cow—same way that random people might crowdfund a project on Kickstarter—allowing a larger number of people to buy a smaller amount of superior beef. In short order, after visiting some ranches and constructing a website, Crowd

1040 East Union Street
Seattle, Washington
tel: (206) 900-8699 • restaurantbateau.com

One can have no greater respect for a restaurant than one that reveres the cow so much that it commits to a program of raising its own beef, as well as butchering, aging, cooking, and serving it. Very, very few restaurateurs are willing to take on such a labor- and capital-intensive operation. When they do (such as at Spain's El Capricho, see page 62), their restaurants deserve our attention and support.

This is not difficult to offer Seattle restaurant maven Renee Erickson, whose other triumphs include the Walrus and the Carpenter, an oyster bar. The concept is simple: Erickson, along with chef Taylor Thornhill and talented butcher Tom Coss, brings in whole beef carcasses (some of which they've raised themselves, some of which are raised by trusted small ranchers) and turns them into dry-aged goodness. On a big chalkboard in the dining room, the dozens of steaks are listed first by ranch and length of aging and then by particular cut. Coss is resourceful with the animals, producing many obscure cuts, such as Jacob's Ladder, Merlan, Oyster, Ball Tip, and more—as well as the old standbys. Each carcass offers only a limited number of cuts, and each cut is listed by weight and price. When one is purchased, a staff member takes a long pool cue–like pole with a piece of white chalk at the end and crosses it off, so everyone gets a fair shot at what's remaining. All of the steaks are grass fed and grass finished.

The room is casual but elegant. Cooked in cast-iron pans and butter basted, steaks are given a long rest, after which they are picked up in a hot pan and reflashed for service. They are served with a choice of three different, pungent compound butters: bone marrow, preserved lemon and brown butter, and anchovy.

A hallmark of Erickson's restaurants is her exquisite taste in everything from interior design to cocktails, and this is on full display at Bateau. The wine list is moderate in length but well chosen, and the seasonal sides are pitch-perfect, with gorgeous green salads, vibrant tomatoes, and foraged-mushroom fricassees. You may think salmon when visiting Seattle, but don't sleep on the steak.

Cow launched, selling its first cow out in a day. The spirit of Crowd Cow is now as much about exploring the rancher and the ranch as it is about just selling delicious beef; Joe and Ethan want to show that in beef, as in wine and chocolate, there is *terroir*. The two founders have even put out a book, *Craft Beef: A Revolution in Small Farms and Big Flavors*, chronicling their philosophy and tales of beef sourcing.

Indeed, the sourcing side of the job has become the most compelling part of it: Joe and Ethan have become steak hunters, that is, they now travel around the country and the world in search of the tastiest, most ethically raised, distinctive beef. On their site you can purchase shares of cows (as much or as little as you want, and when the order fills up, the cow "tips" and the meat will be harvested and sent out) from everywhere from Washington State to California, Montana, Missouri, and Pennsylvania.

Crowd Cow has even broken open Japan, where, among its several super-marbled triumphs, it has found the ultimate cult beef: olive-fed Kuroge Washu-breed Wagyu from a tiny corner of the country, the only place in the region where imported olive trees were planted. The beef is extraordinary. Joe shared one of the first samples with us, which we and a few of our steak-obsessed friends cooked up in Jordan's mom's backyard in Austin, along with a bunch of different steaks from other producers. With an oleic acid content of 65 percent (for reference, olive oil itself tends to run 55 to 83 percent) and bursting with juice, the steak's featherlight fat belied its richness. It simply melted in the mouth, leaving a light, nutty flavor and disappearing with a resonant smack of umami.

Marketed Meat: The Truths and Myths of Branded Beef

Branding cattle with a hot iron is (rightly) seen as cruel these days and is hardly practiced. But what's called "branded beef," well, that's one of the biggest trends in the world of beef in the last twenty years. Simply put, it's just beef with a name, be it Creekstone or Niman Ranch. That name could stand for something like a real place or stringent standards, or it could be totally made-up and functionally meaningless. The simple act of putting a brand name on meat is a form of marketing. It suggests to the buyer that this beef stands for something, implying some aspect of quality that, if the brand is purchased again, will remain consistent. That suggested quality might be tenderness (Tyson's Tender Promise) or environmental and animal welfare (Publix's GreenWise).

In many cases, the brand does stand for something, as every branded beef program proclaims its own standards, based on things like locality, aging, genetics, and grade. To become certified in the United States, the program must be accepted and monitored by the USDA, which verifies that the claims of the brand are backed in every carcass. Not all brands are USDA certified, meaning that those that are not are held only by their own standards. American Branded Beef programs tend to fall into three major categories: breed specific, place specific, and company specific.

BREED SPECIFIC

Breed-specific programs focus on one particular breed. Most famous of them all, Certified Angus Beef (CAB for short, founded in 1978) promises that all of its meat comes from Angus cattle. There's also a Certified Hereford Beef program for that breed and even a Certified Texas Longhorn Beef program. HeartBrand sells Akaushi cattle, a subset of Japanese Wagyu. In each of these cases, the genetics of the cattle used in the program are maintained and considered central to the quality of the beef.

Today, many, many brands peddle the ever-popular Angus breed, including Niman Ranch and Creekstone. In addition to the guarantee of breed, some of these brands support further standards, such as vegetarian diet, no hormones or antibiotics, and humane treatment. With the certification in 1978 of CAB, the general thought about branded programs would be that they were based on breed. But a decade later, the USDA began approving brands based on qualities other than breed.

PLACE SPECIFIC

Other brands are based on place, often launched by a coalition of like-minded ranchers to leverage teamwork and size to compete better in a brutal market. Oregon Country Beef is a good example. This brand doesn't claim to be USDA certified, but it is non-GMO verified and GAP certified (a nonprofit that promotes animal welfare) by third parties.

While we don't have designation of origin—another type of brand, in its own way—for beef in the United States, other countries do. The most famous in the beef origin world is arguably Kobe beef, a special kind of beef from Wagyu cattle that can only come from the Kobe region of Japan. Over the years, misuse of the name Kobe beef has been a constant problem for those protecting the brand. Merchants in the United States

have repeatedly sold beef as Kobe that wasn't from the region or even from Japan. (If you're offered Kobe beef at a restaurant, be skeptical, exceedingly little real Kobe beef comes into this country, and it is tightly controlled.) Other famous beef designations of origin lie in the European Union, such as Spain's Carne de Ávila, France's Boeuf charolais du Bourbonnais, and the United Kingdom's Scotch beef.

COMPANY SPECIFIC

New categories of branded beef were based on a single company. For instance, Cargill, one of the country's big four beef companies, introduced its Sterling Silver program, becoming the second USDA-approved brand after CAB. Cargill differentiates its Sterling Silver beef not by breed but by a promise of marbling and maturity.

Then, of course, there are the grocery store brands—those weird labels you find in big grocery store chains that vaguely sound like something significant but that you've never seen anywhere else. They try to stand out against generic beef, though they may not be much better. A good example would be Safeway's Rancher's Reserve, which began in 2001 and was Select grade beef supplied by Cargill. The claim of Rancher's Reserve was tenderness because, as a Safeway executive explained in a 2006 article in *Beef* magazine, "Every focus group we conducted indicated the most important aspect of beef-eating satisfaction was tenderness."

The power of branding allowed Rancher's Reserve to fetch a higher price than normal Select-grade commodity beef. And it worked splendidly. In only a few years, Rancher's Reserve was moving a similar amount of tonnage as the vaunted Certified Angus Beef. However, the tenderness

**1401-255 Shinbeppucho Maehama
Miyazaki 880-0834, Miyazaki Prefecture, Japan
tel: (+81) 985-28-2914 • rest.miyachiku.jp/miyachiku**

In the United States, the most famous high-end beef from Japan may be Kobe, but in Japan the beef that has been winning awards and that many consider the country's most decadent is from the region of Miyazaki, located on the southeastern coast of the southern island of Kyushu. While this area is flush with water from rivers and an abundant coastline, it's the nearby mountains where the black Wagyu cattle are bred that are of importance to us. These grain-fed animals produce some of the most marbled, tender, and tasty meat in the world.

Several restaurants in Miyazaki serve this beef, but none does so with the care and integrity of Miyachiku. The style here is teppanyaki, meaning the beef is cooked on a flattop. This is where Benihana's shtick came from, but in Miyachiku and the other area restaurants, you simply sit at a counter built around the cooktop while the chef cooks small cubes of this expensive, rarefied beef in front of you. The meat is served in only small portions because any more would be almost indecently filling. And to the side, in fat rendered from the steak, the chef cooks vegetables and mushrooms, which are also served in small bites. Every now and then, the chef pours a few drops of alcohol onto the meat and sets it aflame to get a seared crust.

All in all, it's a far cry from the lusty, carnal American steak experience. But in its precision, restraint, and pinpointed pleasure, it's very Japanese. When you have those small bites and the steak literally melts in your mouth, almost disappearing into a wisp of profoundly beefy essence, you understand why they do it this way.

Everyone should know bad beef when they see it . . . or rather smell it. If you're wondering whether to cook a piece of meat on the edge, go with your, er, gut. But we'll lay it out for you, as bad beef is both unpleasant and potentially unsafe. Most beef spoilage comes via bacteria introduced at processing, as the meat of a living animal is typically microbe-free. But once the animal is killed, bacteria from the hide or processing facility can get in there. Indicators the meat has spoiled are a slimy surface and the aroma of rotten eggs, which occurs because the bacteria is breaking down protein molecules and releasing sulfur compounds. Also, the surface tension of the meat will have disappeared; rather than be resilient to the touch, it will feel flaccid and dead. "Most of these [bacteria] are harmless but unpleasant," notes Harold McGee, but it's best to avoid the experience.

If you've got beef in a Cryovac bag, it's undergoing what is called "wet aging" (see page 86). The amount of time meat is wet aged is much shorter than for dry aging, as the moist environment (even in a really cold refrigerator) is a happy one for bacteria. Wet aging should not go on for more than three weeks. Whatever the beef gains in tenderization will be finished by then, and there are no flavor gains to be had. Indeed, the beef will start to deteriorate. In working on this book, we tasted some Cryovac-aged meat that had been bagged for somewhere between thirty-five and forty-two days. It didn't make us sick or anything, but its texture lost some integrity, and the flavor had a touch of funk that was nothing like the delicious taste of dry-aged beef. For safety and taste, don't keep unfrozen meat in Cryovac bags for more than twenty-one days in the refrigerator.

standard for Select beef was difficult to maintain, both accurately and consistently. The only reliable test of tenderness, Safeway meat scientists found, took forty minutes to process, making it unrealistic, so they came up with their own rating system that presumably worked faster but was less reliable. The brand was retired in 2015, as Safeway recast its image with upgraded meats and produce overall. Safeway simply started selling USDA Choice-graded meat, a higher-level product.

Branded beef is something to be aware of, and USDA-certified brands actually involve a third-party guarantee (in this case, the government) that you're getting something that lives up to certain standards beyond the USDA grades. You can look them up on the USDA website to learn

what criteria are being imposed. However, plenty of brands—notably grocery store versions—are little more than names attached to beef to make it seem more specific or significant than it is.

Grade School

The grading of beef can seem both incredibly simple and contentiously complex, and your relationship to it depends on how far down the rabbit hole you want to go.

If you want to remain on the surface, there are only three USDA quality grades you'll ever confront: Prime, Choice, and Select. Categories below Select exist, but you won't deal with them for steaks.

Grading is done by the US Department of Agriculture, a service paid for by the meat packer or producer; companies can opt to sell their beef ungraded. (That's not the same as uninspected. The USDA inspects facilities as part of its taxpayer-funded mandate.) Many slaughterhouses—especially the biggest ones—employ full-time USDA agents who grade every carcass as it passes through.

Beef is graded to create an estimate of the satisfaction consumers can expect from a piece of meat. This is done visually by the evaluation of marbling, the amount and distribution of intramuscular fat (see page 41 for more on that) between the twelfth and thirteenth ribs. From that glimpse at a tiny part of the cow, a grade is given to the entire carcass.

In the simple worldview, Prime is the best, accounting for about 5 percent of all graded beef, according to the USDA, which describes Prime beef as having "slightly abundant to abundant marbling and is generally sold in hotels and restaurants."

Second best and accounting for around 70 percent of all graded beef, Choice is "high quality, but has less marbling than Prime." Both grades are "well-suited for broiling, roasting, or grilling."

Third best is Select, noted by the USDA as "normally leaner than Prime or Choice. It is fairly tender, but because it has less marbling, it may not have as much juiciness or flavor. Select beef can be great on the grill, and is also good for marinating and braising." Select is about 20 percent of graded beef, with the balance falling into five lower categories that sound more like punishments than anything you'd want to cook: Standard, Commercial, Utility, Cutter, and Canner.

(The truth about Select is that grocery chains often create their private brands of beef in order to avoid customers having to see "Select" on a label. Generally, if any beef grades high enough to earn a Prime or Choice grade, it will be marketed under that designation.)

There you have it. That's the simple version. But you don't have to be Sherlock Holmes to reckon it might be *too* simple. And indeed it is.

Prime Suspect

As the USDA wrote in the just-noted definition, Prime beef is unusual enough that it generally goes straight to high-end hotels and restaurants. It's true that it's still pretty hard to find Prime-rated beef at your average grocery store, hence the rise and cachet of the steak house: the meat you could get there used to be substantially better than what you could cook at home and worth going out for. But you'll notice we're using the past tense there. In the age of the gourmet grocery store, top-level beef gets disseminated much more evenly. Furthermore, the mail-order business has grown hugely in the last twenty years. (Today, the best way for steak houses to add value is by dry aging, which is covered in chapter 4.)

But how do we know Prime-rated beef is all it's cracked up to be? The short answer is we don't. That shouldn't be all that surprising, now that we know grading is done by the eye test of a fallible human.

"In my father's day," says butcher Bryan Flannery, "probably 20 percent of the cattle raised was classified as Prime. That was in the full-blown corn phase." (Here, Bryan is referring to the then common practice of feeding cattle corn

diets that made them fat, which is still the primary diet today. But in the 1960s and 1970s, he says, the cattle came from many fewer places and were in general much more consistent.) "But about ten years ago it was down to about 2 percent." That's a precipitous drop, fueled by a number of factors. First, market demand was down. Fat was the enemy in the 1980s and 1990s, and the country wasn't calling for well-marbled meat. (This also marks the ascent of chicken in the American diet, which has taken a huge swath of market share from beef in the last thirty years.) To combat this fear of fat, in 1987, and for the third time since creating grading, the USDA lowered the marbling standard for Prime, eating into the category that was once Choice. It also changed the name of the third-tier category from Good to the suave-sounding Select. (We think there should be a grade called "Meh.")

While industry conventional wisdom has Prime grading up in recent years to 3.5 percent or even higher, Flannery is suspect of those numbers. "I think that right now, in my experience, it's probably down to 1 percent. We order Prime-rated beef all the time and end up downgrading it because it doesn't meet our standards of Prime. Probably 15 percent of what we buy as Prime we don't sell as such. And we can't return that. We take the loss. If the government slaps Prime on a piece of beef, there's no recourse."

So, if the reported supply of Prime-graded beef has almost doubled in the last twenty years, but someone like Bryan Flannery, who orders only Prime beef, attests it's lower than he can remember, what gives? It seems the Prime grade has slid down the sliding scale. "A lot of meat graded today as Prime wouldn't have qualified in the past," Flannery says. "And I understand. If the inspector is looking at one thousand head

and has in his mind that twenty to thirty of them need to be Prime rated to fall into the accepted percentage, he's going to grade them Prime, even if they might only barely qualify or not qualify on traditional standards."

If you can't trust the grading system, how can you know whether or not your meat is up to par? The easiest way, of course, is to find a trusted source, like Flannery, who you know can vouch for the quality of his or her product. But what if it is not just the grading system and the Prime conspiracy that are the problem? What if it's the *criteria* by which we've been taught to grade beef that's actually bunk? As you'll discover when you're reading this book, there are lots of things we like to be contrarian about (tempering, resting . . . just wait, you'll see). But perhaps the biggest and most controversial one is the question of *marbling*.

The Truth about Marbling

All this fuss over grading really comes down to marbling—to intramuscular fat. Not the big lips of fat that cling to the exterior of muscles and divide them from one another, but those little rivulets and wisps of white that disperse out into the lean red meat like veins in a leaf. That's the marbling we can see. It also exists as microscopic little cells of juicy goodness that melt as the steak is cooked and explode in our mouths when we burst them with our teeth.

"Fat is flavor" is one of those memorable aphorisms for meat, much like "location, location, location" is to real estate. We've been told over and over that marbling is the key to everything. It causes the burst of juiciness we love in moist steak, and it carries—no, it embodies!—the deepest, most savory flavors. It is simply the essence of great steak. This is why Japanese Kobe beef, which shows more marbling than lean meat, is considered the world's greatest steak delicacy. As Mark Schatzker writes in his book *Steak*, "Sensory evaluations have proven the supremacy of marbling time and again. American meat scientists believe in marbling the way American physicists believe in atoms and American biologists believe in cells."

But is marbling *truly* the key to steak? *Is* fat flavor? There are reasons to doubt these assertions, reasons you don't need scientists to prove. Well, do as Schatzker suggests: take a big bite of fat. Does it taste like beefy delicious steak? No, it doesn't taste like much of anything. Now, the external fat does have a different composition than the intramuscular fat, but not *that* different. Even when you do have a big, juicy bite of liquefied marbling, say in a bite of real Japanese highly marbled Wagyu, the sensation you get from the liquid is not that of overpowering beef essence. (If you want to get scientific about it, it's the flavor of soft, slightly nutty oleic acid.) Jordan has tasted what he (and many others) consider the beefiest-tasting steaks in the world, the ones from eight- to twelve-year-old oxen in Spain that have been grass fed and have been active their whole lives. The meat is not at all what we'd consider "heavily marbled," yet there's no denying its beefy flavor.

We're sorry, but we've all had Prime and Choice steaks that have very little flavor, despite an abundance of juicy, unctuous fat. Perhaps the cow was fattened up exceptionally fast; plied with hormones, antibiotics, and beta-agonists; and then harvested at twelve months of age. It may have fat, but it simply won't have as much flavor as an animal that was on pasture for most

of its life, lived drug-free, and was harvested at twenty to thirty months.

None of this empirical evidence seems to support the idea that fat is flavor. More likely, it seems reasonable to assume that flavor comes from both muscle *and* fat. The genetics of the cow, what the cow ate, and how it lived all matter. We know that grass and a diverse forage show up as flavor in both the milk and the meat of a cow. Animals that move more in their lifetime develop not only more toughness in their muscles but also more flavor. Age contributes to flavor, too: the longer the cow lives, the more phytonutrients and beta-carotenes and other compounds get stored away in the muscles and the fats. And finally, how the animal was treated affects the flavor. Cattle that are stressed or fearful tend to have off flavors. If you really want steak with great flavor, you have to seek out meat of character—not just graded Prime.

Other Steak Labels and What They Mean

Producers love to plaster their meats with labels and certifications. From various labels, you can learn whether the steaks came from animals that were raised on open grassland, fed organic food, raised free of chemical additives, and treated humanely—allegedly. Of course, as with many food terms these days, these labels often mean less than you might think. Here's a brief guide to them.

GRASS FED

It may be the most meaningful movement happening in the steak world these days, but when it comes to the label, "grass-fed beef" doesn't

1208 South Howard Avenue
Tampa, Florida
tel: (813) 251-2421 • bernssteakhouse.com

Of all the old-school steak houses in America, Bern's, improbably located in Tampa, Florida, is king. Founded in 1956, it offers the decadent clubbiness of the classic steak house but with a baroque eccentricity that distinguishes it from the far-too-common soulless, corporate steak temple. For instance, the restaurant is a vast, multichambered, warren-like space, with each of its windowless dining rooms uniquely appointed with one-of-a-kind decorations that range from oil paintings to classical busts to images of European vineyards.

Although the décor may be quite theatrical, the food is highly serious, with a DIY spirit that reaches into every corner of the kitchen. Bern's not only operates a farm that grows some of the produce on offer but also roasts its own coffee, cellars its own cheese, buys its spices whole and grinds them, and, yes, ages and cuts to order every steak.

All of the steak served is Prime and aged five to eight weeks. Ordering it can be a little daunting, however, as the specificity on the menu is reminiscent of a spreadsheet. Filet mignon, Chateaubriand, strip sirloin, Delmonico (ribeye), porterhouse, and T-bone are all offered in at least four options based on width and weight that correspond to recommendations for number of people served and proper doneness. You can even choose from eight different degrees of doneness, such as very rare (no crust), very rare (with crust), rare (cold center), and so on. It's a complicated but loving and respectful testament to the supreme value of steak. Take some time to explore the steak section of the Bern's website—it's remarkable.

There's much more to the menu and the quality of offerings at Bern's than can be covered here, but we'd be remiss not to mention the wine program, which boasts the largest restaurant cellar in the world, harboring around seven hundred thousand bottles, and a remarkable two hundred wines offered by the glass. Because Bern's long ago bought not by the case but by the pallet (fifty-six cases), huge supplies of high-quality wines dating back to the 1960s and 1970s remain, not to mention rarities from the eighteenth and nineteenth centuries.

Tampa may not be a destination for most people, but if you find yourself in Florida—or even in the southeastern United States—it's worth a detour for a great steak dinner and a fine bottle of wine.

have a lot of meaning. In 2016, the USDA's Agricultural Marketing Service dropped any official definitions of the term *grass fed* from its regulations. The USDA website still defines the grass-fed standard as requiring "ruminant animals be fed only grass and forage, with the exception of milk consumed prior to weaning . . . cannot be fed grain or grain by-products and must have continuous access to pasture during the growing season." However, this term is not rigorously enforced or inspected. That is, producers who want to label their product as officially grass fed and earn the "USDA Process Verified" tag have only to submit $108 and documentation stating their animals are fed solely on grass and they'll receive the label. No inspection is required.

The upshot • Real grass-fed producers complain all the time that many ranchers simply cheat the system—they have the grass-fed label, yet don't feed their animals only grass. Furthermore, there's consternation that other producers don't actually graze their animals, but instead confine them to a feedlot and give them concentrated grass pellets that contain none of the wholesomeness or diversity of true, well-managed pasture. Plus, this label focuses only on diet and doesn't take into account whether or not the animals were fed hormones or antibiotics or how they were treated. In essence, the USDA's grass-fed label is toothless.

Fortunately, much more rigorous and serious third-party grass-fed certifiers exist who actually do annual audits of producers. The gold standard among them is the American Grassfed Association. If you see the circular, green "American Grassfed" logo on a product, the cows were fed only forage, were raised on pasture and not in confinement, and were never treated with hormones or antibiotics. Another organization is the Oregon-based A Greener World, whose "Certified Grassfed by AGW" label also requires documentation and annual audits of both farms and plants (if applicable) and goes as far as requiring forage testing for the nutrition of the feed.

ORGANIC

The organic seal from the USDA is quite thorough. For meat, it requires that the animals were raised on certified organic land—meaning it's been free of most synthetic fertilizers and pesticides for at least three years—have year-round access to pasture (although they don't necessarily have to be grass fed), were fed 100 percent organic feed and forage (which can include grain), and were not administered antibiotics or hormones. This is regulated by documentation and an annual audit from a USDA inspector.

The upshot • Although this says nothing about grass fed, and the list of allowed organic and synthetic substances within the organic designation is incredibly long and full of all sorts of chemicals, this is the most highly regulated and demanding of the USDA labels.

PASTURE RAISED

The USDA doesn't conduct third-party "Pasture Raised" certification, but it does have to approve any product that bears this label. In this case, pasture raised, or variants like "pasture grown" or "meadow raised," refers only to the living conditions of the animals and not to what they were fed. The USDA requires meats bearing these labels to come from animals that had a minimum of 120 days a year of continuous free

The meat case of a good grocery store can be a tempting place or a minefield. A good way to increase your chances of having a decent steak for dinner is choosing the right piece of meat. Unfortunately, the clerks behind the counters are less likely to be able to offer good guidance as they may once have been. Grocery store beef these days is often cut at a central processing facility and delivered to the stores, meaning the counter people just lay it out without needing to know anything about the cuts. Here are a few tips to take out some of the guesswork.

- **Take your time and really inspect the cuts on offer.** Every piece of steak is different, so it pays to make sure each one is great. You wouldn't buy an expensive pair of pants without first trying them on, would you?

- **Choose the freshest steaks.** All the meat in the supermarket looks red. This is because special packaging is used that allows the myoglobin in the meat to combine with oxygen to "bloom," or turn a bright, attractive shade of red. (Incidentally, harder-working muscles like chuck or flank contain more myoglobin and will thus appear redder than rib and loin steaks.) However, if you detect brown or gray on the steaks, it means the iron in the myoglobin is oxidizing. That's not necessarily a sign of spoilage, but rather just a steak that's been sitting around longer.

- **Go for thicker steaks.** Even if the outside shows more oxidation, a thicker steak will have a greater proportion of fresh, unexposed meat.

- **Prepackaged or under glass?** Not always, but usually, grocers put their best meat in the case. The case generally holds a better selection of cuts as well.

- **Do look for fat.** The whole point of our marbling screed was that marbling is not the *sole* source of flavor in a steak, but it *is* a good indication of what will turn juicy and sweet. Exterior fat, while you don't want to pay for too much of it, can help the steak cook more evenly and slowly.

- **Avoid connective tissue.** Look for steaks that have large, single muscles or muscle groups. When you can see several individual muscles in a piece of beef being offered as a steak, pass up the cut. The connective tissue separating the muscles will toughen during fast cooking, making large parts of the steak inedible.

- **Avoid the fancy store-created brand names.** This is how stores have learned to sell lower-grade meat. Go for well-marbled, upper Choice for the best quality-to-price ratio.

access to the outdoors. This is "desk regulated," meaning that these labels only require the submission of documentation.

The upshot • Given that the labels only require access to "the outdoors" (whatever that exactly means) for only about four months of the year and that the access is not physically verified by a compliance agent, these labels can be considered essentially meaningless. Any farmer serious enough about pasturing his or her animals and wanting to communicate that to the general public would seek more stringent certification than what the USDA provides.

RAISED WITHOUT HORMONES OR ANTIBIOTICS

Products bearing this USDA certification can have no antibiotics or any added hormones—ever. The USDA certifies these labels by reviewing documentation sent in by the producer. No in-person audits are made.

The upshot • Concerns about giving cattle antibiotics, the widespread use of which is considered very likely to contribute to the rise of antibiotic-resistant bacteria and create dangers of superbugs that can't be controlled, or added hormones, whose negative effects on health have not been substantiated (though they're banned in Europe), are legitimate. These labels are helpful, but, once again, enforcement is light, and it's generally up to the producer to stand by the claims. The best way to ensure the absence of hormones and antibiotics in your beef is to buy organically certified meat or to research the producer yourself.

"PRODUCT OF THE USA"

In 2015, Congress repealed the Country of Origin Labeling law (COOL, for short) that required beef labels to state where the animal was born, raised, and slaughtered.

Industry groups who lobbied against COOL (and won) said that tracking, labeling, and verifying the movement of beef wasted a billion dollars a year for an industry that's already tight. The anti-COOL forces also said that there's no regulation against meat companies offering that information voluntarily, and customers can vote with their dollars by supporting the companies that do.

But now, without COOL, imported beef can misleadingly but legally bear a "Product of the USA" mark if it's been processed in this country. So, a side of beef raised in Australia but processed and packed at a facility in Kansas can be called American beef, which is outrageous.

Luckily, the USDA seems to think it's a serious enough question to revisit the issue. They were scheduled to open up the topic for debate starting in August 2018. We shall see what they decide.

In the meantime, be wary of beef that is being heavily promoted as a US product. As with someone who doth protest too much, it may not be from here at all. And there's really no way to know.

Bryan Butler of Salt & Time in Austin, Texas

CHAPTER 3

Steak Cuts

Recalling some of the steaks we've bought in the past can be a little cringe inducing. Aaron flashes back to the commodity briskets he bought for ninety-nine cents a pound at H-E-B when learning how to barbecue. When he was broke all the time, he, like most people, ate cheap commodity steaks—you know, the ones in those plastic-wrapped Styrofoam trays in the grocery store cooler. That meat could be from anywhere. For Jordan, it's similar, but he remembers buying really cheap chuck and flank meat and thinking he could cook it like steaks. It would always smell really great when it hit the pan, but then you had to chew a piece for five minutes to get it down. Jordan and his roommates would study up on the Heimlich maneuver when they bought beef, just in case.

Hey, we've all been there: who among us hasn't bought that cheap, dull gray slab of organic matter sealed beneath a shiny layer of plastic wrap on top of some flimsy polystyrene foam back? But when the beef craving strikes, there are better ways to indulge it.

In the previous section, we talked about what makes for good beef, but we didn't specifically talk about all the other kinds of decisions necessary to get steak on the table: What individual cut do you want? How do you want it cooked? Where should the meat come from? Should it be fresh or aged? What should you do with it?

To secure the tastiest steak, you need a good provider. You need a place where you have choices and where you can ask for more information about the meat you're buying and about what to do with it once you've got it. Does that sound like Costco, Walmart, or Kroger? Not at all. Even at many high-end grocers like Whole Foods, it's almost impossible to find anyone who can tell you anything about the meat or give sound advice on how to prepare it.

That's not how it used to be. Before the massive scaling and industrialization of groceries, every local store had a butcher, and the good butchers could tell you all you needed to know to get dinner on the table that night.

Luckily, the tradition of the local butcher is coming back. Many cities now have one or more small, artisanal butcher shops where whole carcasses are broken down and the meats are handled with care and experience. (Shout-outs to some awesome butcheries across the United States: McCann's Local Meats in Rochester, New York; Clove & Hoof in Oakland, California; Taylor's Market in Sacramento, California; Purely Meat Co. and Butcher and Larder in Chicago; Porter Road in Nashville, Tennessee; the Organic

Butcher of McLean, Virginia; Fleisher's and the Meat Hook in New York City; Gwen Butcher Shop in Los Angeles; and Chop Butchery & Charcuterie in Portland, Oregon.) Austin is very lucky to have a few such shops. The most ambitious among them is Salt & Time, a butcher shop and *salumeria* opened by two friends on the east side of town in 2013.

Many good butchers exist across the country now, but it is hard to imagine two who are more talented, thoughtful, driven, and passionate than business partners Ben Runkle and Bryan Butler. Aaron remembers Bryan when he was just a butcher about town working at the Wheatsville Co-op on Guadalupe, though they didn't really meet until Aaron started going in as a customer. Jordan first encountered them as a customer too, but quickly introduced himself as he was so impressed by their commitment to local producers. They have a badass restaurant attached to their shop, incredibly sourced and butchered meats, and some of the tastiest charcuterie in the country. This is why we asked them to be a part of this book to help us talk about steak cuts: where they come from, how to choose them, and what to do with them.

A Good Butchery

A massive, long-bearded hulk of a man, S&T's Bryan Butler is the partner who breaks down the whole carcasses (Ben has the skills, but as a wizard of charcuterie, he's happy to defer to Bryan's passion and prodigious talent for whole-animal butchery.) Despite his years of training and his enthusiasm for the art, Bryan had considered getting out of the business on several occasions. As Ben observes, "I really

think Bryan's career arc is like what happened to butchery in America in a nutshell."

In 1996, straight out of high school and seeking a trade, Bryan went to a formal two-year program for whole-animal butchery, meat-market management, costing—the works. His was the last graduating class, as the school then shut down due to low enrollment (remember, this was well before the craft-butchery boom of the last few years). Bryan found work at some small mom-and-pop places, all of which were struggling just to stay open against the onslaught of cheap meat sold by the likes of Walmart, where he would ultimately end up employed for a short run. There he faced the horrors of working from (excuse the pun) inside the belly of that monster, a dehumanizing experience. Bryan quit and found work with smaller, independent grocers, before joining Ben at S&T.

Today, Ben and Bryan are inundated with people who want to learn how to butcher, as a wave of new-school butcheries became one of the more compelling food trends of the last decade. Butchery was almost completely lost as a skill, as assembly-line, low-wage meatpacking plants dominated. It was a trade maintained by only a handful of obscure folks scattered throughout the country who, like Bryan, lacked career opportunities and considered abandoning the profession. When this new wave came around— thanks to the slow food movement, a new reverence for artisanship, and a growing love and appreciation of fine cooking at home—enough customers were willing to spend more money for better meat.

As Ben says, "As a personal consumer of meat, there's a number of qualities I consider in the question of whether I want to buy it, and cheap is nowhere on my list. Obviously, value matters, but cheap is not the same as value. When you're talking about something as complicated with as many factors that affect how it tastes and what it does to your body and what it does to the world around it, cheap is not the way to go about thinking about good meat."

Today, the small, artisanal butcher shop still represents an economically challenging model— Walmart and Costco haven't gone anywhere— but as the interest in quality, well-raised meats continues to rise, craft butcheries will remain our country's small, ecumenical temples to meat that matters.

Speaking of the skills, in 2018, Bryan was part of the first-ever United States team to compete in the World Butchery Challenge, an international competition that pits teams of butchers in a timed contest of breaking down a variety of whole animals (to be precise, three and a quarter hours to do a side of beef, a side of pork, a whole lamb, and five chickens). They must produce salable, beautiful cuts, and create a slew of preparations, from patés to sausages, and products while being judged on cleanliness, appearance, professionalism, and efficiency.

The American team, which finished sixth (a satisfying result, considering it was their first go-round), received an interesting comment from one of the judges at the end. Noting their paltry amount of waste afterward (which was dwarfed by the amount of waste produced by rival teams), the judge said incredulously, "That's all your waste?" Bryan's American team had offered in their presentation some thrifty things that clever American butchers do (like creating a bougie pet food from scraps, or packaging and selling bones for home chefs). So impressed were the judges that they mentioned they might look for ways to emphasize thrift in the future.

Thrift is an essential aspect of the butcher's art. It's an important quality in and of itself, but it's also the whetstone that keeps a butcher sharp. A butcher's main job is to buy a carcass and figure out the best way to get the most money out of it. Each animal is a complicated mass of muscle, tendon, bone, and fat that can be taken apart in almost infinite ways. It's the knowledge, skill, and desire of each butcher that determines how much he or she gets out of each carcass. A skilled one can produce a panoply of steaks and other cuts, as well as enticing preparations (pâté, tartare, terrine, sausage) made from trim or less exciting cuts. If the butcher is lazy or lacks vision, he or she can cut up the obvious steaks, grind the not-so-obvious stuff into hamburger meat, and waste all the rest.

Salt & Time is a butcher shop that goes the extra mile, but this isn't just an endorsement of two men. It is recognition of the hardworking artisanal butchers trying to get a foothold everywhere. Ben and Bryan know all of the cuts and are deft with the knife in preparing them. They buy whole carcasses directly from farmers, almost always from places they have visited so they can speak to the way the animals are raised. And they both have a great touch in the kitchen, an underrated skill for a butcher, to whom the most common question asked is probably, "How would you recommend cooking this?" But most of all, they understand bovine bone and muscle structure: they know every cut, from the renowned to the obscure. Following, we're going to go over our favorites with them.

Bryan Butler (left) and Ben Runkle (right)

1. **Do ask: "Where is the meat from?"** • If you're going to go out of your way to go to a butcher shop instead of a grocery store, you should be able to know that. Not every place is going to be local, but the person behind the counter should know a good bit about the supply chain and where the shop's beef is coming from. We take a lot of pride in our sourcing and believe any steak—any meat, really—is all the more enjoyable if you know something about it. So go ahead and ask us about the farm, what the cow was fed, anything.

2. **Don't ask: "Is that cut any good?"** • People come in and don't seem to have much confidence in us or even in their own taste. We don't carry bad meat. And in our opinion, every cut can be good if the meat itself is good, if the animal is raised with integrity.

3. **The most expensive cuts are not necessarily "the best."** • If you're going to go to a butcher shop, don't get hung up on ribeyes and strips. Ask us what our favorite steaks are or which ones we love to turn customers on to. One of the biggest differentiations between a real butcher shop and a grocery store is that at a butcher shop you have all of these other options. Even if the ribeyes at our place are a lot more expensive because they're super high-end, we probably have three or four cuts you might like better than the anonymous grocery store meat.

4. **Look beyond grade.** • A lot of people ask, "Do you have Prime?" without really knowing what that means. They assume it means something about more wholesome or more natural, whereas it has a pretty narrow definition. Furthermore, USDA Prime and Choice are not the only measures of quality in beef. Not all beef is even graded. Marbling is important, but other factors can influence tenderness and flavor, and we always select our beef for those things. So if it doesn't say Prime on the card, don't be put off.

5. **Know your portion sizes.** • Before coming in, you should have a rough idea of how much meat you want. When we ask people how much they want of a particular cut or tell them how much it weighs, they usually have no sense of how much to buy. But there's a big difference between a three-ounce piece and an eight-ounce piece. We can help only so much, so it's good if you have some idea of how much you want per person.

6. **Ask our opinions about how certain steaks are best cooked.** • On one end there are people who overcook their steaks to medium-well or well, but on the other end, there are people who undercook some cuts because of, say, the machismo of cooking it as rare as you can. Not every cut benefits from that; some cuts are better cooked a little further to render the fat or to break down the connective tissue. Tell us how you like to eat your steak, and we can tell you which cuts are best that way.

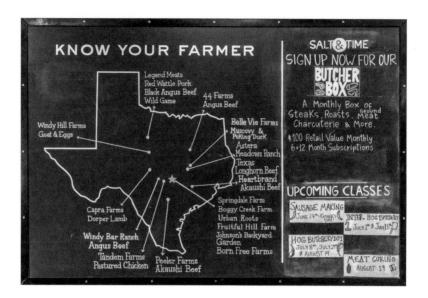

7. **Tell us what you want to make, and we'll sell you the right cut.** • We butcher, but we also cook. So if we know what you're making, we can help you out with the right meat. It may not always be exactly what's written in the recipe. For instance, if the recipe asks for a pound of lean-end brisket, well, we're not going to just trim a pound off and leave the other ten pounds unsold. But we can steer you to any number of cuts that will work just as well, if not better, for the dish.

8. **Be adventurous.** • There are lots of delicious cuts and techniques that go beyond steak. Steaks never disappoint, but knowing how to use the rest of the animal is important, too, not to mention usually economical and delicious. So instead of just defaulting to the standard, let us help you discover new cuts and techniques.

9. **Don't forget to ask about bones and fat.** • Two things that tend to set the professional kitchen apart from the home kitchen are cooking technique and pan sauces. For instance, cooking in animal fat rather than vegetable oil and the depth of flavor that adds. You can always ask us for a little extra beef fat to season your pan or grill for cooking your steak. We sell stock, but if you want to make your own, ask for some bones to make a stock for a nice, thick pan sauce. You can make a steak that much better by using the fat and stock from the same animal.

10. **Feel free to make requests.** • If you don't see it in the case, it doesn't mean we don't have it. As with most small butcher shops, our display space is limited, and we often have a number of interesting things in back. Just ask!

Know Your Steaks

If you've never bothered to consider it, here's something obvious: steak—and meat in general—is the muscle of an animal. Steaks are simply what we call the fast-cooking portions. All steak cuts—whether everyday or esoteric—come pretty much from the middle of the cow. By contrast, meat from the front and back legs and their attendant muscle groups in the chest and haunches is better served by slow cooking, because those muscles are tougher (after all, they do literally tons of work moving around the bulk of a thousand-pound animal).

A cow uses the middle of its body far less for movement. Rather, the muscles there protect and reinforce vital body parts and structures, like the spine, the heart, the rumen, and the other organs. Because the muscles are less strained in contraction and extension, the muscle tissue will be softer and less sinewy. Softer tissue means you can cook the meat faster without sacrificing tenderness, hence steak. Knowing a bit about the individual steak cuts, where on the anatomy they come from, and their use to the animal only makes things easier when deciding how to cook them.

In American butchery, a side of beef (half of a cow split lengthwise right down the middle), which may be six feet (or more) long and weigh several hundreds of pounds, is subdivided into seven more manageable sections, broken down according to bone structure. These are called primals, and there are seven of them. Starting at the head and topside of the animal, the primals are chuck, rib, loin, and round. Starting at the head and underside, they are brisket (the pectorals), plate, and flank. Given the length of

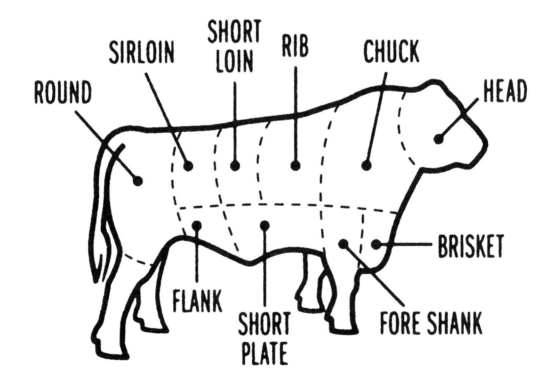

the spine and rib cage of the animal, divisions between the rib-containing primals are made by counting ribs. Saw and knife in hand, the butcher will count five ribs from the front of the rib cage to separate the chuck from the rib section, between the fifth and sixth ribs. The top of the ribs (rib primal) near the spine will be separated from the bottom section (plate primal) ten to twelve inches from the spine, sawing crosswise straight through the ribs. The hindquarter is separated from the forequarter between the twelfth and thirteenth ribs. The loin and sirloin are removed from the round (the leg and haunch), and the flank, which is the underside, is separated from the loin and ribs up top.

The steaks that we'll be focusing on here come from the middle sections: the **rib**, **loin** and **sirloin**, **plate**, and **flank**. All of the other meat is (usually) too tough to cook like a steak.

KNOW YOUR STEAK LINGO

Chine or chine bone • The vertebral column; in some rib roasts, this may be left on. For most steaks, butchers remove it.

Chuck steak • Any steak cut from the beef chuck primal. Some may have more specific titles—e.g., the flat iron—but sometimes these steaks are just generically called chuck steaks.

Côte de boeuf • the French term for a thick-cut bone-in ribeye; usually serves two.

Cowboy steak • A chined, bone-in ribeye with a short, Frenched rib bone.

Culotte steak • A flavorful steak from the sirloin cap, also known in Brazil as the *picanha*.

Dark cutter • Term for when the lean muscle has a dark appearance, typically caused by stress to the animal prior to slaughter. Also, when plural, the name of Aaron's new band!

Delmonico steak • Over the generations it's had a bit of a shifty meaning, but generally acknowledged today as boneless ribeye steak.

Dry aging • The process of aging meat in closely controlled cold temperatures for a period of days or weeks to increase tenderness and flavor.

Filet mignon • A thick-cut piece of the tenderloin without any fat or connective tissue.

Frenching • The process of removing all remaining meat and connective tissue from a bone until it looks clean, slick, and white.

Marbling • Intramuscular fat, or the white streaks inside the lean, red meat.

Pepper steak • Preparation in which steak is rubbed with coarsely ground black pepper, from the French *steak au poivre*.

Primal cuts • The seven major subsections of a side of beef in American butchery. Separating these are the first cuts a butcher makes on a carcass.

Subprimal • The next division after primals. For instance, the loin primal can be divided into short loin and sirloin.

Tomahawk steak • A chined, bone-in ribeye with a long, Frenched rib bone.

THE RIB STEAKS

The rib primal offers some of the most tender, marbled, and flavorful meat on the entire animal. This is, of course, the source of the rib roast; of, when subdivided, the ribeye steak— what old-timers call the Delmonico—and of the French thick, bone-in *côte de boeuf*. The entire rib primal, rib bones and backbone and all, is known in the meat trade as the 103 (all cuts have a processing number). It's a massive and impressive cut that often gets dry aged as a whole, as we do in the home-aging fridge. Depending on how or whether the meat is taken off the bones and how much of the rib bones is left on, you get a variety of different steaks.

When the rib roast is kept in one big piece, it's known as prime rib, a popular special-occasion or holiday cut. It's an impressive hunk of beef, but because it is roasted whole and served in thin slices, it is not a steak. Therefore, unlike a steak, the emphasis is the internal meat, not the crust. The standing rib roast, on end with all the bones sticking out, is an equally majestic sight.

"This 103 is one of the most labor-intensive areas," says Bryan, as he turns it on his table. "During the holidays, I do a dozen or more of them, which involves frenching the bones. (Frenching is when all the meat and sinew is peeled off the bones, leaving them bright, white, and clean.) Over the years, I've adopted more of a culinary approach to frenching. Most cut around the bone and scrape it lightly. I put in a little more time and get it completely clean," he says, tugging all the interior membrane from the bone, like peeling a tube sock off a foot. "The reason why is if you rush it, there will be dry little bits on the bone, and

we want that stark white alabaster bone. It just looks more appealing that way."

Ribeye

Prime rib is nice, but we prefer this long roast when it's been divided into individual steaks, called ribeyes, simply because when you cook individual steaks, you have exponentially more surface area to turn into a beautifully browned Maillardian crust (that is, the crispy, tasty exterior of a well-seared steak, explored further on page 154).

If you take the meat off the bone as a whole, you get a boneless rib roast or, when cut crosswise into steaks, boneless ribeye steaks. The butcher may choose to leave some amount of the rib bone intact. If a short section of the rib bone is left and cleaned, you get the cowboy steak. And if the entire length of rib remains, meat removed, you get the famously long-handled tomahawk steak.

Despite its immense popularity, the rib steak can be a little challenging to cook and to eat because it's not just a single muscle like the loin, but rather a collection of four muscles connected by a little tender sinew and fat. The muscles are the ribeye, the heart of the steak also called the *longissimus dorsi*; the ribeye cap, aka the *spinalis dorsi*; the *complexus*; and the tail, which is just a little tip, often removed.

When cooking a ribeye, the fat and sinew between these four muscles render, occasionally making a ribeye something of a floppy mess—or it can even fall apart. Also, because the grains of these muscles run at slightly different angles, you need to take special care to make sure you're always cutting against the grain. This isn't usually a problem because

American ribeyes aren't so big, which means you can simply slice in one direction across the steak and easily remain perpendicular or some transverse angle to the meat's grain. But if the steak happens to be huge. . . .

The tastiest and most tender and juicy piece of the cow is the ribeye cap, or *spinalis dorsi*. Somehow, this muscle has the most intense beefy flavor of any part. It's possible to deconstruct the rib roast not as steaks, but as individual muscles (creating ribeye fillets that look like large tenderloins), and thus preserving the *spinalis* as an entire steak unto itself rather than just the outside ring of a ribeye steak. But that's so impossibly decadent and selfish to deprive the rest of the ribeye steak of its best part that almost no one ever does it. But if someone did, we'd hope for a call.

Best way to cook • Depending on whether they are thin or thick, bone in or bone out, ribeyes warrant different approaches. Thick-cut, bone-in *côte de boeuf* (the French love to serve this cut for two people) needs to cook hot to gain the sear and then to spend a little time in ambient heat to get the proper internal temperature. Reverse searing works great. In contrast, thin, boneless cuts do well in a cast-iron skillet just on top of the stove. Remember that fat slows down the cooking, so this marbled cut can be forgiving, allowing flexibility in the searing of the outside, because the inside will unavoidably take longer.

Opposite page: Aaron trims a chined, bone-in ribeye, leaving the bone long to create a "tomahawk steak." This cut is great on the grill, and you can even use the bone as a handle to flip the steak!

BONE IN OR BONELESS?

One of the eternal questions when buying steaks is whether you want them bone in or boneless. It's a tough question mainly because people don't really know what the bone is good for and it seems like one more thing to stress about. But believe us, it's not. The answer is always bone in.

The reason for this is not, however, the one you most commonly hear, which is that the bone provides flavor by somehow infusing the meat. Rather, the bone provides structure and insulation to the steak, meaning that it can affect the rate of cooking (usually the impact is slowing it down, making it easier to get even cooking). Different bones have different densities. The lighter the bone, curiously, the better an insulator it is; rib bones are lighter than leg bones, for instance. That's because the lower-density bones contain more air, which is a poor conductor of heat. So, for steak purposes, the bone will heat up more slowly than the meat and fat around it, slowing down the cooking.

This is a good thing, leaving a small streak of rarer meat at the bone, which a lot of people like. Just remember to measure the internal temperature of large steaks away from the bone, as closer to the bone will likely read ten to fifteen degrees lower than the rest of the meat. That is to say, if you get the meat adjacent to the bone to a perfect medium-rare, the rest will be well overcooked.

The other advantage of cooking on the bone: someone (or some dog) gets to chew on all that delicious meat.

Parade de la Vega
Jiménez de Jamuz, León, Spain
tel: (+34) 987-66-42-24 • bodegaelcapricho.com

Some people like to slice their own steak. They want the whole slab of meat on the plate in front of them to enjoy the primal experience more fully. But if you're hungrily awaiting the delivery of your steak in the dim crypt that is the dining room of El Capricho, that won't be an option.

It's difficult not to call El Capricho the greatest steak house in the world simply because above all else, it is an act of passion. The fact that the destination is in the middle of a bleak nowhere, three hours northwest of Madrid, makes it all the more remarkable.

Every year, chef-owner José Gordón scours northern Spain and Portugal for high-quality, three-year-old oxen—two-thousand-pound beasts with giant, fearsome horns—that he brings to his sprawling ranch, where they are condemned to a gentle, roaming life of leisure. They feed on pasture—much of it wild thyme and lavender—and have grain supplement available, but only if they desire to eat it. He visits his oxen twice a day, inspecting their health and bestowing affection, and starting when they reach age eight, he begins to select individuals who are ready for sacrifice, as he says. They may become as old as fifteen before their time comes. After sacrifice, he ages the meat for 120 days before serving it in his grand, subterranean restaurant. This is the ideal steak: pasture-raised, older animal, lengthily dry aged.

Coming from giant, older oxen, the ribeye steaks he serves are enormous—around five pounds, bone in. They are grilled in the Basque way, reverse seared (see page 165) over hot charcoal with healthy handfuls of coarse salt, and then sliced at the table. The deep, transcendent beefiness of these steaks is almost indescribable, but savoring one of them is probably the most primal, resonant beef experience anywhere. Given that Gordón is responsible for the whole animal—not just the ribeyes—the rest of the menu is an ode to the remainder of the beast.

Start with a plate of *cecina*—this is nonnegotiable—thin slices of Castilian cured beef that has been salted and aged for at least eight years. It's like Spain's famous *jamón ibérico*, but with the depth and richness of beef. Don't miss the beef tongue, which has been brined, smoked, cured, and boiled before being served in thick medallions at the table. A crunchy, bracing watercress salad, simply dressed with olive oil, balsamic vinegar, and salt, is all you need with the steak, except for a good bottle of wine, and El Capricho has an excellent and well-priced list.

When the main event, the steak, comes to the table, the first thing you'll notice is that the mighty rib steaks are two to three times larger than anything you've ever had before. Indeed, they're bigger than your entire plate. So it's easier for everyone if chef Gordón or one of the servers slices the meat at the table, which is what they do on a little stand they bring to the table when the steak arrives. Gordón shows up with his long, curved breaking knife (a butcher's tool for breaking down carcasses) and carefully but quickly cuts the meat. Instead of just cutting across the grain of the ribeye in one direction, however, he treats each of the constituent muscles individually. The ribeye gets sliced on its own and arranged on the platter. Then he shifts and cuts the *complexus* at a slightly different angle to slice it as perpendicular to the grain as possible. Next comes the tip, which he cuts into little morsels. After that, he takes the whole long *spinalis dorsi* (ribeye cap) and first slices it lengthwise into two plump strips and then slices it across into bite-size chunks, allowing everyone to get an equal piece. Finally, he takes the fat that separates each muscle, cuts it into manageable bites, and leaves it in a little pile. "Don't forget to taste the fat," he reminds diners in his broken English. "A lot of flavor in there."

If you love steak—and because you're reading this book you probably do—it is incumbent on you to make the pilgrimage to this otherworldly temple of steak.

Porterhouse

THE LOIN STEAKS

Moving from the head of the cow toward the rear, after the rib primal comes the loin, separated from the rib between the twelfth and thirteenth ribs. The muscles in the loin connect the front and back of the animal and support it, but they aren't responsible for direct movement, hence the tenderness of these cuts. Indeed, before the current fashionability of the ribeye, these were the most celebrated and desired cuts of steak: T-bone, porterhouse, and tenderloin.

T-Bone and Porterhouse

To understand these cuts, let's talk a little bit about cow anatomy. In the loin, we're still working at the top of the cow, right along the edge with the muscles that protect and surround the spine. When a cow is split into two sides of beef, the spine is cut through the middle. The spinal cord is surrounded by bones that spur in each direction—up and down and to the left and right. If you think of it in cross section, it looks like a plus sign, with the intersection of the two lines being the spinal cord. The top quadrants (the northwest and northeast) are filled with the *longissimus dorsi* muscle, which extends toward the head into the rib primal as the "eye" of the ribeye, though here it is called the strip. The lower quadrants (southwest and southeast) are occupied by the tenderloin muscle, or *psoas major* for you Latin speakers. You can see how these important muscles protect the all-important spinal cord but don't do much work of their own. So as you split the carcass in half vertically, you get two halves, each with a T-shaped bone running through it. This is the bone that gives the T-bone its name.

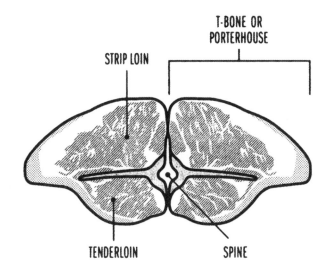

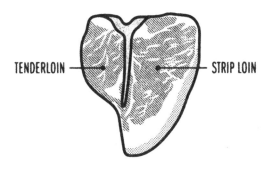

It's also the same bone that defines the porterhouse. The T-bone and porterhouse are just names for steaks taken from different ends of this bone segment. These cuts are renowned because they contain meat both from the tenderloin, prized for its namesake tenderness, and from the strip, prized for its strong beefy flavor.

So what's the difference between T-bone and porterhouse? The tenderloin muscle has a severe taper—imagine a baseball bat—starting from a point near the rib and enlarging in diameter as it heads toward the rear of the cow. At its most severely tapered end, when its diameter is, say, only as big as a quarter or even less, it's too small to enjoy as its own steak, so it's left on the spinal bone, with a portion of the strip on the other side of the bone. When the portion of the tenderloin is just a smidge—less than an inch and a quarter in diameter—you're looking at a T-bone steak. As the tenderloin increases in diameter heading back toward the rear, the overall steak becomes larger and more luxurious, offering a sizable portion of both tenderloin and strip. That's a porterhouse, which some consider the greatest of all cuts. In Italy, this is the famed *bistecca fiorentina*. Not only do you get both tenderloin and strip on the same cut, but you also get substantial portions of both.

Best way to cook • The T-bone is usually a thinly cut steak, and it's best taken right from the refrigerator and thrown onto high heat to get a good sear and a medium-rare interior. Porterhouses are thick-cut, luxuriant steaks. Because of this, some attention must be paid to getting the interior to medium-rare as well as the outside well browned. Try the reverse sear (see page 165): Start slow, cook to doneness, rest, and then finally, sear really hot. The meat closest to the bone will be the rarest, but part of the pleasure of the cut is having different shades of doneness on the plate. After the steak has rested, cut both sides off the bone, then slice them and present them with the bone.

Tenderloin (aka Filet Mignon)

Of course, you can take the tenderloin off the bone as a complete muscle. As just noted, it will be long and tube shaped, with a narrow section at one end expanding to a much thicker, baseball bat–like opposite end. We see this cut sold whole more commonly with pork—the famous pork loin. With beef,

butchers usually slice individual round steaks from this tubular muscle. Prized for their soft texture and mild flavor, these steaks are called tenderloins and are the most tender cut of the whole animal. The other names for this cut are filet mignon and Chateaubriand. The former usually describes the narrow rounds, while the latter is reserved for the plump, larger end and is sometimes offered as a steak for two. (Bern's, the venerated steak house of Tampa [see page 43], cooks the filet mignon and Chateaubriand differently: The filet mignon is broiled with the grain running up and down, perpendicular to the heat, so it cooks faster. The Chateaubriand is cut from the thick end of the tenderloin and cooked with the grain

Tenderloin

parallel to the heat, so it cooks slower and allows the development of a significant crust.)

Oh, and what about the really narrow end that's too small to be served as a steak? Well, that end can be cut up into smaller pieces for kebabs or finely diced for tartare.

Tenderloins are generally rather lean, soft, and, again, mildly flavored. These qualities used to make them popular among a certain dainty set. But in today's world of macho meat, the fillet has fallen in esteem, probably equal to and opposite of the rising popularity of the ribeye. Aaron, on the other hand, is a true believer. For him, it all comes down to texture. People regularly assume fattier meat is better meat, but it's not always true. It's also the quality of the fat, and in the tenderloin, there's no heavy marbling; instead, all of it is well integrated. There's a reason this cut is called the tenderloin: it eats like butter. And speaking of butter, Aaron always augments his tenderloins with some. In the pan, he adds a tablespoon or two and bastes it over the top while the tenderloin is cooking. On the grill, he'll often take a stick of butter and rub it on the warm steak as it cooks to help build the crust, a technique he picked up from his dad.

Best way to cook • Given its leanness and relative delicacy, this cut is best cooked in a heavy-bottomed pan on the stove top or an outdoor grill. Tenderloins don't have a lot of interior fat, meaning they cook quickly. A pan gives you more flexibility and greater control. Plus, add butter as Aaron does and do a little pan basting at the end, which helps make up for the lack of fat in the steak (also consider adding herbs and garlic to the butter to boost the flavor of this mild-tasting cut).

Strip

If you remove the whole tenderloin in one piece, you're left with a bone with the *longissimus dorsi*, or "strip" muscle, attached. Butchers have a choice here. They'll often remove the entire strip loin in one piece from the bone and then cross-cut the loin into boneless steaks of a desired thickness. These are called boneless strips or New York strips. They may also be called Kansas City strips. People argue about whether there's a difference between the two. One side says there's no difference, that the cut was called the Kansas City strip until Delmonico's restaurant in New York decided it would be more attractive to customers if it was called the New York strip.

Strip

Some say, however, that there is a slight difference. The Kansas City comes with a small portion of the bone attached and perhaps a bit of tail fat at the pointy end of the steak. These can also just be called bone-in New York strips, however. No matter the name, this is a flavorful, luxurious steak that has a tight grain, not too much fat, and a lot of flavor. If it's possible that one of the most iconic of all steaks could be underappreciated today, the New York strip is it.

Best way to cook • Most strips are thin enough that cooking them conventionally on a medium-hot grill or stove-top griddle should allow the formation of a nice crust without over- or under-cooking the exterior. Medium-rare is the goal. These are great as individual steaks: they're not too big, feeding one person generously.

THE BUTCHER'S CUTS

Some people call them "off cuts" or "new-school cuts," but the term *butcher's cuts* seems the most apt. These steaks are some of the most flavorful, affordable, and satisfying cuts from the entire animal, yet because of their appearance, lack of mind-blowing tenderness, or unimpressive marbling, they are overlooked and unappreciated by the masses. So if they didn't sell, these were the pieces the butchers took home for themselves (or, perhaps more accurately, if the butchers never put them out for sale, they could always take them home).

In some ways, the steaks that follow are fundamentally different from the luxe cuts we've just discussed. The famous steaks—ribeye, strip,

THE DIFFERENCE BETWEEN THE RIBEYE AND THE STRIP

Okay, so the two most luxuriant and reigning celebrities of the steak world come from opposite ends of one muscle, the *longissimus dorsi.* So what makes these two steaks different?

Let's start with looks. The ribeye is a rounder steak with a rounder shape. Remember, it incorporates parts of other muscles, too, the *spinalis* and the *complexus* for two. These muscles are part of the ribeye steak as a whole and are separated from one another by seams of fat and membrane. The strip steak, on the other hand, is just one muscle, and its shape is narrower, a little more wedge-like and pointed.

Flavorwise, both are potent and beefy, with the edge in beefiness and depth of flavor going to the strip steak. Marbling, however, usually falls in the other direction, with ribeyes tending to

be fattier and juicier than strips, though sometimes they also contain big, annoying interior clumps of fat where the different muscles are connected. Texturewise, the ribeye is usually the more tender and juicy, while the tighter grain of the strip can give it more chew, which to some of us is not a bad thing. Price? Usually similar, with the ribeye, due to its current popularity, maybe slightly more expensive.

So, head-to-head, which should you choose? It is hard to award an advantage. The ribeye does have the *spinalis*, the greatest cut on the steak, but it can also be somewhat of a mess and contains big pockets of fat. On the other hand, the strip is less flashy but more solid. For our money, advantage strip.

porterhouse, tenderloin—are all long, tubular muscles near the spine from which the individual steaks are cut thickly and across the grain of the whole. These butcher's cuts are all thin and relatively flat and long. Called thin meats, they have long, coarse muscle fibers that run in one direction, and you can usually see that grain. The steaks are cut with the grain, though to eat them, you must cut them across the grain to make them chewable and tender.

People who favor tenderloins say they love the texture, but Ben Runkle takes a slightly contrarian view. "People actually love the *absence* of texture. We've been taught to value the lack of texture as silkiness—the idea that having to chew a little bit is a sign of inferiority." Indeed, the more tender the steak, the more quickly it goes down, and the faster and more of it you eat. Mainstream Americans seem to like that. But think of the advantages of a little extra chewiness: more tooth means more chewing, with each bite releasing more juice, more flavor.

So these aren't thick-cut luxe steaks but rather thinner, grainier steaks with a huge amount of flavor, a satisfying amount of chew, and prices that reward the thrifty.

Hanger

For a long time, no one in the United States but the butchers knew about the hanger steak. Then, about twenty years ago, it started to appear on menus at restaurants. Even then, it didn't become a widely known cut until recently. But now the secret is out. The hanger is one of the most fully and uniquely flavored steaks on the whole cow, and it's still relatively cheap for such a rich, savory cut. Shaped like a long tube or almost like a baguette, it's easily cooked and sliced.

It's an unusual piece, as there is only one hanger per animal, as opposed to all of the other muscles, of which there are two symmetrically oriented on both sides of beef. It's called the hanger because it actually hangs off the inside of the carcass when the carcass is hung. According to Bryan, it hangs predominantly on the left side and is difficult to remove from the carcass. "It hangs inside the gut, so if you pierce the stomach or anything [else] when removing it, it becomes immediately contaminated," he says. "To remove it you almost have to climb into the carcass like a tauntaun." (That's a reference from *The Empire Strikes Back*, if you're wondering.) "You can't do that until the cow is eviscerated, then you reach up into the cavity with a knife and cut it freehand

Hanger

without being able to look at it. It takes real skill, and we realize it's something you should pay a little money for because if the butcher messes it up, it just goes to trim."

Bryan also notes that the aorta runs right through it, which is a big reason why there's such a strong mineral and iron-like flavor: it has blood pumping through it at all times. If you like full flavor at a good price, this is the cut for you.

Best way to cook • A dense piece of meat, the hanger cooks well over medium heat to a solid medium-rare. Too rare and the meat is tough to chew. Too well done and it becomes notably stringy and tough. The smoke and char of the grill are wonderful complements to the intense, bloody flavor of this cut.

Bavette

Aaron's favorite cut, the bottom sirloin flap (aka flap meat) is perhaps the greatest of the so-called butcher's cuts. But much more poetic is its French name, *bavette*, which means "bib" and describes the broad, flat shape of the steak. The bavette is, along with the hanger, the apex of the flavor and price ratio, though its taste is a little more conventionally beefy and its texture a little more tender. Aaron will take a well-cooked bavette over a ribeye most days. That's because it's not as rich, which he likes, and the flavor's usually stronger.

Bavette comes from just below the sirloin and adjacent to the flank. "I call this area the onion of the cow," says Bryan, "because it's in the belly of the animal and inside of here you keep peeling off all these great cuts—flank steak, bavette, and it's near the skirt."

The bavette is really just a flap muscle that supports other muscles on the side of the cow. It

doesn't do a tremendous amount of work, and thus remains relatively tender. It's not highly marbled, but nevertheless filled with flavor, and its grain is quite wide and slack. This is the quintessential bistro steak.

If you have a whole bavette flap, one end will be tapered and thinner than the thick, heavy end. You can cut it (with the grain) into individual steaks or cook it as a big whole. If you opt to cut, be aware that the thinner ends will cook faster.

Best way to cook • Bavette cooked on the stove top is good, especially if it's been divided into small steaks, shaped sort of like those tall strips of salmon. But when cooked in larger pieces,

Bavette

it's great on the grill over a medium-hot fire. The density of the meat means it cooks rather slowly, and it's essential to bring it to medium-rare or medium, as a really rare bavette is too chewy. It will form a big crust—sometimes almost too crusty and dry—so make sure you have enough heat to cook the interior without leaving the steak on the fire too long.

Flat Iron

We're now going to talk about an area of the cow we haven't touched on before, as it is not known for producing steaks: the chuck. Otherwise known as the shoulder clod, the chuck is a big, heavily worked muscle that does a lot of lifting and supporting—not exactly a recipe for tender meat that you can cook quickly. But that was before the "discovery" of the flat iron steak.

"Before the flat iron," says Bryan, "the chuck was generally taken as a whole piece, the seven-bone roast, etc. Or [it was] used for ground beef." But a couple of meat scientists at universities in Nebraska and Florida changed that. Working under funding from a national beef trade organization specifically dedicated to finding new ways to increase the value of a cow, the two searched through thirty-nine different muscles of the chuck and round (rear of the cow) in 144 carcasses (meaning over fifty-six hundred muscles tested in all) for tenderness and flavor. They eventually discovered the flat iron, a muscle in the shoulder blade that had previously been consigned to ground beef or stew meat because of the presence of a brutally tough tendon running through it. The scientists showed that if a butcher takes the time to remove the silver skin and then the connective tissue in the middle of the muscle delicately, he

or she can end up with two neatly shaped flat (but not thin) slabs of rectangular meat.

Turns out this meat rates as the second most tender in the entire cow (after the tenderloin). And for the price, which is way under that of the tenderloin, and the flavor, which is way over, the flat iron is a fantastic deal. In England, the flat iron is known as the butler's steak; in France, it's called the *paleron*; and in Australia, it's the oyster blade.

It's best to have a good butcher remove the seam for you. Jordan recently was at someone's house and got tasked with cooking the steak, a flat iron from Costco. The butcher there (or wherever) had done a terrible job trimming out

Flat Iron

the tendon, so it took Jordan another fifteen minutes to find and remove all the sinew, and the steak still looked rough. A good butcher can clean it up in just a few minutes.

Best way to cook • This tender steak is exceptionally forgiving. The rather fine grain and decent marbling mean that you can cook it rare, though it's at its best between rare and medium-rare. The neat, rectangular shape makes it easy to handle. A dense muscle, it can take a lot of high heat, making it great on a wood-fired grill, but it also cooks up with an exceptional crust in a pan. One flat iron is usually enough to feed three, or even four, people, especially if you've got a number of tasty side dishes.

Skirt

The skirt is one of the most confusing steaks of all because it's not actually singular. There are two skirts, and they're different. The inside skirt is called that because it lies inside the body cavity, where its job is to compress the abdomen. The outside skirt is attached to the diaphragm, which it moves. Both are long, thin, and ribbon-like, with the inside skirt being about 30 percent wider. "Any of those diaphragm muscles do work," Bryan explains. "They expand and contract millions and millions of times [over the life of the animal]. That's how they get flavor."

But the two skirts are not created equal. "Of the two skirts on the carcass, the outside is the one you want," says Bryan. "It's much more tender than the inside." Both have flavor, but the outside skirt, in addition to being more tender, has even more flavor. Although these are usually very cheap cuts, the outside skirt of a cow that's been raised well can have significant marbling.

Best way to cook • Best used for fajitas or stir-fries, the inside skirt inevitably needs marinating or some other form of tenderization (pounding, perhaps) to make it easier to eat. At Salt & Time, after marinating, the inside skirt often gets rolled into a pinwheel, tied with a string, and sold as spiral rounds, which can be cooked like steaks, but "only if it's high-quality meat," cautions Bryan. "Also, it should get some mechanical tenderizing, lots actually—like a mallet or meat tenderizer device. Most skirts sold at grocery stores come tenderized already. [And] a good marinade with high acid helps." After cooking the pinwheel, just unwind the meat and cut it into thin, easily chewable slices (though the meat

Skirt

will still be chewy). The outside skirt, if it is high quality, doesn't need special treatment. It can be cooked simply as a steak, though it shows best when cooked medium-rare to medium on the grill.

Flank

Another flat, broad steak, the flank comes from the belly of the animal, where, as part of the abdomen, it does quite a bit of work. "Flank steak can be tough," says Bryan, "but if you get a good marbled one, it's delicious." The flank is notable for the distinctly coarse grain running down its length. Judge a good one by looking for telltale white marbling generously dispersed through the grain. Although it can be tough, the flank's got good flavor, and precise cooking makes it extremely easy to eat. If it's lean or tough, just slice it more thinly than you normally would for serving.

Best way to cook • The flank's big flavor and obvious grain take especially well to grilling, as the licks of fire and smoke penetrate into the heart of the meat. As long as you don't cook it past medium-rare, it's rewarding. Flank steaks are cheap and great for parties, as they cook quickly and consistently. Just don't forget to slice them thinly for serving—and only across the grain.

Tri-Tip

Some may debate whether the thick, dense tri-tip is fairly dubbed a steak, as it takes quite a while to cook, sort of like an outdoor roast (and it's almost always cooked out-doors). But conventional wisdom generally hails this large piece as a steak because you can cook the whole thing slowly over direct

Flank

heat. "Underrated," says Bryan. "It's a hybrid between a steak and a roast."

The tri-tip is so called because of its somewhat triangular shape, though it also looks a bit like that arrowhead-shaped Star Fleet insignia from *Star Trek*. The muscle is right in between the bavette and the ball-tip roast in the lower sirloin of the cow, so it's thicker than most steaks and usually very lean, requiring careful cooking. The cut became popular in the 1950s in California, the state with which it's still most closely associated, and it's the signature of Santa Maria (a town on California's Central Coast) "barbecue." Barbecue is in quotation marks here because Santa Maria style calls for cooking the tri-tip on big grills that can be hoisted up and down over a coal bed to adjust heat exposure, rather than slow smoking over many hours. The meat is usually rubbed with some sort of spice mixture. While it's a big, heavy cut, resist the urge to divide a whole tri-tip into smaller pieces. It cooks most easily as a whole, so just plan to feed six to eight people with a good-size one.

Best way to cook • The reason Santa Maria cooks use a height-adjustable grill for the tri-tip is because it should not be cooked too fast. You have to go fairly slowly to give the outside heat time to penetrate to the middle of the steak. Reverse searing (see page 165) works well. The grain of the meat shifts a little across the steak, so pay attention when slicing and shift directions along with the meat to ensure you slice against the grain.

Tri-tip

If you go into a butchery in France or into, say, the shop of a good French butcher in America, such as Olivier's in San Francisco, you may see a number of little steaks you've never seen before. At Olivier's, odd muscles that hang from the racks in the back of the cooler are offered at inexpensive prices. These cuts symbolize the stylistic differences between French-style and American-style butchery.

If you wanted to boil it down to its essence, the classic American way is to use a band saw and the European way, also known as "seam butchery," is to use a number of different knives. The American method prizes efficiency and speed but is cruder. The approach is to slice through whole clusters of muscles in one cut, with each muscle separated by fascia. The result is a hodgepodge of different muscles and a lot of gristle. For instance, "Americans will render a square chuck," says Bryan, referring to the act of cutting out a big, cube-shaped hunk of the one-hundred-pound shoulder clod (chuck) regardless of individual muscles. "This cuts through the flat iron, cuts through the mock tender, cuts through the clod and the chuck eye." In contrast, he says, "The French tradition maximizes the profit by separating each individual muscle—tracing the seams and membranes. For butchers, it's a point of pride to be able to pull these muscles cleanly, follow the seam, and not cut into the muscle."

One of the challenges of seam butchery, of course, is that butchers end up with all of these very small, obscure micromuscles—such as the *gousse d'ail* (garlic clove), *l'araignée* (spider), *poire* (pear), *surprise*, and *merlan* that hang at Olivier's—that are hard to put on a restaurant menu because you're only going to get one or two per side and each one is only an ounce or two of meat. Ben Runkle points out that the cruder American method of just breaking down the side of beef into larger chunks while paying no heed to individual muscles is probably a reflection of burger and fast-food culture. "If you're grinding most of it up, why spend the time to isolate individual muscles?"

At Salt & Time or Olivier's or any good butcher shop, the approach is usually seam butchery. "Our philosophy is that we don't want to grind up good cuts into ground beef," Ben says. "And we don't need to, because as skilled butchers, we end up with enough trim. If you're fabricating beautiful steaks, you're going to end up with a couple of pounds of trim for every ten pounds of steak. But if you're selling how many billions of burgers, you need a lot of ground beef."

Some of Our Favorite Cooking Approaches

In part 3, we'll dive deep into the mechanics of how to cook a steak perfectly. There is, of course, no single path to perfection, and no one way to cook a steak. But now that you have a sense of all of the different cuts out there, we want to get you thinking about some nice ways to cook each of them. Again, this is not meant to be the final word for any of these cuts. They are just some approaches that have served us well in the past.

CUT	IDEAS FOR HOW TO COOK
Bone-in ribeye	While good in a pan, it's always better on the fire, which doesn't need to be too scorching, as a thick-cut bone-in ribeye needs time to cook the interior to medium-rare. That bone holds the thing together, and if it's long like a tomahawk cut, it gives the option of using it like a handle if you want it to go right onto the coals.
Boneless ribeye	Boneless ribeyes are great for the pan. Without the bone to hold the different muscle groups together, these steaks can get floppy on the grill and leak fat into the fire, creating flare-ups. In the pan, they develop a perfect crust, too. Plus, they're delicious all the way from rare through to medium.
T-bone	Thin-cut weekday steaks work great in a hot pan, as they take just a few minutes to cook. But a searing fire gives a great crust and keeps the interior pink.
Porterhouse	The bone-in wonder steak, the porterhouse is meant for the grill. Cook the fillet side to medium-rare and the sirloin side will be fine. Remember, the meat near the bone will be a little rarer in order for the center of each side to be perfect, but that's part of the pleasure.
Tenderloin	The tenderloin likes to be babied in a pan over medium heat, with a good dose of butter in the pan to add back a little of the fat that's inherently missing from the cut. Tenderloins are best on the rare side of medium-rare, as the meat is so silky.
Strip	All-around crowd-pleasers, strips (whether you call 'em New York or Kansas City) are especially good on the grill, as their deep beefy flavor loves a dash of wood smoke. Always aim for medium-rare on this one.

CUT	IDEAS FOR HOW TO COOK
Hanger	The hanger delivers big flavor from a big muscle that runs close to the internal organs. Pan cooking tends to take too long and can result in stringy meat if the water can't escape fast enough. It is best on a hot grill, cooked to solid medium-rare. Too rare and it's tough.
Bavette	Works in a pan, but is better on the drier environment of the grill. The open grain releases a lot of water, which can cause steaming in the pan, making it hard to form a thick crust. On the grill, you get a great crust. Cook to solid medium-rare.
Flat iron	Great on the grill or in a pan, and forgiving on either side of medium-rare. The flavor really comes out in the cooking, though, so don't go too rare.
Skirt	Inside skirts need marinating or tenderizing and are best cut thinly for fajitas or stir-fries. Outside skirts have excellent flavor and can be cooked fast as a steak but still like marinades. Best cooked superfast on the grill.
Flank	Great, inexpensive cut with lots of flavor. Won't wow you with tenderness, but loves some smoke from the grill. Don't overcook or it's too tender. Just fast sear it to medium-rare.

Part II

NEXT-
LEVEL
BEEF

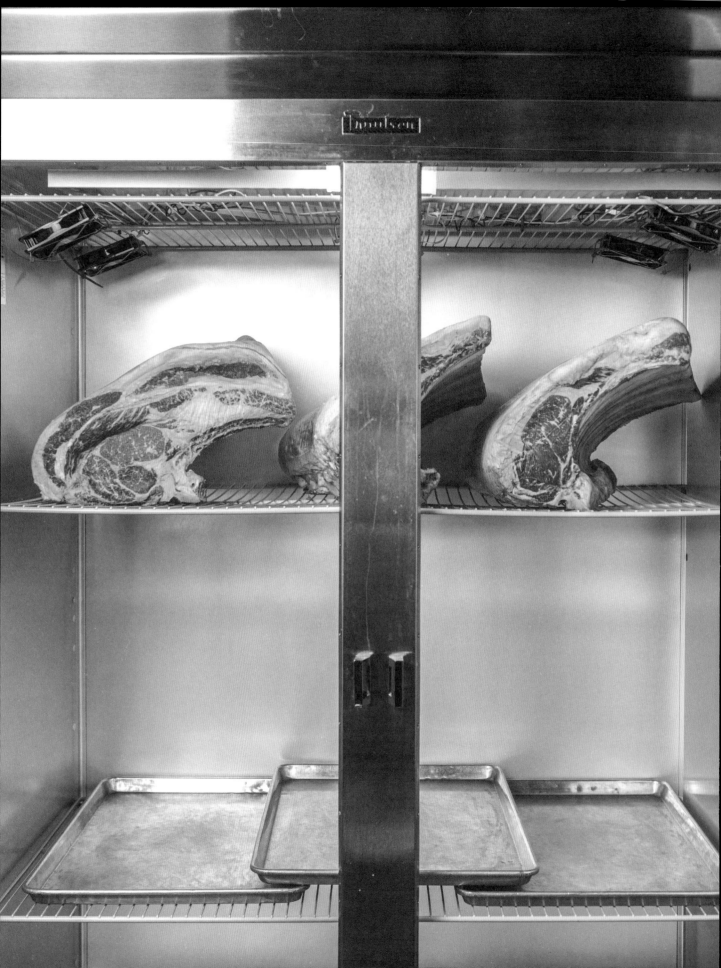

CHAPTER 4

Dry Aging

The term "old meat" does not sound appetizing. But "dry-aged meat"? Well, that's different. Now we're in the realm of finely aged wine or a cheese served at the peak of ripeness.

No bigger trend exists in steak these days than dry aging. What used to be a rare, dark art has now become a mainstream dark art. What used to be a rumored delicacy and difficult-to-find product has become popular—and by consequence less difficult to find. And its popularity is no surprise. When you can transform an ordinary, delicious piece of steak into something that retains all original deliciousness but becomes even more tender, more complex, more savory, why wouldn't you do it?

Aaron had his eyes opened to the wonders of dry-aged steak a few years ago at John Tesar's Dallas restaurant Knife (see page 84). Tesar gave Aaron a tasting that ranged from a 45-day steak all the way to over 200 days. Man, that was some beefy, beefy beef. He'd never had anything like it. Some of the older stuff was almost too funky and intense, but the midrange had just the right amount of gaminess. Jordan's first memorable encounter came in Spain, where a 120-day dry-aged rib cut blew him away (see page 62). Afterward, he had to find more beef like that. Years later, he can still remember the taste.

Because finding great dry-aged beef isn't always easy, in this chapter, we're going to tell you exactly how and why it works and how to do it. Neither of us had any experience aging steak before writing this book, but lots of conversation and advice from friends showed that it's definitely something you can do at home. But before we get into that, we want to offer a few words on the differences between "old meat" and dry-aged majesty from someone who knows.

"I inherited a dry-age program at this facility from the people we bought it from," says John Kosmidis, chief operating officer of Prime Foods Distributor, an important New York–based beef supplier to such esteemed steak houses as the high-end chain Smith & Wollensky. "Our predecessors had built a new establishment for dry aging with all the modern tools. But although they had a successful business and were highly regarded for their dry-age program, when we took over, I and my partners hated it. We thought the beef was terrible. We would look at each other and say, 'Is everyone here brainwashed?'"

Kosmidis and his partners realized the answer was yes. "The brainwashing had gone up the chain from the producers to the processors to the further processors to Michelin-starred chefs to the media to the end consumer," he says. "Everybody accepted something that if found in any other product would get you fired. But if you put it [spoilage] on the beef, it was prime dry-aged product. We thought that was so wrong."

What Kosmidis is describing happened several years ago, when he and his partners founded the business. But it also describes something about dry-aged beef. If it doesn't taste good to you, something is probably wrong. The tolerance for dry-aged chicanery in this world is great, as beef can get weird if it's not properly aged. People might eat it anyway, find it off or too funky, and then say they don't like dry-aged beef. Kosmidis sees this as the result of bad and irresponsible practices. "Other packers post photos of their dry-aging rooms [on social media], and we just shake our heads," says Kosmidis. "They have meat piled up on meat, on racks that obviously haven't been cleaned or moved in years, [and] there's no air circulation. If you have mold growing because of bad conditions, your beef will be different colors. It can have purple, yellow, green, peach fuzz and hair. It's not aging. It's rotting."

Kosmidis et al. decided to fix the situation. But for the art of dry aging, there's no manual, no textbook, not even any real experts or scientists. You can't just hire a dry-aging wizard from the Internet to come in and fix your program. You have to start from the ground up. Over the next few years, the group revamped their procedure time and time again, spending millions in the process. They learned they had to pay attention not only to their aging conditions but also to their suppliers: how the meat was brought to them (full carcass or Cryovaced), how it was

1680 Vine Street
Los Angeles, California
tel: (323) 416-1280 • aplrestaurant.com

Nothing made us happier than the 2018 opening of Adam Perry Lang's long-awaited, long-toiled-over Hollywood steak house APL. No other accomplished American chef has ever been as associated with steak as Lang. Along with a Michelin three-star background at Guy Savoy in Paris and Daniel in New York and some respectable barbecue chops (Aaron has made custom smokers for him), Adam has serious steak credentials. More than anyone, he's responsible for the surge of dry aging across the country, an art form he mastered at programs he created at Robert's in New York and Carnevino in Las Vegas.

His beautiful new restaurant at the corner of Hollywood and Vine fulfills the dream of doing it for himself. The achievement here is purity: incredible steaks, done simply and perfectly. To that end, Lang is involved in every step of the process. He built a one-thousand-square-foot dry-aging room under the restaurant and tracks all of the meat himself. Everything is butchered on the premises (at the time of writing, by Lang himself) and cooked in a high-powered broiler. Every aspect of the experience has been considered, down to the steak knives, which Lang makes himself, having learned to forge and shape steel for this purpose (the knives are listed at nine hundred fifty dollars on the menu, the lowest cost of a felony in California; he's serious about people not stealing them).

The menu is impressively simple: dry-aged steaks with a couple of sauces, as well as some classic sides, a lovely fish selection, a few pastas, and some starters. It's rather minimalist, putting all of the focus back on the quality of the meat, which is impressive. The aging is done just long enough to create that savory, funky bite, but never gets in the way of the carefully sourced, deeply beefy steak.

5300 E. Mockingbird Lane
Dallas, Texas
tel: (214) 443-9339 • knifedallas.com

In his previous incarnation at Spoon, chef John Tesar was known for fish. That makes his reinvention as a master of meat all the more remarkable, especially because in no time his steak became some of the very best in the country. Tesar is known as a skilled technician who can cook anything, so his touch with simple, dumb steak is impressive. Here, it's really the quality of the beef he chooses and the flavors he coaxes out of his dry-aging room that make eating steak at Knife worth a diversion.

The lengthy, diverse menu is well executed across the board (don't skip the bacon-crusted bone marrow and caviar), but the steak menu—divided into New School, Old School, and Exotic—is the place to mine. The New School category lists such butcher's cuts as the flat iron, culotte (sirloin cap), and skirt, all grilled over red oak. These all come from 44 Farms, an Angus ranch between Dallas and Austin that serves as Tesar's main supplier and muse. Old School cuts include ribeye, filet mignon, and such. The Exotic menu comes from the dry-aging room and features 240-day and 110-day steaks, among others. Tesar has become known for pushing the dry aging to new distances, and sometimes he'll have the odd 360-day pieces back there. Meat sources in the aging cellar also include HeartBrand and Creekstone. A variety of sauces—béarnaise, au poivre, Bordelaise, *chimichurri*, and *salsa verde*—are available on request.

fabricated, how long since its slaughter date. They learned they had to pay attention to their refrigerated rooms: how much new meat was going into the same room as meat that had been there for a week or two. They had to clean. They had to have air circulation and rotate the meats. "It was the school of hard knocks," Kosmidis says. "Trial and error. We took notes. We learned from our mistakes and paid for all of them." But today, their steaks set the standard for dry-aged perfection.

Nowadays, Prime Foods keeps something like seven thousand subprimals of beef in its massive aging program. To be that large and precise is an achievement, and the lessons are well learned. And it turns out that all of the professionals who are dry aging meat for sale to customers or at their restaurants voiced the same refrain as Kosmidis: you have to learn by doing.

"We're still learning as we go along," says Bryan Flannery, who runs the famed Flannery Beef with his daughter, Katie, in Northern California (see page 33). "We've got a system we like right now, but it's changed over the years as we've grown and changed and learned more about the aging process." For the Flannerys, getting enough air movement and making sure it was reaching every corner of their dry-aging room was key.

"You've got to figure out what works for you," adds chef Adam Perry Lang, the reigning king of restaurant dry aging, from the vast room underneath his new APL Restaurant in Hollywood (see page 83). Lang can largely be credited for popularizing (or repopularizing—after all, hanging beef for tenderization has been around for centuries) the dry-aging trend, as he's done in New York, Las Vegas, and now at APL, his signature, personal spot. "There's no manual for this. No teacher," he continues. "But when

you determine what you like in an aged piece of beef, it just takes time and experimentation to learn how to make it happen."

That's true in the restaurant and commercial realm, but it's also possible in the home. It's an undertaking, to be sure, but if you're a serious and passionate steak lover with a little extra room in your place, it might be worthwhile.

What Is Dry Aging?

Dry aging is a complex but natural process that's essentially an early-stage degradation of meat in which chemical processes alter its fundamental nature, making it more tender and more flavorful. As great food scientist and writer Harold McGee wrote in an essay in the bygone food journal *Lucky Peach* (issue #2), raw meats don't have much flavor in their natural state, which is why we cook, season, and transform them.

"But sometimes we can get our food to make itself more delicious," he says, "by treating it in a way that creates favorable conditions for the enzymes that are already in the food to work together in a certain fashion. Enzymes are molecules that exist in foods—and in microbes intimately involved with food—that can transform those basic, bland building blocks. They're nanocooks—the true molecular cooks. Dry aging, ripening, and fermentation are all processes that take advantage of enzymes to make foods delicious before cooking."

Every meat ages, but none quite as well as beef. As *Modernist Cuisine*, the incredible multivolume tome on the science of cooking, explains, "For reasons having to do with the relative activity of enzymes in different muscle-fiber types, red meat generally matures more slowly than white meat. Large animals require more time than smaller animals. And meat from younger animals ages faster than the meat of their more mature kin." Fish see almost no benefit from aging, chickens for only a handful of days, and pork and lamb for a week or so. But beef? Beef needs two or three weeks to tenderize properly. Flavor development usually starts at anywhere from twenty-eight to forty-five days and can be taken into the hundreds of days.

This process has been around for centuries and likely longer, as there's a thin line between intentionally aging meat and just trying to keep it from spoiling until your clan can finish it all. Of course, people have known how to preserve meat with smoke and salt for tens of thousands of years. But in the nineteenth century, McGee writes, beef and lamb would be hung at room temperature until the exterior flesh actually rotted. This result was desirable, probably because of the gains in tenderization and flavor, but also for matters of practicality, as the lack of refrigeration meant that a side of beef simply aged until it was fully consumed. Of course, we don't desire rot today, but by controlling the simple variables of time, temperature, humidity, and airflow, we can guide the aging process to transform meat into something truly stupendous.

So what's going on here? After slaughter, naturally occurring enzymes in the meat go to work. When the animal was alive, those enzymes were controlled by the living cells. But after the cells die, the enzymes are uninhibited and go to work on other compounds in the organism. They break down larger, flavorless molecules and chop them into smaller bits we can taste. In particular, they start to chop up fats, proteins, and a carbohydrate called glycogen into sugars, amino acids, and fatty acids. One of those

amino acids rendered is glutamate, aka umami. And umami is, well, everything—or at least a primary reason savory things are so delicious.

Dry aging also forces beef to lose moisture. It's not much but significant, as the remaining juices and tissue become more concentrated. Evaporation further concentrates the newly created enzymatic sugars and umami-boosting protein compounds. It makes beef beefier and, on cooking, creates even greater Maillardian cascades (remember, Maillard is the set of reactions that occur when the surface of the meat is browned during cooking). It's an orgy of flavor, thanks to microbes that have been let off the leash.

WET AGING? MEH . . .

Inevitably, all the talk of dry aging brings up the topic of wet aging. This is when beef is Cryovaced and kept in the plastic bag for a few weeks, sitting in its own juices. Some people claim it is not only as effective but also more efficient than dry aging. After all, if it's the enzymes that are acting, can't they do so in a bag without any of the moisture loss that occurs during dry aging? The answer is yes, and it turns out that wet aging in a sealed bag does yield the same gains in tenderizing after about fourteen days. However, there appear to be no attendant flavor gains. In fact, after more than about four weeks maximum, research has shown tasters find wet-aged meat to be "flat" and "metallic." Indeed, dry aging in a windblown cellar seems vaguely healthful. Who would want to be smothered in a wet plastic bag for weeks?

The other great benefit of aging is tenderization. A couple of enzymes called calpains and cathepsins sever the bonds in certain proteins, weakening connective tissues and reducing pressure, resulting in more tender, silky meat that's also juicier because the relaxed meat has squeezed out less moisture during cooking. It's a win, win, win—more flavorful, more complex, more tender.

The Challenges of Aging Beef

So if aging beef is so great, why isn't everyone doing it all the time? There are a number of factors. On the commercial scale, dry aging takes time. And time equals money. If you have to lay out a lot of cash for beef you're not going to sell for weeks or months, you're taking on a big negative on your books for a significant amount of time, not to mention running an aging cellar requires space (additional rent), climate control (higher bills), and attendance (more labor costs). There's also risk. What if something goes wrong? It could mean tens of thousands of dollars or more in losses. As long as people aren't demanding it, as long as they're satisfied with a simple, conventional unaged steak, why bother?

For the home dry ager—which you could become—the challenges are analogous. You need room for an extra refrigerator and to be able to afford the bills of running it full time. You need humidity gauges and wind-force producers to have the confidence that the meat is not going bad on you. You need to have a source where you can buy a large subprimal of meat. And most of all, you need patience.

How and Why to Age Beef at Home

Despite all the previous talk about the dry-aging school of hard knocks, it's not that hard to age beef at home. And indeed, if you're a steak lover, eat it regularly, and have a spacious abode, all the reasons in the world implore you to do this. After all, in most places, it's difficult if not impossible to buy dry-aged meat to cook at home. Restaurants may have it, but they don't sell at retail. And if you can find such places, dry-aged meat is expensive—not just the meat but also the shipping if it's coming from a seller outside of your area. That said, dry aging beef is a commitment, so you have to really want it. On the other hand, as complicated and edgy as dry aging sounds—it's really neither.

1. CREATE A DRY-AGING FRIDGE AND TRICK IT OUT

Beef aging can only occur in a highly controlled environment, which means temperature control is imperative. Maintaining a sufficiently low temperature without freezing is what decides the difference between aging and rotting. It's the low temperature that keeps the spoilage bacteria at bay while allowing the enzymes to do their work. If there's too much heat and moisture, the bacteria go crazy, and you've got a big hunk of rotting meat on your hands. A proper aging fridge should give you at least two feet across, though three feet is better, and about five feet of height, enough for two or three separate racks. The point of having a large enough fridge is that if you're going to age large subprimals (big pieces of meat containing several steaks that you'll slice off yourself), you need to have a couple going at any one time so you don't run out and have to start from scratch and wait

months every time you want an aged steak. Also, this is not a fridge into which you're going to throw some extra bunches of celery and leftover risotto. If you want to be serious about dry aging, only beef goes in here.

Any sort of fridge will work as long as its reliable and has adjustable racks. Commercial refrigerators with glass doors are cool because you can see the meat transform (in slow motion) before your very eyes. But it's certainly not necessary. Aaron bought a Traulsen two-door fridge from a restaurant supply store (he needed it anyway) and put it in his home garage (with plans to move it to a new facility later). But you don't necessarily need restaurant-grade equipment. A good-quality used fridge purchased on craigslist will do the trick as long as it's consistent and reliable. Whatever you buy, after you get it home, thoroughly scrub down the interior with water and bleach to disinfect it. Once the whole thing—top, bottom, sides, and racks—is wiped down, it's fine to start decking it out.

2. BUY SOME FANS

Besides the proper-size fridge itself, you need to account for humidity and airflow. Of the two, airflow is the more important. Without constant air movement, the air stagnates and moisture hovers, creating a ripe environment for bacteria and mold to propagate. They love a moist and somewhat warm environment. As you dry out that exterior layer of beef, it forms a bulwark, preventing the interior from losing moisture. So air movement is a hero: it stifles bad bacterial growth and protects the juicy interior of the steak.

You'll need at least one fan, but two or more are better. As Kosmidis said about his professional dry-aging cellar, "Every piece of meat is getting

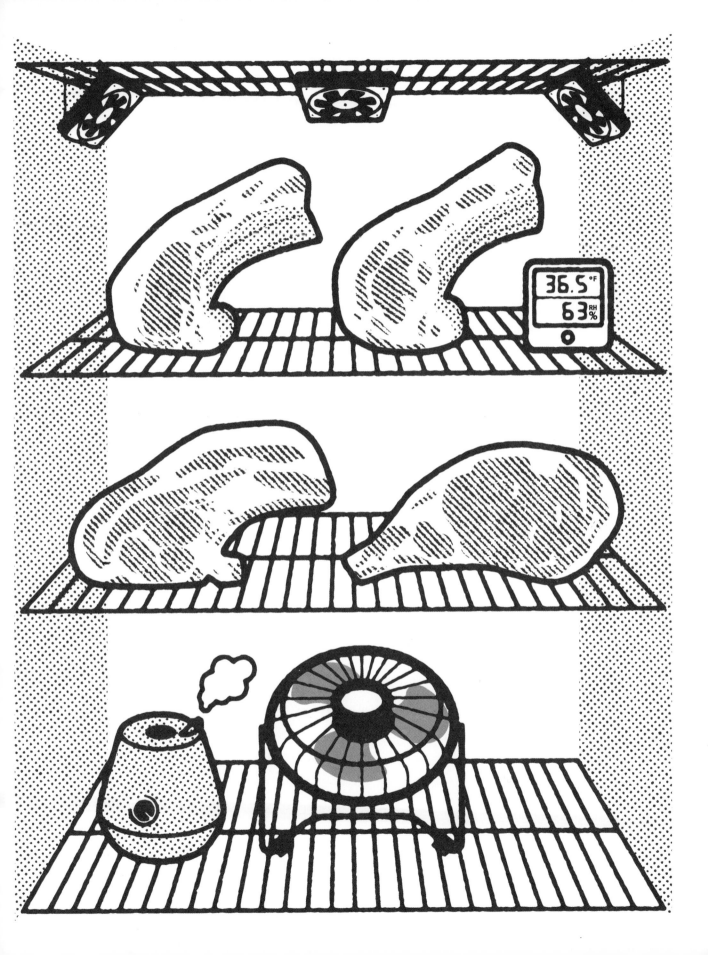

hit by air from at least eight different directions." That's overkill for the home setup, but good circulation is key, not unlike the dynamics inside a barbecue smoker. To get maximum air movement in a small space, Aaron set up several small but powerful fans to create an array. He bought a few small twelve-volt CPU cooling fans at a computer store, wired them in parallel, connected them to a power source, and then hung them from wires at the top of the refrigerator. But now he says that was overkill and he wouldn't bother going to that much trouble again. It's cheaper and easier just to get two or three small Vornado or other desk or room fans and point them from different directions at the meat. The result is a swirling chaos of air that ensures moisture is swept away. Professionals talk about necessary wind velocity in measurements of linear feet per second, but without getting so geeky, this setup has worked well for meat that's been steadily aging for months.

3. HUMIDITY AND TEMPERATURE

Humidity is a concern in dry aging, though it is not as big a deal for the home dry ager as for the people working on a commercial scale. The crucial aspect of humidity is making sure it's not too high. Too moist an environment and bacteria will grow, so drier is better. But the drier it is, the more moisture evaporates from the meat, causing the meat to lose weight. Indeed, after a standard forty-five to sixty days of dry aging, a rib rack of beef can lose up to 30 percent of its weight in water. So large meat packers—people who sell meat by the pound—typically like to keep the humidity as high as possible to retain water weight without courting microbes.

For those interested foremost in quality, however, that shouldn't be a concern. Kosmidis

says, "We experimented constantly. At first, we were at high humidity, around 80 percent. In the beginning, we accepted the thinking that if you're dry aging, your first priority should not be to minimize your yield loss but to produce a proper product regardless of loss."

The figures generally cited as necessary for maintaining a safe environment are 70 to 80 percent humidity. If you have a restaurant with a giant room full of aging meat with fresh, wet meat being introduced on a weekly basis, managing humidity to maintain sterile levels becomes more of a challenge. But in a typical refrigerator, staying below 80 percent humidity is not a problem.

Home refrigerators are programmed to be dry: to condense humidity and then dispose of the water periodically. This is because the frequent opening of a refrigerator door introduces humidity into the environment, which makes fridges less efficient because it takes more energy to cool humid air. That means if you have a fridge dedicated to meat aging and you're rarely opening the door, it's going to dry out in there, to the tune of humidity levels in the 30 percent range.

Very low humidity doesn't appear to be a severe problem in aging meat. You might think that low humidity will cause the meat to eventually shrivel up and dry out, but luckily it doesn't seem to work that way—at least not over the few weeks or months most people will age their meat. Rather, and amazingly, dry-aged meat is usually quite juicy. Scientists debate why this is so, but some have referred to the exterior drying of the meat as basically closing off the channels through which water contacts the air, sealing moisture in.

Temperature in a refrigerator generally takes care of itself. Standard temperatures for aging beef run between 34°F and 39°F. This is generally easy to maintain, especially if you keep the door closed all the time.

Aaron added a humidifier to keep his dry-aging fridge from getting too dry and set the temperature at 38°F. He also added a basic sensor, easily purchased at any hardware store, to monitor the humidity and temperature. After just a few days, the rig stabilized in a range at which it seems comfortable: 36°F to 38°F and 60 to 64 percent humidity. The beef happily aged for months.

4. BUY SOME BIG HUNKS OF MEAT

Aging individual steaks doesn't work. Sure, you can let them sit out in the refrigerator for a few days, but these loners will dry out before any of the significant chemical changes from aging take place. If you left that steak in the fridge for, say, twenty-eight days, by the time you trimmed off the rock-hard, dried outer shell, you'd have nothing left to cook. Thus, aging has to be done on bigger pieces, large enough that you can trim off that crusty pellicle and still have plenty of delicious, juicy meat. So what cuts, er, make the cut?

First of all, you want well-marbled cuts with bones and fat caps, so this factors out most steak cuts. Pieces like skirt, flank, bavette, and even tenderloin are all too small and lack bones and much exterior fat. Also, you want high-quality meat that has been handled well since it was fabricated (the meat industry's term for cut). It should be fresh, pristine meat that hasn't been punctured or opened up in any way. This all ensures the integrity of the interior of the meat, as the exterior pellicle that develops during dry aging will all be trimmed away.

Bones and fat caps are essential for a few reasons. First and foremost is that they lie on the exterior and protect the meat. As the enzymatic aging occurs within the meat, these components are slowing the loss of moisture from the exterior. But there's also a flavor component to the fat.

A good deal of that "funk" people love about dry-aged meat, that somewhat gamy, mushroomy, cheesy, nutty aroma that layers on the irresistible umami, is dependent on fat. As *Modernist Cuisine* notes, "The oxidation of fat and other susceptible molecules also contributes to the aroma of dry-aged meat. In the case of meats high in saturated fats, beef being the prime example, the aroma can be pleasantly nutty, with mild cheesy notes. Indeed, it is the combination of concentration and oxidation that further enhances the flavor of meat as it continues to dry age beyond the point at which enzymatic tenderization has come to a halt."

The upshot of this is that tenderizing is accomplished within about two weeks. Further aging is for flavor, and a healthy fat cap and lots of marbling provide that. The most profound expressions of the aged flavor occur on the perimeter of the steak; the interior will taste less intense. Perhaps this is because the interior meat isn't exposed to oxygen and thus the fat doesn't oxidize. But it does mean that as much of the outer part of the steak as possible should be left on while cooking. You may take off most of the fat cap, but consider leaving on some of the fatty scraps. And definitely keep the bone. All of these parts—especially the rib-cap muscle, or *spinalis dorsi*, which takes on the most intense aged flavor of any part—will contribute flavor and aroma to the final, delicious steak.

So with their processing numbers and a brief description, here are the large cuts that offer

Long bone 103 rib

maximum efficiency, return, and character for dry aging.

- First, you can do an entire **rib primal**, known affectionately as a **103**. It's the works: ribs six through twelve, with chine and blade bones intact, covered with a fat cap and "lifter" meat (the latter, also known as blade meat, is made up of thin muscles, often removed, that line the extended rib bones). The 103 is what you see in the home aging fridge in Austin (pictured on page 80). Its cousin, the long bone 103 rib, is pictured at left. It meets all the criteria but is incredibly heavy and unwieldy—not an easy carry from the fridge to the countertop. Also, when it comes time to cut steaks off of it, cutting through the chine is a lot of work.

- The **107** is a smaller version of the 103, with blade and chine bone removed and rib bones shortened; everything else is intact.

- The **109A** has even more rib bone removed as well as some of the exterior "lifter" meat that's always removed on ribeye steaks, making it a nice and tidy package. This is an excellent cut to age because the bone and fat cap protect the meat during drying.

- The **109 Export** is similar to the 109A, but the fat cap is removed. Along with the 109A, this is the easiest big rib cut to age because of its size and ease of handling. However, the missing fat cap is a downside, as the fat protects the outer layer of meat, which in this case is the precious *spinalis*. Without the fat, the *spinalis* will dry out.

- The **112A** is a boneless rib roast and will still age well, but it's better with the bone. If you have less space and aren't planning to age for too long, the smaller package of the 112A can be handy. But in general and for longer aging, you want to age on the bone, as it protects the meat from moisture loss.

- The **loin primal** ages well, too. Remember, this is the area that has both the tenderloin and the strip loin on either side of the T-bone. In this case, most people age only the strip, as it is better marbled than the tenderloin and thus develops more flavor. Recommended for aging are the **175**, which is the bone-in strip loin, and the **180**, which is boneless. Again, if you have the choice, go bone in.

When it comes to sourcing your meat this should be obvious: try not to buy anything that's been previously frozen. If you have the ability to procure primals and subprimals that haven't been Cryovaced, do that, as the freshness of the beef is an asset. However, if the meat's been in plastic for just a short time, it's okay. What you want to avoid is meat that has wet aged for more than a week or so, as the degradation that occurred inside the plastic doesn't translate well to the dry-aging environment. The meat will tend to dry out without much flavor development. The way to source these cuts is by talking to a butcher at a specialized shop or a good grocery store. These large cuts won't be offered at the counter, but the butcher should be happy to get them for you from his or her supplier or at least connect you directly to the supplier.

5. STORE YOUR MEAT

When you put the beef in the dry-aging refrigerator, make sure it sits on standard wire shelves (as in Metro shelves) that allow air to pass through them. Remember, the idea is for air to be blowing on all sides of the meat at all times. Make sure there's five or six inches between cuts of meat, as the evaporating water needs some place to go and fresh air needs to circulate freely around the cuts. Every week or so, shift the angle or position of the meat just to even things out.

6. WAIT AND MONITOR YOUR PROGRESS

Okay, you have your fridge plugged in and chilling. You've set up an array of three or more fans and have cold air blowing like mad throughout the fridge. You've purchased your beef and placed it on one or more shelves in the fridge. What's next? Now is the easy part: you just wait. But for how long?

How long you age your beef is entirely up to you. But here's a handy guide to the general cutoffs. Remember, every animal is different, however, so every piece of meat is different. Also, differences in temperature and humidity can have a profound effect on the rate of these chemical transformations. There is no precise accounting for any of this. And even if you're getting a piece of meat cut from a fresh carcass that has never seen the inside of a bag, the likelihood is that the meat is already at least a week old. Cooling, processing, and transportation all take a certain amount of time, so it's almost surely not "fresh" meat that you're getting.

In the first 14 days of aging, you'll start to experience tenderization of the meat, but no flavor change. From 14 to 21 days, the meat will continue to tenderize, but that process should technically end around the three-week mark. From 21 to 28 days, you may get the first hint of an evolution of flavor, though not much. The advent of that dry-aging funk only starts to kick in after 28 days, when it should become noticeable the moment you open the fridge door and take a whiff. Flavor development will continue indefinitely and then becomes a matter of taste. At 45 days, you might get that telltale whiff of blue cheese that some people talk about, though in our experience, it's more of a gamy, mushroomy quality. Many people consider 45 days of aging a sweet spot; some

people think of it as just the beginning. It's not unusual to find meat sellers taking steaks to 60, or even 90, days. You can expect quite a bit of funk after 90 days. And flavor keeps developing, albeit more slowly. Nowadays, chefs are taking aging to ever more distant extremes, up to 220 or 360 days—and sometimes up to 400 days. A butcher in Paris even sells vintage steaks that are over a decade old, though it sounds like he uses a special freezing technique (ice-cold air is blown at high velocity over the meat), so it's not quite the same.

In general, you may have diminishing returns from aging more than 60 to 90 days, and we don't recommend going beyond that. The meat will just dry out and become hard and crusty. You'll have to cut the dried parts off, as they become basically petrified and harder to eat. Over time, that dried pellicle will simply increase and you'll lose more and more meat. At 60 days you can have both great flavor and great tenderness.

7. FINISHING

Whew, you've made it to the end of your journey and successfully aged a large chunk of beef. It smells funky-delicious, and the exterior meat has dried and turned a glorious color of dark reddish brown. Now it's time to slice off a couple of steaks to taste the results.

Pull the big piece from the fridge and set it on a clean cutting surface. Have a very sharp slicing knife handy. If there's any bone like the chine (spine) bone on your piece, also have ready a saw—we recommend the twenty-two-inch Weston butcher saw—as you can't slice through a heavy beef bone with a knife. Then decide how thick you want your steaks and slice them off cleanly. It's all basic, no matter what subprimal you're using. Just visualize the kind of steak you want and cut through the bone. Now, if there's still a lot of meat left on the piece, it can be returned to the refrigerator to continue aging. Or you can just plan to consume the rest over the next week, keeping it in your kitchen fridge.

After you've got the steaks, you'll want to clean them up a by removing the hardened exterior crust. Do this carefully, and not too generously, as you want to keep as much good meat and fat as possible. If you cut too deeply into the steaks, you'll discover meat that's as bright and fresh and red as you'd find in a grocery store meat counter. Instead of going that far, just remove the driest bits, as the rest cooks beautifully, softening in the pan (or on the coals) as the fat around it melts and wets it. These will be some of the tastiest, meatiest bites you'll have.

DON'T SCRAP THOSE SCRAPS!

After you've trimmed your steaks, you'll find a little pile of trimmings sitting on the cutting board. Given however many weeks you dedicated to aging the meat to perfection, don't you dare throw those bits away. That's valuable stuff right there! There are a number of things you can do with the scraps. For the fat, you can render it down into a liquid and baste or spray the meat with it during and after cooking, as you would with butter. This way, you're simply dressing this delectable meat with some of its most flavorful bits. Any shards of meat bark you slice off can be saved along with the bones and turned into deep, savory, rich stock, which could then be reduced again to make an aged-beef demi-glace for aged beef.

You can't talk dry aging without bringing up the subject of mold. A good cellar with great air movement and moderate humidity should grow little to no mold as the beef ages. However, for long periods, even at low temperatures and moderate humidity, some species of mold will eventually form on the exterior of the beef. Is it something to be afraid of?

In an email, Harold McGee agrees that the meat's own enzymes are key, but microbes play a role, too. "I do think that the changes in flavor and texture are mainly due to the meat's own chemistry," he writes, "but there is evidence from dry-cured hams that surface microbes can affect the external muscles. What we easily see is the molds, but there are yeasts and bacteria in there as well, and apparently their *Gemisch* of enzymes can penetrate to some extent. Of course, hams are aged for months to years, so that effect may not be relevant to dry-aged beef. . . . I haven't found any real research on this."

The most common molds are harmless and even beneficial. As a 2016 paper published in the *Journal of Animal Science Technology* noted, several molds can appear on the surface. "*Thamnidium,* which is the most desirable, appears as pale gray patches called 'whiskers' on the fatty parts of aged beef. These organisms are important because their enzymes are able to penetrate into the meat. In fact, *Thamnidium* releases proteases and creates collagenolytic enzymes which break down the muscle and connective tissues. As a result, these actions bring about tenderness and taste in the dry-aged beef."

In general, a little mold is natural and will get trimmed off before cooking. The dried crust of the meat protects the interior meat from mold-based spoilage. And beef will also usually be seared at a very high temperature for several minutes, making it difficult for any microbial life to survive. The mold in all the best dry-aging cellars we've seen has taken the shape of a sort of white film, similar to the mold you'll find on the exterior of a salami. It always gets trimmed off and the interior meat is fine.

Exterior mold is not usually dangerous. But if there are openings in the meat into which surface microbes could have entered and found a moist environment, throw away that piece. Likewise, if the beef has developed slime or off-colored molds or any sort of bad aroma, throw it away.

To try to preempt the mold question, some people have taken to introducing a tried and proven mold at the beginning through innoculation. Adam Perry Lang brought out some aged meat to inoculate his Las Vegas dry-aging room at Carnevino and then again when he built APL, his palace in Los Angeles. John Tesar got some scraps from Adam to inoculate his dry-aging room at Knife. Even so, Tesar's steaks taste different from Perry Lang's, suggesting that the source of the meat is far more important than whatever culture grows on the outside. But even cellar mold can have a proud provenance. To do this for your home dry-aging fridge, simply find your favorite dry ager of steak and ask for some scraps and fat trimmings. Take those scraps and leave them in your own fridge for a couple of weeks, then toss them. If it works, you'll have introduced a microbial culture that will thrive and take up residence. We didn't do this for our first dry-aging runs and the beef was fine. Indeed, it didn't develop much mold at all. But in future cycles, we're going to inoculate. After all, better the mold you know than the mold you don't.

CHAPTER 5

The Grill

There's a saying in the steak business: show me how you cook a steak, and I'll tell you who you are. Well, actually, there isn't. But there could be. How people like to cook their steaks is a very personal thing. And it is more than just about cast iron versus grill. Are you a techie or a Luddite? Do you like to tinker or do you like things neatly prepackaged for success? Are you a stickler for family tradition or a free DIY spirit? Steak tells all.

When it comes to cooking spaghetti or making an omelet, few options exist. But a steak, though a simple food, offers many ways to get it to the table, each with its own set of advantages and challenges. Steak eternally provokes curiosity. "How do you cook a steak?" is cocktail banter that rarely fails to incite discussion—at least in carnivore circles. And for those who care, the answers are always telling. Many folks just default to the old Weber grill on the back patio, while others throw a cast-iron pan into a super-heated oven to get it ready for a stove-top sear. Tech-minded people get out a plastic bag and start heating up a bin filled with water to sous vide the cuts.

And unlike noodles or omelets, with steak, each cooking method leaves an impression on the meat. A finished steak is as much a product of how it was cooked as what was cooked. And this is why it's a personal matter. As an expression, your steak-cooking rig is not unlike your car. Are you a hot rod or a Prius or a Mercedes SUV?

In this chapter, we're going to look at the various kinds of cookers and methods most commonly used today to get a steak from raw to medium-rare (hopefully) and offer some thoughts on each. Now, this book is mostly about cooking with fire, so we're going to focus on that. But we'd be remiss if we didn't mention other energy sources, like gas and electricity, before we get to wood and charcoal. And just maybe we can learn something about ourselves in the process.

Stove-Top Cooking: Indoor and Classic

The classic method will never go out of style, whether your stove is gas or electric (hopefully the former). With a good pan, this is one of the best techniques to get a thick and dense crust on the steak, which is always desirable. The magical browning potential of a cast-iron pan is only one of the attractions of stove-top cooking. The fact that it's an indoor method means you can do it any time, including in the middle of winter or at 2:00 a.m. if the craving for a late-night steak hits (as it does).

The drawbacks to this method are ancillary— more like inconveniences. For one, cooking a steak in hot fat for several minutes generates smoke, which, even when employing a consumer-grade stove hood, will fill a house or apartment with thick, gray clouds and likely set off the smoke alarm. This is something you don't want occurring at, say, 2:00 a.m., as happened to Jordan one night after the bars closed and he and a couple of friends found themselves at his house and hungry. His (formerly) sleeping wife, Christie, had some choice (or were they prime?) words after being piercingly jolted from sleep by an alarm to find a massively beefy cloud of smoke, a heavily steaky aroma (not her favorite), and a few drunk dudes.

Also, cooking this way generates a lot of sizzle, and it's common to find the stove and anything within a three-foot radius (and sometimes far beyond) of it splattered with a sheen of steak grease. Some people think this is a bad thing, such as, again, one's spouse! Stacy Franklin has been known to comment sarcastically after indoor steak cooking about the veneer of grease that somehow coats kitchen cabinets even all the way across the room. It's easy to clean up but not so attractive if it sits around a day, attracting lint and dog hair.

Those people are the ones who worry the relative lack of heat generated by most conventional home stoves is a serious limitation. They may go to such lengths as preheating a pan in a 500°F oven for thirty minutes before pulling it out with a heavily oven-mittened hand and putting it on the stove top over an equally high flame. This attempt at high heat ensures that you're cooking at 500°F, though that's still far below the broilers most steakhouses use, which cook on both sides at temperatures between 800°F and 1200°F. And, yes, this method is almost guaranteed to set off any home smoke alarm.

Although some cooks believe the average home stove's inability to generate higher heat is a drawback, that might not be so. A lot of people cook their steaks too hot, overcooking the exterior while undercooking the interior. If you're cooking a two-inch-thick rib steak with a bone, you won't be able to finish it on the stove top anyway. You'll want to brown the outside and then finish it in the oven until your desired internal temperature has been reached. In this case, superhigh heat doesn't really help that much. The same browning can be achieved at lower temperatures.

Another advantage of the cast-iron pan is the transparency of flavor. Say you've got a piece of well-aged steak whose intense beefiness you want to highlight as cleanly as possible. In this case, you may not want to cook it over coals and layer smoky flavor on top of the hard-earned savor of good dry aging. Thus cast iron over a flame (be it from live fire on a grill or your gas range) is the best bet, using just some neutral oil or tallow in the pan to give the most transparent version of the steak. Conversely, if

you've got a relatively mild cut like a tenderloin without any age on it, doing it in a pan allows you to pan baste it with butter, garlic, herbs, or any other sort of aromatic, "cooking in" the seasoning, so to speak.

To cook on the stove, any pan will work, but the heavier the better. Heavier pans retain more heat from preheating, which lets them deliver it to a big slab of meat without cooling down too much. You also want a large skillet, so the meat is not crowded by the sides of the pan. Moisture from the meat needs to be able to escape rapidly during cooking to get that nicely browned crust; in a crowded or tight pan, the steam hangs about and steams the meat. One of the problems with most cookware, especially the fairly crude category of cast iron, is the microscopic unevenness of the pan, leading to differences in diffusivity on the surface, or hot spots and cooler ones. One way to circumvent this is to move the steak around while you cook it and to flip it frequently. Another is Aaron's method.

Aaron uses two pans. He places a large, square, flat griddle (no grill grooves) directly on the burner and on top of that he sets his cast-iron skillet. Then he heats them both up simultaneously for at least twenty minutes. The griddle underneath serves to double the thickness of the metal being heated (making it similar to a *plancha* or French top you'll see at a restaurant), which compensates for the unevenness of a single pan. It also doubles the heat-holding capacity of the metal, meaning that when he drops the steak on it, there's much more thermal mass to transfer the heat to the steak. This gives the steak a good wallop of heat at the beginning and prevents the cast iron from losing too much heat to the steak. Plus, the pan makes a quick recovery, powering the steak through the rest of the cooking. If the steak then has to go into the oven, he keeps it in the top pan and leaves the underlying griddle on the stove to cool.

WHEN TO USE THE OVEN

For thick steaks, the oven is your friend. We need the stove top to build the all-important crust, but if your steak is more than an inch or an inch and a half thick and you want it medium-rare at the center, you'll probably need to finish the steak in the oven. In there, the ambient heat will now keep the cooking going until the interior of the steak comes to temp, but the browning of the exterior will come to a halt so the steak doesn't burn. Determine if the steak needs to finish in the oven by checking the temperature with a meat thermometer. For thick steaks that came straight out of the fridge, the interior might still be at 70°F or 80°F by the time the crust is finished, so make sure the oven is turned on to 250°F or so before you start searing the steak on the stove top. You can go straight into the oven with the pan you're already cooking the steak in. Or if you want cooking on the exterior to slow down, move the steak onto a different ovenproof pan.

Gas Grills: Charmless Convenience

Yes, yes, gas grills are handy, but we still find ourselves indifferent to them. Why? Well, they're the Prius of grills. They're effective and efficient at their job, but there's also something soulless and clinical about them. Car analogies aside, among tools people love, the gas grill tends to rate way down on the list, falling somewhere between a (nonriding) lawn mower and a

> ### A NOTE ON HEAVY PANS
>
> Cast-iron pans are great, but they are not the only skillets you can use. Anything thick bottomed and heavy will do the job. The reason you want something heavy and dense is that it retains a ton of heat, so when you put the cool steak into the hot pan, the pan will take only a slight dip in temperature before recovering and continuing to cook the meat. The great thing about cast iron and carbon steel is that these metals love the fat in the steak and actually bind it to the metal, creating a lovely thin, almost nonstick sheen.

washing machine. It earns your grudging respect by getting the job done, but it's not a treasured tool that you scheme how to take with you when the waters rise.

The advantages of gas grills all have to do with practicality. Without a doubt, they are convenient, as they effortlessly fire up at the flip of a switch. You can be grilling in ten minutes. This is perfect for getting a solid dinner on the table in a timely fashion on those nights when you don't have time to light a proper fire or when you have a dozen screaming kids hungry for hot dogs. (*Timely* is the key word in the above sentence, as the goal is to avoid what Jordan's mother-in-law, Linda, terms "martini meat," otherwise known as horrendously overcooked meat due to a surfeit of predinner gin cocktails that, in addition to resulting in sloppy grillwork, tend to slow everything down until the cooking occurs in the dark, another potential pitfall.)

Gas grills also afford the same kind of control that a gas burner does on a stove, as you can

raise or lower the heat just by turning a knob. This allows a level of precision cooking hard to attain with live fire. Cleaning gas grills is a breeze, too. Rather than have to shovel out piles of ash from the depths of a sooty pit, you can just remove the heating plates and grills and scrub them under a hose with soapy steel wool on a sunny day.

The downsides of gas grills are nothing more than crucial counterarguments to a couple of the previous points. Yes, turning a gas flame up and down provides precision, but there's no real skill involved in that. It's as basic and intuitive as turning the volume up and down on your car radio. Learning to use live fire properly is an art and a skill that cooking on a gas grill will never provide. Also, what you don't get on a gas grill is smoke or any of the flavor that comes from a real fire. For many, the taste of the fire is part of the primal appeal of steak. Lastly, gas grills tend not to get as hot as wood or charcoal grills, which can present a challenge if you want that fast, deep sear.

Sous Vide Equipment: Steak by Spock

A long time ago, people had to relieve themselves outside. Then there were rusticities like outhouses and chamber pots. Modern plumbing arrived and we had toilets in the house flushed by pulling a chain. Next, a little handle was introduced. Today they flush themselves. And then there are Japanese toilets, with blow dryers, seat heating, and more. Are these better ways or just different, foolproof, equipment-driven changes?

The same could be asked about sous vide. Sous vide steaks are a modern phenomenon, and the tech bros and gals have flocked to this technique because it involves gadgets and some general smug sense of "hacking" or "disrupting" traditional cooking methods. As gas grilling took the effort out of grilling, sous vide takes the guesswork out of gas grilling. Now, don't get us wrong, we like a good gadget. Aaron loves his digital moisture meter for randomly checking the water content of post oak logs; Jordan is attached to his Sony digital voice recorder. And the sous vide method makes sense in some situations. But much like gas grilling, it's a results-based approach, not process based. And as much as we love a good result, we love it that much more when it's the product of a process in which we've been deeply engaged.

For the uninitiated, here's the deal with sous vide. It's essentially a reversal of the traditional method for cooking steak, accomplished with the precision of technology. It begins by cooking the inside, and the finishing touch is cooking the outside.

The term *sous vide* is French and means "under vacuum." This refers not to the actual cooking, but to the fact that it involves food (in this case steak) in a vacuum-sealed plastic bag, which prevents moisture loss and oxidation. The bag is then submerged into a heated water bath, which is kept at a precise temperature through the use of an immersion circulator, a device once found only in laboratories but now sold at (not inconsiderable) retail prices for the home chef. This nifty gadget circulates the water, warming it to the precisely desired temperature. Over time, thanks to thermodynamics, the meat comes to the same temperature as the water—your desired internal temperature.

For steak, sous vide has been a game changer. Say you want a medium-rare steak. You set the water-bath temperature for 130°F, or just under.

Then you bag your steak and drop it into the water for at least forty-five minutes to an hour or more (depending on the thickness). When the steak is done, it will be sopping wet and look unpalatably gray and unappetizing. Throw away the bag, dry the steak off, and then slap it into a superhot pan to sear the outside until it's nice and brown and crisp. That's it. The inside remains medium-rare while the outside develops a quick, attractive crust.

There's a ton of upside to this. For one, perfect doneness is guaranteed to the exact temperature desired by the chef. The searing at the end happens fast enough that it doesn't alter the internal temperature of the meat. No method is more precise. If overcooking the meat is a profound fear, this is the way for you.

You can see why this can be an excellent idea for restaurants. First, precision is more crucial in a restaurant than in a home-cooked meal. If you overcook a steak at home, shame on you, and you'll probably hear about it from your spouse. Yet at the end of the day, you just suck it up and eat the overdone meat. But if that happens at a restaurant, the steak goes back to the kitchen and the restaurant eats the cost. The customer has had a stressful and unpleasant experience in having to send back food, and the restaurant loses money. The other factor for restaurants is speed and convenience. Rather than figuring out the timing on how to get a thick-cut steak cooked and rested (which can take twenty to thirty minutes when cooking conventionally) on the table the moment you're ready for it, restaurants can now just have steaks prepped in a water bath. When the order comes in, the meat is pretty much done, needing only that final sear, which takes but a minute. A home chef can benefit from this method, too. You

can simply set the steak to cook for an hour while you prepare the side dishes.

So does sous vide have any drawbacks? Of course! First, there's the cost of the equipment. A decent water circulator for the amateur chef runs $130 to $200. You need to have plastic bags, too. And all of this for something you could just as easily cook in a pan you already own. Then there's the notion of juiciness and texture. Sous vide steak in a bag can be kept in a bath for hours and hours without its temperature getting too high. Technically, you could put the meat in the bath before you leave for work and finish it when you get home. However, the texture of the meat starts to break down after more than an hour or so in the water. It gets mushy, losing its chew. It also loses its juices into the bag, not on the plate. Therefore, mushy *and* dry steak is a possibility if the sous vide is not done with maximum integrity and timing. We've had steaks like this at restaurants, and it's not pleasant.

Even when done well, sous vide steak is fairly obvious. The transition zone in the steak from the outer, seared crust to the internal meat is very thin. One of the pleasures, we've found, of grilled or griddled steak is that spectrum of doneness you get from inside to out: the crunchy, dried exterior crust with a thin band of well-done meat inside leading all the way to a rare or medium-rare center creates a complex textural experience. This is diminished with sous vide.

The plastic bags are another drawback. The vast majority are not reused. Instead, they get thrown in the trash and potentially end up as part of the massive floating garbage island in the Pacific. Why waste plastic when you don't have to? And lastly, clinically preparing steak in a plastic bag in a water bath misses out on the old-fashioned analog pleasures of cooking. You don't get to

work on your skills in cooking the steaks to perfect doneness. You also miss out on many of the smells and sounds of cooking, which impact your perceptions of the flavor, driving hunger and anticipation.

Kamado Cookers: Hot and Heavy!

The luxury SUVs of outdoor cooking, those oval-shaped ceramic cookers known by the ubiquitous brand Big Green Egg (BGE) have been the biggest trend in outdoor cooking for the last ten years or so. The BGE and other brands are examples of kamado cookers, a style that originated in the Far East thousands of years ago. These ovoid cookers are tiled on the outside, have thick, smooth ceramic interiors, and lids that hinge near the top and open like a Fabergé egg. Air intake comes in through the bottom. These grills have become badges of the bourgeois, essential possessions for the suburban backyard set. And all that's a good thing. Kamado-style cookers are excellent devices for cooking many things. Unfortunately, steak is not one of them.

Yes, kamados, which are heated by placing charcoal in the bottom, can sear steaks beautifully at the incredibly high temperatures they are capable of reaching (800°F to 900°F), but cooking the steaks evenly and gently is the problem. Because of their thick ceramic walls, these cookers hold heat especially well, getting very hot and maintaining the temperature easily for a long time. That's a great feature in an oven but not necessarily in a grill. Thus, the kamado "grills" work best for processes with long cook times, where holding a consistent temperature is the name of the game, such as roasting, smoking, and baking.

Kamado cookers are awesome, rock solid, almost indestructible pieces of equipment and do any backyard proud. For smoking briskets and ribs or roasting chickens and pork shoulders, they're amazing. If you want to bake a loaf of bread in the dead of summer without turning on the oven, the BGE is for you. Spareribs? No problem. Even pizza! But the challenges in cooking *steaks* on a kamado are legion. For one, the circular shape of a kamado (especially the smaller models) makes it difficult to have a two-zone setup in which hot coals are placed on only one-half of the grill (see page 147). Especially important for cooking thicker cuts of meat, a two-zone configuration permits you to sear the outside of the meat directly over the coals, but then move the meat off the coals to a warm but not scorching spot where it can cook more slowly, allowing the inside to come up to temperature. In a conventional round grill like a Weber kettle, this is easy to do, as its thin walls don't retain a lot of heat, clearly dividing the hot and cool sides and enabling real contrast. In a kamado, the radiant heat can be so great that even in a two-zone setup, the cool side will still be really hot.

Heat in general can be a challenge in these ovoid cookers. While they have a remarkable ability to hold lower temperatures for long periods, arriving at those desired temperatures can be difficult. Experience has shown us that one of the key skills in using a kamado is to keep it from getting too hot. Once you overload it with even just a little excess charcoal, it can get too hot to use optimally. And kamados take forever to cool down, especially in warm weather. (In cold climates and in winter, however, they can be great assets in outdoor cooking.) Grilling well-marbled steaks in such heat over live coals can cause a lot of fat to render and ignite immediately, creating a flare-up fest and plenty of bitterly charred, overdone meat.

Lastly, kamados are expensive. The smallest Big Green Egg costs four hundred dollars without accessories, and its grill only measures ten inches in diameter, big enough for one good-size ribeye or porterhouse cooked in a single zone. The extra-large Big Green Egg, which has a grill measuring twenty-nine inches, costs around two thousand dollars.

Good Old-Fashioned Charcoal Grill: The Answer We've Been Waiting For

The charcoal grill is an even more ancient technology than the three-thousand-year-old kamado. After all, a grill can technically be as simple as a hole in the ground with a cooking grate over it. Or you can make one at home by putting hot coals in a metal pot and covering it with a cooking surface. A charcoal grill can be improvised out of almost anything that won't burn or melt.

If you value flavor and experience over convenience and speed, a charcoal grill is the choice you make. Learning to master hot coals and manipulating their intensity to your advantage is both a challenge and a pleasure—and an important life skill! But getting really good at charcoal grilling is not easy. You have to practice often to get good. And it requires paying attention throughout the process, from lighting the coals to shaping your coal bed all the way to cooking. The required mental presence and observation can be tough to achieve if, say, you only grill when you have company over to distract you (and watch out for those martinis!).

The only other drawbacks are a lack of precision and, of course, cleaning out the ash. Charcoal grills are unfortunately a bit dirty to maintain.

Even if you can charcoal grill for free using a hole in the ground, better options are not very expensive. The stubby, ground-bound Weber Smokey Joe will get the job done for only thirty-five dollars, and if you prefer to tend the steaks while standing up, the original Weber kettle grill sells for about one hundred dollars. While nothing special, the kettle has a good design and is easy to use, relatively easy to clean, and fairly durable. And with its some 360 square inches of grill space, it's plenty big to cook for a good-size party and to set up for two-zone cooking.

Of course, you can always ascend up the price and quality scale from there. The Char-Broil Kettleman ($150) has a more intricate design, a hinged lid like a kamado, and fancier "TRU-infrared" grates, whose thicker steel and tighter configuration are touted as transferring more heat to the meat while reducing flare-ups.

From there, things get pricier, mostly because the grills themselves are given more elaborate mountings (inset into various carts with countertops) and accessories (like gas-powered ignitions to light the charcoal), timers, and other accoutrements.

A not-too-common subset of charcoal or wood grills is the Santa Maria grill, also known sometimes as an Argentine or Tuscan grill. These setups feature a large metal container open on the top and often a couple of feet deep, which holds wood that's slowly smoldering down into coals. A couple of rods are attached vertically up from the wood container. They house a cable or chain that attaches to the big cast-iron grill. By use of a wheel-like hand crank, the grill can

Stove top

Weber

Kamado

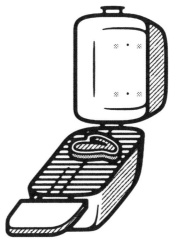

PK

Santa Maria

Chimney

be raised or lowered. This allows the cook to find the perfect distance for the meat above the ever-changing fire. Also, the whole grill can be easily raised when more fuel needs to be added to the fire. The Santa Maria is especially good for larger steak cuts that need a little more time. Tri-tip is the classic example of a steak that can cook with direct heat but needs to have some distance from the fire in order to cook all the way through. Big, chunky bone-in or double-bone ribeyes would also be good candidates.

Hibachi: Easy There, Little Guy!

While the Big Green Egg is a symbol of the modern upscale backyard, how much fire do you really need to cook a steak well? The Japanese answered this question long ago and continue to do so today with their itty-bitty grill we call a hibachi, which they're more likely to refer to as *konro* or *shichirin*.

But since we're Americans, we're just going to hold on to our local jargon. Hibachis are small tabletop boxes or containers resembling flower pots that hold coals and emit heat. In Japan, they have little mesh grates to hold the food or no grate at all when they are meant to cook yakitori skewers of meat, fish, and vegetables laid over the coals. Cute as they may seem, these little powerhouses pack a punch: they're efficient, portable, and versatile, too. Whether you have a tiny studio apartment or a sprawling suburban compound, you may want to consider a hibachi as an efficient everyday solution to low-hassle grilling. One of Jordan's fondest childhood food memories was when he stayed with his grandparents in Seattle, and on warm summer nights, his grandfather fired up a little hibachi on the deck to sizzle one or two steaks for a casual dinner at the round kitchen table.

To grill something like a thin steak (or a couple burgers or fish or chicken breasts) that will only meet the fire for a few minutes, why build a big coal bed and waste a lot of energy when you don't have to? At times like those, the hibachi is a great solution. Just light eight to ten briquettes in a chimney, dump them into the little cooker, and grill away.

Of course, the hibachi's strengths are also its weaknesses. If you need to grill a lot of things over a long period, the hibachi is not your answer. Because it has no cover or lid, long roasting and smoking are out; it can only do open-air grilling. Likewise, two-zone setups are practically impossible in such a small setting. But for efficient one hitters, hibachis can't be beat.

We have a feeling a hibachi renaissance is on the horizon, as society begins to retreat from the giant, charcoal-hungry Webers and kamados and endeavors to cook ever more efficiently. This is why we played around with building a hibachi and why, to our great surprise as we worked on the book, we found that out favorite grill maker, PK (see facing page), is working on its own hibachi version.

FRANKLIN STEAK

110

If you're looking for the ideal charcoal steak grill—incredibly versatile, highly portable, easy cleanup—that will last your entire life and beyond, there's only one choice. Meet the PK Grill. Two of these live in the backyard of Aaron's house and are used pretty much every time a meal is cooked at home. They're not only easy to use but also among the most intuitive grills you'll ever encounter. When you're cooking on one, you feel in the presence of something unique—you feel equipped with a secret tool that no one knows about. And the PK story—about how these near-perfect backyard cookers came to be, developed a following, and then were cast into the ash bin of history only to be rediscovered and resurrected in the early 2000s—makes the experience of owning one all the more special. PK is that trusty classic car that you've kept running for years, learned to tune up yourself, and is a joy to take out in the neighborhood (maybe not too much on the highway, though).

continued

In the mid-1980s, at a garage sale, Little Rock, Arkansas, lawyer Paul James stumbled across an odd, puffy, box-like grill with a silvery cast and rounded corners. He instantly recognized it as the same kind of grill one of his mentors used to cook on way back during James's early days out of law school, which brought back fond memories of good times and good food. He also recalled the reverence his mentor had for the grill, so James bought it, took it home, and started cooking on it. Immediately apparent was that, despite decades of age, it still worked like a dream. The curious appearance and remarkable performance of the grill incited query after query from friends and guests. After some research, James discovered that these odd little grills hadn't been made in years. But in their heyday, they had been manufactured right there in Little Rock.

A little more digging taught him that the full history of the PK goes back to Texas (appropriate for something that makes great barbecue). In 1952, Hilton Meigs, a Beaumont designer, inventor, businessman, local character, and barbecue lover, set out to design the perfect, transportable barbecue pit. He wanted it to be durable, rustproof, and lightweight, yet also able to hold both high and steady temperatures and be easy to use. Meigs chose cast aluminum because it's lighter than steel (the standard material for backyard cookers) and conducts heat better. He called it the Portable Kitchen.

Meigs started to sell his grills, first across Texas (out of his car) and later in greater numbers across the South. Everywhere he went, he won new devotees. In 1958, he sold the business to another man, who moved the business to Little Rock. This was fortuitous, as bauxite, the primary component of aluminum, was a primary resource of Arkansas. The business took off, with the cookers developing a cult following and selling in the tens of thousands in the 1960s. But times change, and in the 1970s and 1980s, gas grills started to edge out pricey little boutique charcoal grills, and cheap, thin steel displaced the more intricate cast aluminum. The PK brand changed hands a couple of more times but eventually went out of production.

James also learned that the intellectual property and brand currently belonged to the Char-Broil company of Columbus, Georgia. Char-Broil had no plans to resuscitate the PK, so James was able to acquire the rights and intellectual property. Over the next several years, he, working with his sister Martha, brought the PK back into production and it began its slow climb back onto the scene. Compared to the big players, it's still a tiny, boutique company. But in 2014, James took on some partners, veterans from the tech world, to help take PK to a new level. That's where things stand now, as PK picks up new devotees every day. To use one is to love it. Let's look at why.

PK makes two styles of grill, the original and the 360. The latter has more bells and whistles and is a little larger, but the basic concept is the same. We mentioned the cast aluminum. Again, it's an excellent conductor of heat, lightweight, and rustproof. That's why a PK will serve a family over generations. Of course, never breaking down or tarnishing might not be the best business model, compared to something that's going to rust out and need replacement after five or ten years. But integrity is part of the plan. "Our entire team loves being involved in a thing that doesn't end up in landfill," says Scott Moody, one of the new PK partners. "I take a lot of pride that I help make a thing that somebody can buy, use forever, and then hand off to their kids, and it's never going to go into a garbage heap."

The design is poetically simple. The two halves of the shell fit together to make a box-shaped clamshell. One end cleverly interlocks to form a hinge, allowing the top to be lifted, but there's no pin or hasp keeping them together. You can even put each half in the dishwasher.

These are handy conveniences. The real brilliance is in the design for cooking. The oblong—instead of round—shape makes it perfect for two-zone cooking, as the hot area and cold area can be clearly defined and separated with enough space to make both zones effective. Rounded corners instead of angular ones allow air to move more fluidly. Interior convective currents and airflow are determined by four easy-to-operate vents, two on the top and two on the bottom. Using these wide open, you can flood the chamber with air to reach high temperatures perfect for grilling. Opening and closing them in combination permits the creation of convective heat for roasting and smoking. That's right—one simple cooker on which you can grill, roast, or smoke. It's simple and ingenious. Conveniently, one end of the grate is hinged, which means more coals can be added during long cooks without having to remove any food on the grill.

When it comes to steak, the PK is literally unsurpassed. A few years ago, it was organically adopted by some of the top competitors in the Steak Cookoff Association and has since taken that scene by storm. In March 2015, Scott Moody gave a couple of PKs to some of the finalists in a cook-off, who took them home and just kept cooking on them. By October of that year, according to Moody, six of the ten finalists were using them. The following year, that number was eight or nine out of ten. "And now it's like our grill is the go-to kit for competitive steak cooking. Anybody that cooks competitive steaks cooks on a PK Grill because they feel that's the only way you can compete."

What makes the PK so good for steak? Mainly, it's the aluminum. Aluminum conducts heat about four times more efficiently than steel. It gets superhot inside. Another advantage is the relatively shallow base. Compared to a Weber kettle and kamados, the coals rest quite high and close to the grates. This allows the meat to absorb maximal heat directly from the coals for a great sear, but without heating the entire chamber too much (for two-zone effectiveness).

When it comes to cost, the PK (about $380 for the original) is more expensive than a base-model Weber kettle. But when you think about the performance, versatility, and unequaled durability, the cost is more than justified. And on top of that, you'll develop a real love for this little grill. And who would put a price on love?

Experimental Build: The Hybrid Hibachi

Given Aaron's experience in welding his own tools, we thought we'd experiment with building a small, supercharged steak cooker for the handy backyard open-fire enthusiast. The idea was to take the efficiencies and small footprint of a hibachi and trick it out with some of the features of other kinds of grills.

Disclaimer • This hybrid hibachi (HH), made of $5/16$-inch steel, is heavy. The density of its material allows it to hold and radiate its heat more intensely and for longer than a traditional model. It also has the added functionality of grates you can raise and lower, like a Santa Maria grill. Thus, you can make a hot fire but still cook more delicately on it by raising the grates high above the flame. And like a fancy restaurant hearth, it's got a wood cage to keep a steady supply of wood coals going, as opposed to a traditional hibachi, which uses some kind of charcoal for fuel rather than more flavorful and aromatic wood coals.

When it comes to fueling our HH, you need fairly small chunks of wood in the cage, and it helps to mix in some charcoal to keep things burning in this confined space. Just keep an eye out for small coals that can slip out through the sides of the cage.

Altogether, this proved a phenomenal little hybrid hibachi. Not much charcoal was required to get it up to screaming-hot temperatures, and it really responded when we added binchōtan charcoal (see page 126) for a long and even burn. You can certainly give these instructions to a steel worker or welder, or if you have basic welding skills, do it yourself.

Aaron's Instructions

This is a simple build. All in all, it won't take more than 5 hours for a moderately experienced welder if he or she works quickly and efficiently. The key to success is getting things done in the proper order so one step builds on the other. A beginning welder can tackle this, too, though it will take a little longer. Also, I'm giving fairly loose instructions, as this crazy cooker was pretty much improvised on a sketch pad and then built from stuff that was around the shop. Be sure to wear safety googles or a face shield and protective leather gloves as you work and to have a fire extinguisher on hand.

EQUIPMENT AND MATERIALS YOU'LL NEED

- Welder

- Grinder

- Steel ruler or measuring tape and Sharpie, for measuring and marking cuts

- Straight edges and clamps

- Drill press or regular drill (former makes the job much easier)

- 1 sheet steel plate, 4 by 8 feet and $\frac{5}{16}$ inch thick (a $\frac{1}{4}$-inch-thick sheet can be used, but $\frac{5}{16}$ inch is better because it retains heat more efficiently and doesn't warp or bow as easily)

- 30 feet $\frac{1}{2}$-inch cold-rolled round steel (for the cooking grate)

- 20 feet $\frac{5}{8}$-inch cold-rolled round steel (for the wood cage)

- 2 spring grill handles, $\frac{1}{2}$-inch rod (available online or at hardware stores)

Step 1: Cut the Pieces

1. Get yourself ready for an easy welding assembly. First, using a steel ruler and Sharpie, mark your $\frac{5}{16}$-inch steel plate for the rectangles, which will become the back, sides, bottom, and front of the firebox. You'll end up using a little over half of the plate. Before you begin, check the square-ness of the plate you're working with because the sheets are not always perfectly square, and you'll need those proper angles.

I lay out my cutting plan so the side pieces, the front piece, and the back piece all have a factory edge. That is, I mark the cutouts along each side of the sheet, so one edge of each piece uses the clean, well-cut edge from the factory. This way, you'll make fewer cuts and what's

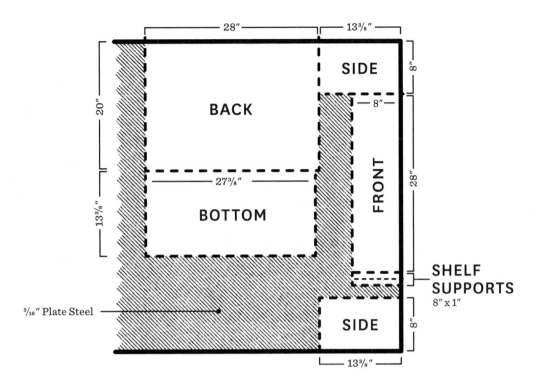

28"   13⅜"

SIDE   8"

BACK

20"

27⅜"   28"

BOTTOM   FRONT

8"

SHELF
SUPPORTS
8" x 1"

⁵⁄₁₆" Plate Steel

SIDE   8"

13⅜"

left in the middle can be used for the bottom, where the exposed edges don't matter.

I used the following dimensions, but you should feel free to make whatever size grill you want. Cut the pieces for the firebox from the steel plate:

2 sides • each 13⅜ by 8 inches

1 back • 28 by 20 inches

1 front • 28 by 8 inches

1 bottom • 27⅜ by 13⅜ inches

2 shelf supports • 8 by 1 inches

2. Cut the following pieces for the cooking grate from the ½-inch round:

2 pieces • 21 inches long, for the grate sides

2 pieces • 16⅞ inches long, for the grate front and back

19 pieces • 12 inches long, for the interior grates

3. Cut the following pieces for the wood cage from the ⅝-inch round:

6 pieces • 6¾ inches long, for the top, bottom, and sides

4 pieces • 13 inches long, for the top, bottom, front, and rear

10 pieces • 11¾ inches long, for the tall vertical pillars and bottom

15 pieces • 3½ inches long, for the short crossbars

8 pieces • 3 inches long, for the sides

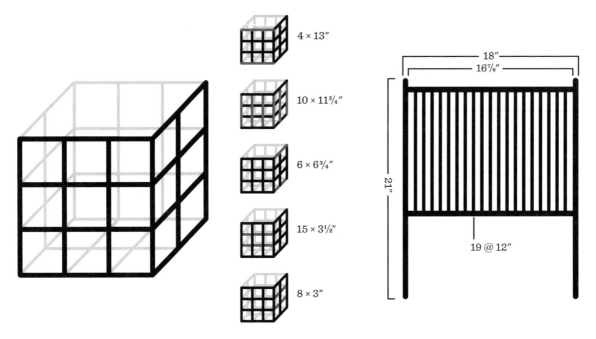

Above left: A side view of the wood cage. Above right: An overhead view of the cooking grate.

Step 2: Build the Components

Firebox • Before assembling the firebox, make the holes you'll need in the back piece, as it's much easier to do this before the box is assembled. These holes are for pegs that will stick out from the back and will allow the grate to be suspended at various heights above the fire.

It's imperative that these holes be even and symmetrical, which means you must mark them and drill them out carefully. I recommend measuring and then clamping a metal ruler or other flat straight edge, followed by a second metal ruler or straight edge ½ inch above it. Use a piece of the ½-inch round and the Sharpie to trace the circle where you need to drill the hole. Make a pair of these horizontal holes a few inches apart at whatever heights you want to be able to lift the grates.

Looking ahead to the next step of building the grates, here is a handy trick: use these first two holes as a jig for the grates, which is better than using the grates as a jig to drill the holes. That's because if something goes wrong with the grate, you can always build it again. But if you screw up the holes, you can't drill new ones. So after you've drilled the holes, take your two 21-inch rods of ½-inch round and place them in the holes—you'll want to grind down those ends a bit and round them off so they fit easily and offer more tolerance when the hibachi heats up—so ½ inch or so of each rod extends through the back. Next, put right angles on the rods to make sure they're straight and then tack in your crosspiece on both sides. All of a sudden, you have the frame for your grate!

Once the holes are drilled, the rest of the firebox is easy. Use right-angle magnets to hold the bottom, sides, front, and back together so the shape is solid and correct, and then use the welder to make little tacks to hold them in place. Finally, make all the welds on the inside so the outside looks really clean.

Cooking Grate • Because you used the holes in the back as the jig for the grates and tacked on the crosspieces (see the previous step), the frame is already done.

From there, draw a line in the middle of the frame and put your first grill grate there, just to mark it. The idea is to start out in the middle and then work your way symmetrically to each side. Don't start on one end and then space everything out from there. If you do that, you'll end up with one gap that fits funny. Just be sure to measure very carefully as you go.

I tacked in that first middle piece and placed a little piece of metal flush next to it, which was spacing for the next one. And after that, I just worked my way down—tack, tack, tack—adding rods of ½-inch round. The tacking is so the grate doesn't warp, because if you put too much weld, the whole thing will bow upward.

Get it together, make sure it's right, and then do your welds on one side. Flip it over, and on the back side, start on the same spot. It's like tuning a drum—there's a counteraction for every action. This is so it's solid, balanced, and doesn't warp.

Now attach your pair of spring handles, and the grate should be ready to go.

Wood Cage • This part is simple. Because your box is already assembled, you should begin making the cage in the bottom of the box so the spacing is correct. I also recommend leaving a wide enough gap between the side of the cage and the edge of the firebox to wedge in a piece of metal or a sheet pan to keep the wind off the fire. If you want, you could even weld a flat piece there. (I didn't, but if I were to build this contraption again, I might do that.)

So, using the ⅝-inch round, start by building your square end pieces in the bottom of the firebox in order to get the spacing and angles correct. Once you've built one square, you can add the vertical rods, using an angle measure to get that perfect 90 degrees. You can then pull the whole thing out and build the rest of the cage outside of the firebox. When you've completed it, place it where you want it in the box and weld it in as lightly or as firmly as you want.

Step 3: Enjoy Your Grill

You're done! Enjoy your own hybrid hibachi, perfect for small fires and versatile cooking. The cage can be used to hold a loose pile of small logs, which will create a continuous source of wood coals for longer cooks. It's easiest to get started by using a charcoal chimney (see page 142). Drag the resulting coals under the grate for heating. Alternatively, the firebox is great for charcoal, wood coals, or binchōtan.

CHAPTER 6

Fuel

When it comes to grilling steak, the fuel source is a seasoning, so you should have some idea about what you want out of your fire when you get started. Do you want a hot fire or a more mellow one? Do you want it to be short and intense or long and slow? Do you want a lot of smoke or just a little? All of these questions will impact the kind of fire you want to create and what you want to burn, which makes understanding your fuel sources critical.

Of course, what we're really talking about here is charcoal and wood. Gas burns clean and adds nothing of itself to the taste of the meat (thank goodness).

Charcoal is amazing stuff, the go-to heat source of the American grill, the flickering fuel of Fourth of July picnics and poolside barbecues. It has many wonderful qualities, which we'll get to in a bit, but wood is fuel for the soul. After all, it powers Franklin BBQ, and the smell of slow-burning oak is the smell of warmth and happiness and dinner. Each fuel has its place and purpose, but whichever one you go with requires learning and practice. This chapter will help get you familiar with both and set you down the road toward mastering your cooking fuel.

Charcoal: Great Bags of Fire!

Every time we grab a bag of charcoal at the store, we fail to consider that we're actually buying an example of one of the most important and oldest human technologies. It's not known exactly when early peoples starting producing charcoal, but it goes back at least tens of thousands of years, if not longer. The earliest example of charcoal being used was over thirty-eight thousand years ago by Cro-Magnons, who adopted it for both drawing on cave walls (they liked to draw beef cattle) and for fire. Around 4000 BCE, charcoal was the catalyst of the Bronze Age: an everyday fire is not hot enough to melt copper, but charcoal along with a forced airflow can reach temperatures in the 2000°F range, the level needed to melt copper.

If you're so inclined, you can do as the ancients did and make your own charcoal, which is not a bad money-saving idea if you have lots of extra wood lying around. Early humans learned to pile wood into a mound and cover it with earth, leaving only slight air intakes on the bottom. They'd light the pile, get it burning, and eventually seal it. Inside, the wood would keep on burning, though slowly and at a relatively low temperature. After several days of smoldering and when the mass had cooled, they'd uncover the mound to expose a pile of dry, crumbled charcoal, much like what we see today when we purchase a bag of lump charcoal. The process isn't too different nowadays; it just takes place in large metal kilns that do the job more efficiently.

If you're scientifically minded, you might wonder what's going on inside that mound or kiln to create charcoal. It starts, of course, with the wood, which at a molecular level is composed of long chains of carbon, hydrogen, and oxygen. When wood is burned, first it dries out, as the free water inside it boils and then disappears as steam. When you hear a fresh piece of poorly seasoned wood hissing in a fire, that's what's happening. Burning along with the water are volatile organic components of wood that, when heated, combine with surrounding oxygen to produce combustion. The products of combustion are light and heat, water, and carbon dioxide. After the wood is completely incinerated, all that's left is the mineral content, which we call ash.

The process of making charcoal involves restricting the combustion so all the carbon doesn't burn away. This is accomplished by limiting the amount of oxygen that reaches the fire. In a fire, the carbon and oxygen molecules in wood combine to become carbon dioxide. If you restrict the oxygen flow, the volatile components and water burn away, leaving mostly pure carbon and minerals, or charcoal.

Charcoal burns much hotter than wood precisely because it's lost all that water, as the energy required to vaporize water is considerable. This is also why charcoal burns without much smoke and without much flame when compared with wood.

The biggest drawback when it comes to charcoal? A yield of charcoal weighs only in the neighborhood of 25 percent of the original wood from which it was made. That is, it takes a lot of wood to make only a little charcoal. An article titled "Peak Wood and the Bronze Age" in the public policy magazine *Pacific Standard* describes how charcoal contributed greatly to the deforestation of the island of Cyprus, a center of early bronze production: "Some 120 pine trees were required to prepare the 6 tons of charcoal needed to produce one copper ingot shaped roughly like a dried ox hide and weighing between 45 and 65 pounds. One ingot, therefore, deforested almost four acres."

The future of charcoal production may lie in looking beyond wood: after all, charcoal can be made from pretty much any organic substance. Some chefs, like Dan Barber of New York's Blue Hill at Stone Barns and Adam Sappington of Country Cat, in Portland, Oregon, fashion charcoal out of animal bones in an effort to reduce waste. They then cook the very meats over those coals. Charcoal made from coconut (see page 128) is big throughout Asia. No matter what the charcoal is made from, however, it's going to give what it does—speed, heat, and consistency. Those are great, but to get the most out of a fire, you have to roll the process back and start with wood.

TYPES OF CHARCOAL, FLAVORS, AND SMOKE

Given how many different brands and types of charcoal exist, choosing what to use can be a bit of a headache. Lump or briquettes? Mesquite or oak? Everyone has his or her preferences, but it's worth remembering that charcoal is nearly pure carbon. That's wood stripped of every substance that made it distinctive. People talk about the unique character of smoke that comes from different charcoals, especially those made from different woods. But unless it's improperly made charcoal that still contains some of the compounds of the wood, the small amount of smoke you get from the coals of various woods will not be terribly dissimilar. There can be differences based on the density and composition of briquettes, of course, but pure lump charcoal is pretty much just charcoal. We'll get to that in a while, when we discuss the different kinds of charcoal you can buy.

Charcoal Briquettes

The charcoal briquette has a somewhat surprising history, going back to camping trips taken by automobile magnate Henry Ford and such buddies as Thomas Edison and Harvey Firestone. More like glamping, these affairs involved a large retinue (including a chef) conveyed in a cavalcade of automobiles, one of which was outfitted as a kitchen. A Michigan real estate agent named Edward Kingsford was invited along in 1919 to discuss timberland with Ford, who needed the wood for Model T construction. Shortly thereafter, Kingsford would broker a huge tract of Michigan forest to Ford.

From top: Thaan-brand Thai-style binchōtan,
lump charcoal, charcoal briquettes

Logging the forest and milling the car bodies out of the timber left much behind in terms of sawdust and wood scraps, which Ford, ever thrifty, hated to see go unused. So he decided to employ a technique invented by University of Oregon chemist Orin Stafford to put sawmill waste to use. Stafford found that by combining sawdust with a bit of tar and using cornstarch as a binding agent, he could make a light, portable fuel, which he named "charcoal briquettes." Edison designed a briquette factory next to the sawmill, and Ford was suddenly in the briquette business.

Unfortunately for Ford, the briquette business was not as robust as the car business. He would have to wait some twenty-five years for briquettes to come into fashion. The Great Depression and a world war didn't leave a lot of people in the mood for cooking out. In 1951, another group bought Ford Charcoal and rebranded it Kingsford, after the man who sold Ford the land. But the product did not take off until an event in 1952: the invention of the Weber grill, which soon made backyard cooking a national pastime and created a demand for little bags of charcoal.

Nowadays, there are many brands of briquettes on the market, and they're all made roughly the same way they have been since Orin Stafford first introduced them. However, that process has been refined. The reason some people stay away from briquettes is the additives used along with the pure charcoal. For instance, the recipe used by Kingsford, which still makes the country's best-selling briquettes, includes wood char, mineral char and mineral carbon (both extra heat sources), limestone (to improve the look of the ash), starch (binder), borax (to help the briquettes slip out of their molds during production), and sawdust (to help the briquettes ignite). Although seeing ingredients like limestone and borax might make you balk, they're both naturally occurring minerals. All in all, despite the laundry list of additives, none of them is terribly concerning. But still, it's hard to get away from the thought of cooking on all those substances that have nothing to do with wood, especially when there are other, cleaner options.

Those options are briquettes labeled "all natural," which contain nothing but char and 4 to 5 percent binder made from vegetable starch. If you care about such things, why not use all natural? There's really nothing to lose. And if you're in the common situation of needing to add more charcoal to an already hot coal bed to extend the length of a cook, a fresh briquette that lacks additives is preferable to one full of additives. So we always choose all-natural charcoal.

Some really great all-natural charcoal briquettes are out there. B&B charcoal, based in Texas, makes some of the best around. Stubb's briquettes are very good, too, as are Kingsford Competition all-natural briquettes. Royal Oak is another good-quality, popular brand.

The advantage of briquettes over lump charcoal is precision. If you've practiced and paid attention to your charcoal use, you more or less know exactly how much heat you can get out of one briquette, allowing you to manage your coal bed to whatever the desired temperature and to know how many more briquettes to add when the fire needs more fuel.

The last thing to say about briquettes is to ignore the kind known as "easy lighting" or "self-starting." These arrive saturated with some sort of lighter fluid, so all you have to do is strike a match and throw it onto a pile of them and they'll ignite. The problem is that lighter fluid is petroleum based and gross, which means you definitely don't want it coming anywhere near your food. Lighting a batch of charcoal in a chimney (see page 142) is easy and effective, making lighter fluid–soaked briquettes unnecessary.

Lump Charcoal

When it came to marketing this stuff, maybe they could have found a better word than *lump* to compete against the more suave-sounding *briquette*. Sometimes this charcoal is called "hardwood charcoal" or "charwood," both an improvement on "lump." Whatever it's called, it's a different, simpler form of char than briquettes: the original, basic, ancient form of charcoal, made solely from pure wood burned in a sealed chamber. No need for binders, accelerants, or igniters.

Because it's pure carbon with no additives, lump charcoal should theoretically burn hotter but shorter than briquettes. That said, it's difficult to compare the fires from both types of charcoal because lump is so varied in size and shape. Even if you weighed out the same exact amount of both lump and briquettes and then burned them, you'd probably get different results each time you did the test. If the pieces of lump are big and awkwardly shaped, the resulting coal bed might be hotter, as more air would likely be able to move through the stack. On the other hand, if the pieces are small and include a bunch of dust from the bag, the fire might be cooler because less oxygen can penetrate the mass.

Some claim that lump gives more flavor than briquettes, though in theory this shouldn't be the case. After all, if the charcoal is properly made, there will be little to no actual wood left in the material. So whether the original material was mesquite or oak should make slim difference. In practice, however, sometimes the wood isn't completely carbonized, meaning some wood compounds are left to burn and provide a bit of smoky flavor. (If you truly *want* smoky flavor in your meat, this whole question is moot: just throw a little actual wood on the coals and you'll get as much or as little of the smoke as you need.)

Lump charcoal does have a couple of drawbacks, both of which arise in lower-quality products. It's not uncommon to find bits of foreign objects in bags of lump charcoal, such as nails, staples, cords, shards of plastic, and the like. First, you definitely don't want these things to be cooking into your food. Second, their presence suggests the wood you're using may not have been pristine logs in the first place, but rather some sort of reclaimed or treated wood from who knows where. Another issue with lump charcoal is that, because of the irregular shapes of the pieces, it tends to have a lot of useless dust in the bag. That's because lump charcoal can grind down against itself in transit and in the store. This dust is useless and can even have the effect of inhibiting combustion if it gets into you coal bed.

Binchōtan

If you've never splurged on a small package of expensive but amazing Japanese charcoal, or binchōtan, you should consider playing around with it, as it's amazing stuff. For instance, it

THE BOTTOM LINE: LUMP VERSUS BRIQUETTES

This is always the great question. You want a lively, somewhat erratic fire that may get really hot but not last long? Go lump. It's perfect for searing steaks. Or do you want something more mellow and consistent that will burn longer and with some predictability? Go briquettes, which are the best anchor for longer-cooking meats.

Here are a couple of other suggestions to help you get to the heart of this debate. When you choose a brand of charcoal—lump or briquette—stick with it for a few months or even a year before you try something else. Get to know its trajectory and heating curves. Note its behaviors. Does it light easily and come quickly to temperature? Or does it start slowly and then maintain a very hot plateau for a long time? Or maybe it reaches a peak and then comes crashing down quickly? Once you have confidence

you understand the way that choice behaves, you can stay with it as your go-to charcoal or endeavor to learn a new one.

Another option in the never-ending debate of lump versus charcoal is to completely ignore the question at hand and change the rules, much like Captain Kirk did when he undermined the Kobayashi Maru test on the original *Star Trek*. Why choose one when you can also mix the two charcoals together? Load a chimney half full with your favorite all-natural briquettes and then fill the other half with your chosen brand of lump hardwood charcoal. This way you get the stamina of briquettes in a dense coal bed. But you also get the flair of lump with its searing highs, and its irregular-shaped pieces will contrast with the briquettes to keep the coal bed well aired without too much ash.

clangs like metal when you bang it together. While it has an eerie whitish gray cast like a White Walker, it in fact burns really, really hot and maintains that heat for hours and hours. And if you don't need a 900°F heat source for a full five or six hours, you can submerge the coals in water, let them dry for a day, and use them again.

Made using a process that goes back centuries to the Edo period (or perhaps much longer, as the record isn't clear), binchōtan takes its name from a single artisan, Binchū-ya Chōzaemon, who perfected the process. Today, binchōtan is still made by artisans, as its process requires much more nuance and technique than Western

charcoal. The finest is said to come from Kishu in Wakayama Prefecture, an area in the southern part of Japan, south and west of Osaka. The wood used for traditional binchōtan is called *ubame* oak (*Quercus phillyraeoides*), a native Japanese species with heavy, shiny leaves and a diminutive stature. These trees don't grow like twisting, gnarled, massive live oak trees. Rather, their branches are relatively thin and wiry, making them not much of a building material.

The wood is harvested in mountains and brought to nearby stone kilns. The branches are generally crowded upright into the kiln, and a fire is started using the same wood. Then the kiln is mostly sealed up, to keep the temperature lower than what is used to make conventional black charcoal. This slow, methodical burning is monitored by the producers for up to a couple of weeks, as they examine and smell the smoke emerging from the kiln. When they can tell that most of the volatiles have burned off, they increase the heat massively and seal the kiln for a short time, which purifies and protects the carbon left in the wood without destroying it. At the right moment, the kiln is opened and the glowing, almost neon-orange branches are raked out (using *really* long rakes, as it can be over 1800°F inside) and instantly smothered under a mixture of damp sand and ash to cool them down quickly. This dusty ash covers the oak, giving it its distinctive white cast.

The result is a product of almost pure carbon, far purer than our black charcoal. Besides its role as a heat source, binchōtan has many other uses. For example, it's a great water purifier: just drop a small piece of it into a pitcher of water and it will instantly start burbling the water through its negative space, filtering out the impurities that stick to the vast, microscopically porous surface of the charcoal. It can do the same filtering magic for the air in a room.

Because of its long life, you see it used at yakitori grills in Japan, as a handful of pieces can last an entire six-hour service. Also, because they're practically pure carbon, binchōtan coals burn with almost no smoke. Jordan loves nothing more than ducking into a little Tokyo bar or *izakaya*, ordering a draft beer (the Japanese major labels like Asahi and Yebisu taste so much better over there) or a Hibiki with a cube, and then sitting back to watch the cooks grill skewers of everything from pork to chicken skin, closely above the glowing-hot binchōtan coals. There's no smoke, and the

meat is so near the heat that the evaporating meat juices are captured and spritz back up onto the meat. It doesn't create flare-ups, just vapors of oils and other compounds seasoning the meat. Of course, fatty beef *will* create flames, so be careful. When cooking beef over binchōtan this way, most chefs use very thin slices that need the ultrahigh, clean heat to sear the outside but leave the inside nice and juicy.

One additional note about binchōtan: It's hard to light, as it takes long, intense heat to get going. The easiest way to do it is to light a chimney half full of regular charcoal and place the binchōtan above that for twenty to thirty minutes. And, as mentioned, if you don't need sustained high heat for five or six hours, you should submerge the binchōtan in water, dry it, and use it another time.

Coconut Charcoal

Charcoal made from coconut shells hails from Southeast Asia. Its fans love it for a number of reasons: It burns hotter than American charcoal and with very little smoke and ash, and it burns for a long time (though not binchōtan long). Some say the vapor it does emit has a sweet smell. Made from the spent hulls of coconuts, it's more eco-friendly than other forms of charcoal, as the process recycles a natural waste product—no trees are cut down. It's more expensive than conventional charcoal, but half the amount gives the same heat for the same length of time.

To make the charcoal, carbonized coconut shells (after about a day of cooking in sealed pits) are ground into a powder, which is mixed with starch (usually from the root of the cassava shrub, also the source of tapioca) and a little water to bind it. Perhaps the cassava starch is what produces the sweet odor. This mixture is extruded into thick-walled tubes and then baked again to remove the water. The result is very dense, heavier than conventional wood char. Like charcoal making everywhere, coconut charcoal doesn't seem to be a particularly highly regulated industry, so quality varies from brand to brand and sometimes even within single brands. When not well made, coconut charcoal can feel messy because it produces a ton of ash while still fetching prices well above conventional wood charcoal. So, if using it, pay attention to its performance and demand better if you think it's producing too much ash and burning uncleanly.

Coconut char is perfect for grills operated by street vendors in places like the Philippines, Malaysia, and Thailand. These cooks, who transport portable grills on the backs of their bicycles and motorbikes, are ready to whip up a fire at any time and grill narrow strips or skewers of meat. Only a small amount of charcoal is needed to fire these grills, which makes dense, hot, long-burning coconut charcoal the perfect solution. Because of the cost and large amount of space required, it's not economical to think about firing the vast cooking surfaces of American-style grills, unless you're grilling a variety of things over a period of an hour and a half to two hours. However, coconut briquettes have been embraced by some American cooks doing long or overnight cooks on their home grills. The lack of ash and the extended cook times make the briquettes ideal for a low-and-slow approach.

Wood: Hug a Tree Today

Enough about charcoal. Even if charcoal has been a species-altering technology (much as the cow was a species-altering animal), using it will never be the equivalent of cooking with wood. When Jordan asked Victor Arguinzoniz, a chef who cooks everything on his menu over wood and whose restaurant, Asador Etxebarri (see page 131) in the Basque Country of Spain, is one of the greatest in the world, to name the most important factor in cooking a steak well (and he makes a great one), his answer was simple: "Use only wood."

You'd have to be blind to miss—as backlash in the wake of molecular gastronomy and the advent of sous vide—that one of the biggest restaurant trends in the last ten years has been the construction of wood-fired hearths. They seem to occupy a central space in every other fashionable restaurant opening these days. Chefs such as Francis Mallmann of Argentina and his rustic, remote mountain hearths and campfire coziness have captured the imagination of a new generation of chefs and diners alike.

Fire has a powerful pull. No other fuel offers the savory, smoky, spicy flavor of wood—not to mention the primal sense of warmth and community, romance, and mental and physical engagement. The smell of sweet wood smoke causes people in the area to snap their heads up when they catch a whiff. The crackle of gently burning wood reminds the ears that this fire is its own living thing. It's also a beacon of civilization and safety. Jordan remembers as a little kid backpacking through the mountains of Washington with his family and feeling terrified by the vastness and loneliness of the peaks, forest, and night sky towering above him. But once his dad or his uncle got that fire crackling, all fear, isolation, and forlornness lifted away, like smoke to the stars. Yet given all the wonderment of fire, most of the time we content ourselves to cooking over charcoal. Why?

As any good scout working on a merit badge knows, a good wood fire is a commitment, and not a small one. Not terribly different from a great affair of the heart, a fire-stoked affair of the hearth brings pleasure but also pain. Indelibly etched in Aaron's brain are thousands of nights spent around a fire. At this point, he has probably spent more time tending fires than doing anything else. The sound of the crackling, the smell of smoke, and that jumpy light are as comforting as cracking open a beer. He's fallen asleep next to fires more times than he can count. (He's not that good at counting, probably because he's also lost so much sleep staying up to make sure the fire keeps going.) He constantly smells like smoke and can't always shower it out of his hair. But he likes to think that cavemen might have been a lot like that, too, except they didn't have shampoo.

An energetic, blazing fire isn't easy to create—it takes planning and time—and can be just as difficult to control. It has a mind of its own and often the muscle to defy you. It can be dangerous and wasteful. It's a commitment of time, attention, and physical engagement. It's an agreement that you and everything you're wearing will smell like smoke until the next shower and washing. It's an acceptance that you're going to get slightly dirty and will have a good bit of cleaning up and ash removal to do. Furthermore, wood can be expensive, and you go through a lot of it in the effort to create and maintain a good coal bed.

But we all know it's worth it—every grimy smear of ash on the brow, every shower you have to take to get the smoke out of your hair, every singed eyelash. Wood fire makes it up to you by creating the most delicious meals and offering memorable experiences that bring people closer to one another and to our own natures.

CHOOSING WOOD

Remember, steak is the ultimate piece of ingredient-driven cuisine, and the fire is a key ingredient, so think of wood as you would any crucial component of a dish. You should choose it with the same care you choose the meat. Follow the same guidelines as you would for smoking: hardwoods over softwoods, good seasoning over green, and sourced from healthy trees over sick.

Hardwoods come from deciduous trees (ones that shed their leaves annually) and produce some sort of nut or fruit. Examples include oak, cherry, maple, hickory, apple, almond, and many more. Softwoods are conifers and are to be avoided. They have needles instead of leaves and include cedar, pine, fir, spruce, and redwood. Hardwoods have a much slower growth rate and much higher density than softwoods and thus cost more. They also have a resistance to fire that makes them slower and more even burning.

Of course, nothing is ever that simple. Some softwoods are harder than hardwoods. Balsa, for instance, is technically a hardwood, but anyone who's done arts and crafts knows that it's way softer than pine. Of course, you never want to cook with pine, as it has highly flammable resins that, when burning, give off a noxious, sooty smoke that's the last thing you want landing on your food.

Plaza de San Juan, 1
48291 Atxondo, Bizkaia
tel: (+34) 946-58-30-42 • asadoretxebarri.com

It is no surprise that we talk a lot about Spain in this book, seeing as it boasts a legendary carnivorous nature and is home to the greatest steak culture in Europe. Across the country—but especially in the north in Basque Country—are hundreds of little *asadors*, grills that specialize in steak. Unfortunately, the secret is out on the greatest of them, Asador Etxebarri (etch-a-bar-ee), in the small town of Axpe, about an hour outside of San Sebastián in the foothills of the Pyrenees. In the 2018 version of the *The World's 50 Best Restaurants*, Etxebarri clocked in at number 10, which is absurd considering it's open only for lunch except on Saturdays, and there's no fancy cooking, no spherification or gelification or foams or even sous vide. Rather, Etxebarri is one of the most primitive restaurants anywhere—everything is cooked only on wood coals. This is chef Arguinzoniz's way. A quiet guy, he grew up in a farmhouse that lacked electricity, so everything was grilled, everything kissed by smoke. Eventually, he bought an old, run-down restaurant in the center of town and started cooking the same way.

But Arguinzoniz's culinary ambition soon grew, and he began to devise little mesh baskets in which to cook things like tiny eels and caviar over fire. He built a collection of mini-grills, each with a Santa Maria–like raising and lowering cable to control heat. And he purposed two ovens in which to keep a constant supply of wood coals at the ready, one for oak coals and one for coals made out of grape vines. After each service, the grill grates are scoured back to perfectly clean stainless steel. Victor wants no lingering bitterness from char passed on to his ingredients—whether langoustines, tuna, or porcini—all of which are impeccably sourced to display a purity and vibrancy we rarely if ever experience. Seasoning is only salt, olive oil, and delicate smoke. It's not unreasonable to compare Victor's mastery of the grill to Mozart's of the musical note or Serena Williams's genius with the tennis racket. Each dish gets its own little mound of coals, perfectly calibrated to cook with absolute precision. Items emerge from the fire vibrant and fresh, with the line between raw and cooked hard to comprehend. It is as if they still bear some energy, some lingering soul from when they were alive.

The savory finale of each meal (before the smoked ice cream) is a *txuleta*, or rib steak from a superannuated, locally raised dairy cow, sometimes fifteen or eighteen years old at slaughter. Tender, juicy, and intensely beefy, the steak bears only oil and some crunchy crumbles of sea salt. For most who taste it, it's the best steak they've ever consumed.

SEASONING GRILL WOOD

Seasoning is the amount of time a log has had to dry out. It's perhaps even more important in grilling than in smoking. In an offset barbecue pit, if you've got a raging fire of 750°F in your firebox, including a poorly seasoned log every now and then is not going to make a decisive difference. However, if you're grilling and burning basically one log at a time, green wood can drive you crazy. First, the wetter the wood, the worse the smoke. Then, evaporating all that excess water in the wood costs energy and will keep the temperature of your fire down. For complete combustion and the good fine smoke you want, you need well-seasoned wood.

As always, when you go out to the wood pile, you'll find logs of varying weights and shapes. Hopefully, most of them will be cut to pretty much the same size. Pick up several different pieces in your hands. Some will weigh more than others, often considerably so. You'll be surprised that two similar-looking logs can feel so different in heft. The idea is to get a sense of the ranges and choose something in the middle. If the log is too heavy, it's not well seasoned. Leave it on the pile for another few months (or years, depending on the climate). If it's too light, the wood is extremely well seasoned and will go up like a match, which lends an unpredictable and charged quality to any cooking fire. Use that piece in the fireplace in winter or throw it on early in your fire and let it burn down before cooking.

(Note, too, that much of the prepackaged firewood sold in grocery stores is kiln dried, a process that speeds up the seasoning. It's good for getting your living room fireplace hopping, but most of it is overseasoned for grilling purposes. We don't recommend it.)

TYPES OF WOOD

Any hardwood can be great for grilling if you age it long enough. That said, different species of hardwoods tend to display different characteristics. They are subtle, for sure, but if you work with one kind of wood for long enough, you do get to know it. As with charcoal, we recommend that you commit to a type of hardwood for a few months or perhaps a year. Even without trying—you don't need to keep a journal or a spreadsheet detailing your experiences—you'll develop a keen knowledge and sense for the wood.

Alder

Most famous as a vehicle for salmon, alder is hardwood carrying a mellow, slightly sweet profile that goes well with fish. Jordan has cooked with it a bunch in the Pacific Northwest, where his family's from, and knows that alder also sets a good fire and can be used effectively to gently season steak. When camping out in the San Juan Islands in Puget Sound, you can find seasoned alder, build a fire, and grill local oysters over it before throwing on some local coastal-raised beef. The wood has a sweetness that goes well with salt. Put alder with the more delicately flavored cuts like the tenderloin. It's also better with steak that hasn't been dry aged too long, as the funkiness from aging clashes with the sweetness of the wood.

Apple

As you'd expect, this classic fruitwood has a bright, fruity, and somewhat sweet character. It's even more subtle than alder, though, and its flavor might get crushed by beefier cuts. Use it on delicate cuts, like tenderloin, or on thinner cuts that spend less time on the grill.

Cherry

A wonderful and fairly rare fruitwood for cooking, cherry has a delightful floral sweetness that we associate with other fruit trees. But there's something else, a little more depth and richness that allows it to work well for both pork and beef. With beefy steaks, it can handle the heavier, more richly flavored cuts, like New York strip, bavette, and flat iron.

Hickory

A specialty of the Midwest and the South, hickory can be counted on for relatively strong flavors, but also for strong and long burn times, which makes it a great foundation for a fire. Aaron has only good things to say about cooking with hickory; it's his second choice after oak. Hickory may be a little sweeter than oak, but it burns just as consistently. The flavor it imparts to the meat gives a sense of depth and umami, a rich savory note, and an abiding sweetness. It's great for the rich, beefy cuts, like ribeye, porterhouse, and strip.

Mesquite

The controversial wood—some love it, some hate it. More than any other kind of smoke, mesquite can always be recognized. It's usually not Aaron's first choice—it doesn't have that softness or sweetness of oak. Mesquite is a hardwood that is indeed very hard and very dense. *Aged* mesquite is a different story, though—it grills great! It just takes a long time to season properly. Mesquite tends to burn quickly and hot, which is why it's popular for charcoal. (Also because it grows in inhospitable places, often as a pest, choking out grasslands for grazing.) Its massive root system makes it

hard to remove, and its thorns can cut through anything, including car tires. It's an ornery wood with an ornery flavor. Used in too great an amount, its harsh, peppery flavor will dominate any ingredient. That's why you don't want to smoke things over it. However, carefully used in short-cooking situations, such as flank or skirt steaks, mesquite can be acceptable.

Oak

May the smell of oak be with you. Even just saying "oak smoke" sounds good. (Aaron likes to joke about coming up with some sort of fragrance line based on oak, like Oak Smoke Joke!) Post oak is the signature wood of Central Texas, and it's the sweetest, richest, cleanest-burning, straight, easy-to-handle wood there is. It's perfect for everything. You can almost never go wrong with any good old oak, however. Red oak, white oak—use anything but green oak. Actually, live oak needs a few years of seasoning before its character is rid of a somewhat intense herbal greenness. Of course, the Central Texas favorite post oak continues to be a blessing. It not only burns beautifully but also offers a lovely balanced flavor. In general, oak brings some undertones of vanilla to a profile steeped in spiciness and sweetness. It's more savory than fruitwoods, but more high-toned than hickory.

Pecan

The pecan is actually a part of the hickory family and closely related to the walnut. The wood has a delicate fruitiness to it, with some hints of nut and spice. It tends to burn long but fairly cool and without too much smoke. In the fall, when the pecan nuts hit the ground, some people even throw spent pecan shells into their

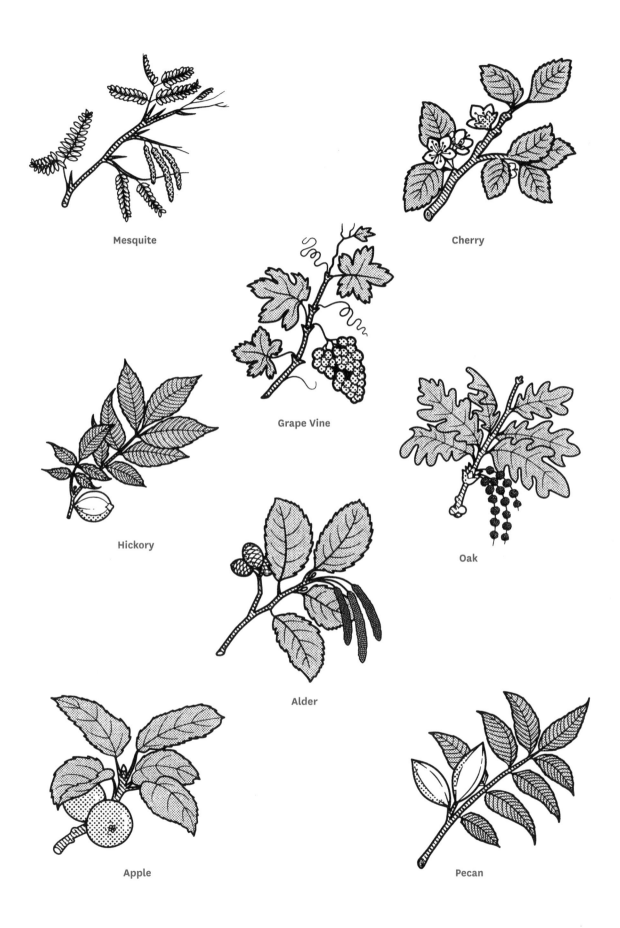

Mesquite

Cherry

Grape Vine

Hickory

Oak

Alder

Apple

Pecan

fires before putting on the steaks to add a spicy, sweet tinge to the smoke.

Grape Vine

Now that nearly every state is producing some sort of wine from grapes, it means nearly everyone has the opportunity to get grape vines for cooking. This is a woody substance, but not from a tree. Using vines is a good way to reproduce some of the flavor of a good steak cooked over fire in places like Tuscany or rural France. Jordan once stayed for a couple of nights in a three-hundred-year-old stone house in the town of Panicale, Umbria, in Italy. The house had a big, old fireplace and was close to a great Italian butcher. He couldn't resist trying to do a *bistecca fiorentina*, the great steak of Tuscany, so he bought a huge, two-and-a-half-inch-thick porterhouse from the butcher and then drove up behind a nearby winery and grabbed a trunkful of old grape vines piled behind a stone barn. Back at the house, he built a roaring fire out of the vines. When the flames died down, he threw on the steak and cooked it until almost burned on the outside. The coals burned out before the steak was done, and it was still raw in the middle. But he didn't mind, as that's the way the Italians eat it anyway. And when you wash it down with some local, tannic Sangiovese, it tastes great.

While it's not easy to find large chunks from thick grape vines (because few are removed each year), vines are pruned of their long canes annually. Most trimmings get stacked up and thrown away. But if you see some or know someone with a winery, don't let them go to waste. Make sure they're well dried, though. They're cut off living plants in the winter, so if you collect them in February or March, bundle them up, and store them through the summer and into fall, they should be ready to go. A handful of dried grape vines thrown on the fire can add a vibrant, peppery spice note. Think of them as seasoning for the fire—add them to another wood, as they are too thin to make a decent fire or create coals on their own.

SOURCING GRILL WOOD

If you want to grill over real wood coals, it's good to buy in bulk and store the wood at your house. If you've got a shed or a covered area, all the better. If you need to stack it on the side of the house, that's fine, but cover it with a tarp in case of showers. You'll want the backlog (no pun intended!) because you'll find yourself going through a lot of wood, and you don't want to have to worry about running out of it.

Finding a good source is necessary. Most areas, even urban ones, are served by a number of firewood delivery services. These are usually companies that are also in the tree trimming and removal business. Much of the time, the landowners just want the wood off their property, so it becomes a free commodity to the sellers. However, wood sellers have to have their own property where they can stack and age it.

Do a little research to find the most honest, reliable companies. For instance, if there's a restaurant you like with a live-fire grill, ask the manager for the source of the wood. Perhaps that firewood vendor would be willing to supply you, too. If people are selling wood on the side of the road, ask how long they've been keeping the wood and what shape the wood is in. For instance, if you live in a rainy area and the wood hasn't been aged long, it may require more aging before it's optimal for using in a cooking fire.

It seems the price of a cord of wood (128 cubic feet, or a stack that's four feet wide and high and eight feet long) has gotten more expensive over the years. We remember a time when it was $75, but in many places now it often runs between $250 and $450. (In Napa, where Jordan lives, it can go over $500 for a delivery—and that doesn't include stacking; a truck drives up and the wood is just dumped in a massive pile in your yard.) And this depends on the type of wood. Softwoods like pine tend to be significantly cheaper than hardwoods. Of course, always spend the extra bucks on the latter.

CUTTING WOOD DOWN TO SIZE

So you've got your firewood delivered and stacked. It's been aged for a few years by the time you bought it, so it's good to go. Now you just need to have it in usable sizes for whatever your grill setup is.

The equipment you'll want is an electric saw and a maul. You could cut your wood down with a chainsaw, but that can be clumsy and dangerous. A better idea is a miter saw (more of a finesse instrument) or chop saw (a bit burlier). These are both saws with circular blades that rotate quickly and can be raised and lowered by hand to cut through whatever's in front of them.

A quick word of warning: These things are dangerous if used carelessly. Always do your wood cutting earlier in the day, and never under the influence of alcohol. Make sure the saw is well anchored and that the log is comfortably and stably resting under the blade. If the wood isn't secure between the base and the side of the saw, there's a real danger it could kick out

violently as it is being cut, putting everything at risk. Please be careful!

Firewood usually comes in 16- to 18-inch lengths. For Aaron's signature setup in the PK (see page 148), he likes to cut that down to a 12-inch log, so a whole log fits snugly in the grill. Then the 4- to 6-inch leftover pieces can be used as small logs for making the base fire in the PK or in another grill.

The 6-inch pieces need to be split so they'll burn faster and more evenly. As always, the tool of choice for splitting wood is a maul, not an ax. This is because we are splitting wood along the grain. (An ax is for chopping wood against the grain; a maul is for splitting it with the grain.) The maul is the lovechild of an ax and a sledgehammer. It is much heavier than an ax, and the point is to use its own weight to crack the wood in half. Once the blunt edge finds the grain in the wood, it effortlessly snaps the wood in two. You can get mauls with 32- or 36-inch-long handles, but if all you're doing is splitting little pieces of firewood into smaller sizes and kindling, a 16- or 24-inch handle will be easier to maneuver.

Once you've sourced your fuel—whether it's a quick bag of charcoal you purchased that morning or some perfectly seasoned wood you bought from a reliable source and cut down to the ideal size, it's finally time to get lit—er, get your fire lit. Since you've perhaps gone to the trouble of buying well-sourced meat, dry aging it to perfection, and seasoning your hardwood for a year or two, a lot is riding on the success of this fire. In the next chapter, we're going to put it all together and end up with something extraordinary to eat.

PERF

Part III

STEAK
ECTION

CHAPTER 7

Firing Up

So, okay, after however many dozens of pages, it's finally time for the main event: putting meat to fire. Well, we're almost there. (This kind of reminds us of the last book, where you're not cooking brisket until the third act.) Anyway, this long-winded display isn't intentional (though we do like to yak), but you've got to walk before you run and you've got to have good fuel and meat before you can produce transcendent steak. And you've also got to have some good tools, as they will make the job better, easier, and less painful. What's a surgeon without a scalpel? What's a painter without a brush? So in this chapter, we're going to look at the basic stuff you should have at hand in order to get a fire rip-roaring, manipulate hot coals and sizzling meats, and do it all without hurting yourself or making too much of a mess.

Then we're going to offer some ideas for grill setups and coal-bed alignments. We're basically making the simple act of cooking a steak more complicated. But it's oh, so good!

Equipment

As with cooking almost anything, being prepared when the food hits the fire is an important key to success. Make sure your *mise en place* (prepped ingredients) is perfect, that all the tools you'll need are nearby. These tools are neither expensive nor hard to find, so no excuses on cutting corners.

CHARCOAL CHIMNEY: LET THERE BE FIRE!

You'd think this simple piece of technology would be so common now that everyone with a backyard grill would have to own one, but surprisingly that's not the case. Every year we meet a couple of people who, on seeing a charcoal chimney, say, "Wow, I've got to get one of those!" Go figure.

A chimney is nonnegotiable. Every home griller should have one. They're not only the easiest, cleanest, and most effective way to light charcoal but also a cooking medium in and of themselves. All you need is some newspaper or other dry paper and a bag of your favorite charcoal. Within twenty minutes you'll have a glowing mound of incendiary charcoal hot enough to grill anything you want.

A chimney is just a thin metal cylinder with an insulated handle attached. The cylinder has two chambers. The smaller bottom one is separated from the top one by a perforated sheet or thin

steel bars, and the top chamber is open to the sky. Air holes have been cut out around the sides.

Here's how to use it • Turn the chimney upside down so the shorter chamber is facing up. This is where you stuff a couple of sheets of crumpled newspaper, a scrunched-up paper bag, or even a few wads of paper torn out of your bag of charcoal. Don't compact the paper too much, as this is what you're going to light and it needs channels for oxygen to power the flames.

Pro tip • To ensure that the paper burns completely, squirt it with a little cooking oil.

Now turn the chimney right side up and set it down on a hard stone surface or even on top of your charcoal grill. Fill the top with charcoal, as much as you think you'll need. For short, small cooks where you don't need too much heat, maybe you need to fill it only halfway or less. A reverse sear (see page 165) on a thick bone-in ribeye is a good example. If you're grilling a bunch of steaks or need extremely high heat, fill it up.

Light the paper in the bottom. In less than a minute, you'll see plumes of thick, white smoke emanating from the chimney. This is the paper burning and starting to catch the bottommost pieces of charcoal (which create a lot of smoke). Within a few more minutes, the paper will have burned out and you'll see a much smaller trail of smoke coming from the chimney. This means it's lit. In the next few minutes, you'll hear popping and crackling and see sparks starting to shoot out of the top like miniature fireworks. If you don't, add some more paper and relight the chimney.

After about fifteen minutes, you'll see coals glowing orange and turning white with ash, a sign they are really heating up. When they are

on the cusp of turning from black to white, dump the contents of the chimney into the space on your grill you want to heat. It's that simple.

The reason to have two chimneys on hand is if you need to start with a larger coal bed or need a quick refresh of hot coals. A standard-size large chimney, like the Weber Rapidfire (at fifteen dollars a very good buy; it holds about five pounds of charcoal and has a helper handle to supply more leverage when pouring the coals out), will fill up only about one-third to one-half of the grill space on a PK Grill. So if

you're cooking for a lot of people and you need a broader coal bed, you'll want to start with more coals. Lighting consecutive batches of coals in the same chimney won't quite do the trick, as the first batch will have cooked down by fifteen to twenty minutes before the second one is ready to go.

TONGS: WHEN FINGERS ARE NOT ENOUGH

Tongs are as essential to a steak griller as a sword was to a musketeer. Like the sharp-tipped sword of a dueler, they allow you to deal with dangerous elements while keeping your distance. As extensions of our hands, tongs are useful for much more than just flipping meat and vegetables. You'll find yourself using them to convey individual coals or even small chunks of wood from one grill to another. You can poke them through the grates to stir up a dying coal bed to get it roaring again. And you can pick up the entire grate, if need be, to add more charcoal or wood to the fire. Have several pairs of tongs handy at all times; you'll constantly find yourself reaching for them.

We've all probably cooked with ninety-nine-cent tongs from the supermarket—and let us remind you, singed knuckles and burned hands are no fun. Spend a few extra dollars for heavy-duty, well-made tongs.

GRILL BRUSH: SCRAPE THIS

Cleaning the grill is an annoying task and therefore one that doesn't get done nearly as often as it should. The less often, the more annoying, as you quickly find yourself dusted in ash and your hands covered with greasy, sooty streaks. Not only is the task annoying, but it's also inconvenient. The best time to clean the grill is immediately after you finish cooking on it, when it's still hot and covered with new oils, fats, and crusts. Of course, the moment you take steaks off the grill, you're inevitably concerned with getting everything to the table, not to mention monitoring your steaks as they rest. Cleaning the grill is the last thing on your mind, which means that it often doesn't get cleaned until the next time you use it. That could be the next day, the following weekend, and even weeks or months down the road.

But clean grates are essential to good cooking. First, they help keep food from sticking. Baked-on sugars and proteins create a surface for your meats to bind to when you put them on even a hot grill. Second, sooty or carbonized grates will add a bitterness to whatever you're grilling on them. And last, the thought of picking up traces of old foods cooked on unclean grills is nasty.

A durable grill brush can grind a grill clean with only a few passes. Find one that holds up to continuous use and won't fall apart (leaving dangerous wire bristles behind) or break. We've had the best luck with brushes designed with a trio of brush extensions coming from a single handle. These allow you to press with the greatest force on the grill without breaking the stem.

To get the most out of your grill brush, scrape the grates when they're hot and the coals are reaching their peak. The detritus you scrape off will simply be incinerated by the coals. If you want to spray some water onto the brush to get the benefit of some steam while cleaning, that can help, too. Scrape often, even after cooking one round of meats and before the next.

TROWEL AND STEEL PAIL: THE BUCKET LIST

If you read our first book, you'll remember Aaron's favorite tool for working the big fires in his cookers was a full-size shovel. So you shouldn't be surprised to learn that small fires call for a small shovel and a bucket. These classic garden tools double as useful props on a trip to the beach, but for the home griller, a sturdy little shovel and a durable bucket always come in handy. A trowel or small shovel can be used to shovel out hot coals or for prodding and working the coal bed, lifting the grill grate, and tidying things up. It's also good for scooping ash when you're cleaning out the grill.

A bucket is one of the most useful tools, not just in grilling but in life. Use it to transport coals from a wood-burning fire to a grill, for instance. Dump ash into it when you need to clean out your grills or fireplace. If your needs are few, fill it with ice and beer. And if nothing else, turn it over and sit on it.

SHEET PANS: YOU'RE GOING TO SHEET YOUR PANS

When you're grilling, trekking between kitchen and grill is inevitable. You need trays sturdy enough to hold a load, yet light enough to be easy to carry with one hand while opening doors. Hence, the good old-fashioned sheet pan will always be your friend.

Equip yourself with a few each of half, quarter, and eighth sizes of commercial sheet pans. Their standard one-inch depth is plenty for collecting any juices a finished steak might leave. Also, purchase a couple of cooling racks that fit inside of them. This setup is good not just for carrying steaks in and out of the house but also for holding the meat (if you've presalted it) for a day or two in the refrigerator or you simply want to dry it off. Sheet pans are great because they're tough enough that you can actually put them on the grill grates or in the fire (handy for the three-zone cooking setup, facing page) and they'll hold up (even if that will likely render them useless for the kitchen again).

SIZZLE PLATTERS: SIZZLE ME THIS

You've seen them before: thin, small, oval metal plates stacked up fifteen or twenty high in hot restaurant kitchens, typically where jet-blasting flames are firing smoking woks and food comes off fast and furious every couple of minutes. They are really just miniaturized sheet pans, and they have much the same function. But they are handier than your ceramic plates at home, as they can go into hot ovens or onto hot grills without being damaged. And if you somehow manage to damage one, they're only a few bucks each at any restaurant supply store.

KITCHEN TOWELS: THE MOST MASSIVELY USEFUL THING

If you don't already have towels in your home, I'm not sure you should be cooking or serving anyone food. Stock up and always keep a generous supply handy. Let's just remind ourselves of some of the many uses of towels. Dampened, they should be spread out underneath cutting boards to offer stability. They can be used instead of pot holders or gloves to pick up hot things or to protect hands from the fire while manipulating tongs. They clean up messes and spills. They dab the edges of sloppy platters. They can be soaked in cold water to wipe the brow of overheated grill cooks or to clean up

the grill itself or any work surface or tool. Find a towel style you like and plan to keep three or four clean ones at the ready.

DIGITAL THERMOMETER: HOT OR NOT?

Because of the short cooking time of steaks and their relatively small size, changes in temperature happen even more rapidly and dramatically than in larger pieces of meat, making a fast and accurate digital thermometer a necessity. Our favorite is still the ThermoWorks Thermapen. It's spendy, running between eighty and one hundred dollars (it goes on sale fairly often), but no other device matches it for speed and precision. When checking the temperatures of ribeyes still sizzling on top of a smoldering coal bed, you don't want to wait seconds to come up with a questionable reading. The Thermapen gives accurate results quickly. It's simply one tool no home chef should be without.

PLASTIC BOTTLE OF COOKING OIL: MAIN SQUEEZE

Surely you already have a bottle of handy cooking oil lingering around your stove. But keeping a plastic, restaurant-style squeeze bottle of cooking oil (Aaron uses grape seed because of its neutral flavor and high smoke point) handy is a low-maintenance, unfussy, easy-cleanup alternative to schlepping around a big glass bottle of oil. Use it to add a sheen to a steak before it goes on the grill, to moisten a paper towel that's about to be used to lubricate the grates before cooking, or to lightly prime the newspaper before lighting the chimney.

Bed Times and Fireside Chats: Setting Up Your Grill and Coals

Okay, *here* is the moment you've been waiting for: prepping your grill and lighting 'er up. At this stage, you have perhaps your biggest decision to make: how to set up the grill. This should always be determined by what you're cooking. For a handy cheat sheet, turn to page 151. But first we encourage you to think about *all* of the variables that go into a successful grill session. Do you have one steak to cook or six? Are they all going to be medium-rare or do some guests want medium and others want rare? Are you also cooking other proteins or vegetables?

Once you've got a sense of everything that's going on the grill, you need to plot out a workflow of when each item is going on, approximately how long it will take to cook, where it's going after it's done, and what's going on next. We're not saying you need to draw Venn diagrams or plot anything out on a computer. But do have a plan.

THE TWO-ZONE SETUP

This is elementary stuff that's been written about hundreds of times before, so we won't belabor it too much. And for those of you who already do a lot of grilling, this won't be anything new. But for those of you who have spent the last couple of decades living in a cave or a city or the Matrix and are just emerging into the world of grilling for the first time, this is the basic configuration you need to know for cooking steaks (and many other things).

You will want to cook any steak significantly thicker than one inch in two ways: quickly and slowly. Quickly uses direct heat radiated by close proximity to a bed of glowing-hot charcoal. Slowly cooks via heat carried by the air circulating around the meat, as in an oven. In the case of a wood or charcoal grill, the quick searing of meat happens via direct grilling, that is, right above a pile of massively hot coals. Slow cooking meat with hot air can also take place on a coal-fired grill, but it needs to happen in a "safe space"—a much cooler spot that makes it hard for the meat to burn or overcook—hence, the classic two-zone setup.

To achieve this, just dump the charcoal from your chimney on one side of the grill. In a rectangular, relatively shallow grill like a PK, this is incredibly easy, as the two sides are well defined. It's a little trickier in a round grill like a Weber; that's why some manufacturers have produced metal separators. And as mentioned previously, this is a pronounced challenge in the Big Green Egg and other kamado cookers: you can put the hot charcoal on one side of the base, but because of the awesome heat retention of the cooker's ceramic walls, if you shut the lid, the whole unit will heat up uniformly. If you *don't* shut the lid, the distance from the coals to the grill allows the heat to spread out, also nullifying the whole point of going with two zones.

THE THREE-ZONE SETUP, GRADUATED AND SPLIT

What could possibly be greater than two zones? Three, of course. Two zones just give you hot and cold. Why not treat yourself to hot, less hot, and cold? With more range, you can achieve greater nuance in the steaks, mimicking a little bit of the flexibility that an adjustable-height Santa Maria grill can offer.

There are a few ways to achieve the mythical three-zone setup. The first is just an elaboration of the two-zone grill, but in this one, you vary the depth of the coal bed to give you more options. A conventional two-zone configuration calls for coals on one side of the grill and nothing on the other. The graduated three-zone grill involves an inclined coal bed, using more coals on one deep end of the hot zone, fewer in the middle, and then nothing on the other half. This is perhaps easiest with briquettes: just pile your hot charcoal three or four pieces deep on one side, then as you move to the other side, slope the coal bed downward using less and less coal until in the middle the bed is just one briquette deep. This offers you very strong intense heat on the far left, declining all the way to indirect heat on the right.

Another variation, the split three-zone setup, calls for piles of coals on both ends of the grill and zero coals for indirect heat in the middle. This unique setup can be especially effective when cooking larger cuts, say two rib steaks two to three inches thick. You can lay the steaks flat on the grill in the middle, exposing them to heat from either direction. Or you can lay them on their sides. Then, to finish, you have two zones for direct cooking already prepared. For some meaty pyrotechnics, try placing a sheet pan or sizzle plate in the middle between the two coal beds. It will heat up quickly and catch the drippings and vaporize them, allowing their meaty mist to curl back up and infuse the steak, much as happens on a gas grill.

CHARCOAL AND ACCENT LOG (THE FRANKLIN FORMATION)

If you bought this book, you're probably wondering what Aaron's preferred grill setup is. Jordan calls it the Franklin Formation. Aaron calls it stickin' a log in there. It may sound simple, but the Franklin Formation (yes, that's what we're going with) is a terrific hybrid of cooking mediums, leveraging the convenience of charcoal while still tapping into the flavor of real wood. This method works especially well on a PK (see page 111) because of the rectangular shape of the grill, but it could be adapted to a round Weber, too.

First, lay a charcoal bed on one side of the grill. Don't leave the other, the indirect side, empty—oh no, this is when you stick a log in there! In the case of the PK, a log trimmed to twelve inches with a chop saw fits perfectly into the cooker's fourteen-inch width. The presence of the log provides a natural boundary against the coal bed. It also makes the indirect side cooler than if there was nothing filling the space, providing more of a contrast from the direct side and allowing even more nuanced cooking. The best part? The point where the hot charcoal contacts the log becomes a small area of combustion. The slightly burning log provides a bit of wood smoke and perhaps some flickers of flame. But because this is a large, dense, and not-too-seasoned piece of wood, there's no danger of it igniting and creating a conflagration, which is what happens if you toss small wood chunks onto the coal bed to get smoke. You can keep this going for a long time, and all you have to do is regularly replenish your charcoal bed; the piece of hardwood will take its time burning down. And it looks cool!

last nearly as long as charcoal, and catching them at their peak and maintaining them for as long as you need is a difficult proposition.

Next, space: A good wood fire needs space to hold enough wood to provide a consistent source of hot coals. This cycle of constant replenishment of wood and coals is why many restaurant grills sport some sort of reinforced metal cage in which logs are stacked high over a coal bed. As the lowest log starts to burn into coals, cooks rake those newly formed embers out under the grilling surface, allowing the fresh wood in the cage to slide down and keep the process going.

In the home setting, there are a number of ways to accomplish this. For instance, you can make a small wood fire in your grill using wood chunks. But once they get going, they burn up quickly, and if you need a stable coal bed for more than fifteen minutes or so, you'll have to add fresh wood to the coals. Fresh wood also produces a ton of flames and smoke, which might be overwhelming if you've got meat on the grill. So the answer is to do as the restaurants do and burn your wood down to coals at a little distance from where you're cooking the meat. But where?

At home, the best solution is to employ two grills. Trust us, it's actually much easier and cheaper than you imagine. If one grill is primarily going to be used to burn down logs, it needn't be fancy. It could be a light, inexpensive Weber with the grate removed so it can hold three or four standard-size logs. It can be handy to have a second grill anyway, for expanded space on the grates or an alternative shape. (If your primary is a PK, for instance, keep a round Weber on hand for things like pizza or paella.) A quick check on craigslist or another local listing

THE WOOD COAL SETUP

The Franklin Formation is handy because it's convenient, yet still has the allure of a wood fire. But we know there are folks out there who are only interested in the purest, most primal and existential grill setup: 100 percent wood fired.

We get it. Meats grilled over wood taste better than meats cooked over charcoal, pure and simple. Grilling over wood showcases the defining components of physical existence, time and space. First, time: When starting with logs, it takes a long time to develop a good coal bed. And *timing* remains a challenge throughout the cook because wood coals burn faster and don't site can often land a used Weber kettle for under fifty bucks. Another option is one of those premade firepits. These round, solid-metal pits are made to burn down logs, and they can double as a backyard campfire site to sit around on cool evenings.

With your trusty shovel and bucket to convey said coals to your primary grill space, you're ready to get cooking. You'll have enough coals to grill thick steaks (or rounds of them) over medium to low heat. Enjoy the fragrant whiff of wood smoke and flickering flames. Wood-fired grilling isn't just a cookout, it's a ritual.

Starting a Wood Fire and Building a Coal Bed

On page 142, we showed you how to light a fire if you plan to use charcoal, using our favorite charcoal tool, the chimney starter. Starting a wood fire is a bit trickier. First, make sure you have a few small wood chunks (four to six inches) as well as larger logs. The easiest way to get it all started is to light a handful of charcoal pieces in the renowned chimney and either put the wood chunks on top of them or simply dump the charcoal into your firepit and arrange the small pieces of wood on top. Throw on some crumpled newspaper to accelerate the process (which you can prime with cooking oil or tallow if you'd like).

Once you have a small fire going, put on a couple of larger pieces, and as the fire gets hotter and expands, some even larger pieces. Aaron does indeed like to build his little log cabins over a few glowing charcoal briquettes. And when he doesn't want quite a log cabin–size fire, he builds a tepee with three logs angled over the coals. The point is to have airflow coming in at the base so the heat catches the logs above.

If you just burn down one or two logs and take the coals to fire your grill, there won't be enough to sustain your wood fire. Instead, burn through a round or two of logs to establish a solid and enduring coal bed. (Hey, we said a wood fire takes time.) This is a philosophical, communal, meditative activity that requires an hour or two to ease into. If you're used to barbecuing ribs or brisket, which take even longer, you get it. Hanging out and drinking a beer as burning wood crackles and hisses and the smoke tickles your nose is one of life's great pleasures. The steaks taste better for it, too.

Grill Setups

The configuration of your grill is the second thing you should consider after what kind of steak you're going to cook, as it will determine what you can and can't do with a fire. There aren't too many variations, but the differences between them are important to note. More detailed accounts of each method were in the previous pages, but we've summarized them for you here.

SETUP	USES
Two zone	The standard setup, good for all steaks thicker than skirts and flanks, or any cut that needs to cook a little longer on the inside without overcooking the outside. The key is to make sure your zones are distinct: one superhot and one much cooler.
Three zone	When you need a bit more nuance, such as the thick tweener cuts between roasts and steaks, like tri-tips and thick-cut bone-in ribeyes.
Franklin Formation	The quick and easy way to cook using two zones with charcoal while getting a steady, even dose of wood smoke and a serious contrast in heat levels.
100 percent wood fire	The best historically, the best today, and the best forever and ever. No combustion-based heat source provides the depth of flavor, the sweet complexity, and the connection to our earthy souls like a coal bed made of real wood.

CHAPTER 8

The Cook

The barbecue mantra of "low and slow" has been in Aaron's head ever since he put his first brisket on a cheap offset smoker. And, indeed, he's logged thousands upon thousands of hours since then, many of them sleepily overnight, gently guiding large pieces of meat into transcendent states of tenderness and flavor. The art of barbecue is very much the art of controlling temperature—how to burn a clean, hot fire while at the same time maintaining absolute temperature consistency inside the cook chamber. But there's something appealing about the fast cook, too. In barbecue, the product is the smoke. You're not using the flame. When it comes to grilling stuff—which he loves to do—the flame is the product and you've got to figure out how to get the most of it without burning everything up. It's a completely different challenge.

Indeed, if slow cooking is like steering a canoe on a lake, grilling is like skimming wake on a Jet Ski. And while slow cooking is art, it's much more forgiving than fast cooking. Fast cooking relays different pleasures, but they require skill to coax out. The most flavorful steak on the planet if poorly cooked is lost to the world. Conversely, an exceptionally well cooked but average piece of meat can still be tasty. In other words, the cooking is super important for steak.

Now, truly, at last, everything is lined up. You have your meat: some excellent steaks you've been waiting to cook. Your equipment—sheet pans, towels, tongs, thermometer—is ready. Your grill setup is dialed in, and your fuel source is nearby. It's time to get grilling.

We've taught you *how* to achieve different grill setups, but now it's time to figure out *when* each is appropriate. This depends on factors like the kind of meat (grass fed or grain fed), the cut (lean or fatty), the size (thick or thin), and whether there's a bone or not.

The two primary goals for great steaks are simple: (1) a robust, savory crust across the entire surface of the meat, and (2) a perfect medium-rare finish (though you can customize this to your own taste).

GOAL #1
A Robust, Savory Crust

The crust is one of the things that makes a steak a steak. No other cut of beef can achieve the steak's deep, glistening, reddish brown crust, with its crystallized bits of protein and fat sparkling like gems and its deep, irresistible beefy smell. It's one of the most compelling phenomena in the entire world of food. And this crust comes from complex chemical processes called the Maillard reactions.

Named for the French scientist who discovered them in the early 1900s, the Maillard reactions are often conflated with caramelization. Although both produce complex molecules and both are referred to as browning reactions based on the color they produce in food, they are different. Caramelization involves the simple breakdown of sugars, whereas the Maillard reactions, according to Harold McGee in *On Food and Cooking*, are all about the thousands of new, distinct compounds created when amino acids react with a carbohydrate or sugar molecule in the presence of high heat. The Maillard effect happens not only to meat but to all sorts of things that brown, including bread, coffee beans, and chocolate. Like caramelization, McGee writes, brown color and deep flavor occur, but "Maillard flavors are more complex and meaty than caramelized flavors, because the involvement of the amino acids adds nitrogen and sulfur atoms to the mix . . . and produces new families of molecules and new aromatic dimensions."

That all sounds very sciency, and it is. But the bottom line is, the true glory of steak is not just a result of the cut itself but also, crucially, of how it is cooked: Maillard reactions when applied to the proteins in beef! Even if you boiled a ribeye, god forbid, to perfection, you'd come out with something far less appealing. That's because Maillard reactions don't occur in the presence of water. Until water becomes vapor, its temperature can't exceed its boiling point of 212°F. That's not hot enough for Maillard reactions to occur. High heat accelerates the rate at which reactions take place and hastens the evaporation of water. That means a dry cooking environment is needed, hence baking, grilling, and frying (yes, frying, that is, cooking with oil, is considered a dry technique, as water is anathema to oil).

So, Maillard is good. But how do you encourage it? How can you guarantee you're going to get a great crust on your meat? Making sure you have a dry environment, a dry surface, and high enough heat (but not so high that the meat burns) are the keys. Maillard browning occurs most optimally between 225°F and 355°F, so an insane amount of heat isn't even necessary. High heat only provides speedy browning before the heat has time to penetrate to the interior of the meat.

The most reliable, foolproof method to achieve a great crust is probably to cook the steak in a pan or on a *plancha* (a thick, steel flattop or griddle, whether fired by gas in a restaurant kitchen or placed on the grill over hot coals). This is because metal is a good conductor of heat, but not *too* good. It enables a prolonged exposure of the meat to heat, allowing a great range of Maillard reactions to take place.

Grilling can also achieve a tremendous crust, of course, but it's a little trickier, as the heat is usually much more intense. Glowing red coals can be so hot that browning on the exterior of the steak can happen too rapidly. Before you know it, you've taken the meat out of the realm of Maillard reactions and into the zone of pyrolysis (a fancy word for burning).

The art of steak cooking is finding the right rate of heating to accomplish Maillard browning without blowing right through it to burning before the interior is cooked to the desired doneness. That brings us to. . . .

GOAL #2
Proper Doneness

So let's get the formalities out of the way: Anyone can cook a steak to well-done. Today, most people—in the United States, anyway—consider that to be overdone, so we're not going to spend time talking about overcooking steaks. Most steaks taste best at medium-rare. Meat has little flavor when raw and is tough and bland when overcooked. Mid-rare is the fine line between them.

There are exceptions, of course, especially when it comes to butcher's cuts (see page 68). In some cases, the cut itself and the type of beef should have a say as to how the steak is cooked. Certain cuts or styles may benefit from a little more or a little less time over the fire. And everyone has his or her own tastes.

Heat-to-meat ratios can be a little counter-intuitive. For the least cooked meat you want the hottest fire. That is, a rare steak is cooked very hot because the outside cooks before the heat penetrates to the interior. Medium-rare takes a little more time and a lower flame because you have to slow it down. A well-done steak (perish the thought!) has to cook even slower over an even lower fire. Some people think well-done should be hotter and longer. That will result in a dry, tough piece of meat. Instead, sear it like a rare steak and then finish it over lower heat.

So how do we heat the interior of the steak to our desired doneness without overheating the exterior? The first thing to remember is that the thickness of the steak is more important than the weight. A two-inch-thick steak that weighs three pounds will cook much more slowly than a three-pound steak that's only a half inch thick. Well-marbled or fatty meat takes longer to reach the desired temperature than leaner beef because heat conduction is slower through fat than through protein or water. Even the grain of the meat plays a role in the transfer of heat. If the heat source is applied parallel to the grain, the steak will cook about 10 percent faster than if the heat is applied perpendicular to the grain.

When you really think about it, the exterior of a steak is vastly overcooked—beyond well-done into the realm of desiccation and near carbonization. We mention this only as a reminder that much of the pleasure of eating a great steak comes not from uniform doneness but rather from a contrast of finishes. That crisp, complex, crunchy crust is sublime in part because it's the opposite of the moist, satiny interior. And between these two extremes are intermediate degrees of doneness, including a thin band of gray, well-done meat just inside the crust meat that gets rarer and rarer as you move toward the center. The best steaks are when that band of well-done meat isn't too thick but also isn't nonexistent (it's all about textural complexity, people!).

Sounds pretty tricky, doesn't it? But really, there's one key: work on the interior of the steak slowly. That's why we spent all that time talking about two or three heat zones. Indirect cooking is your friend.

The only other question is how to measure the interior doneness of the steak. We've already waxed poetic about the Thermapen (see page 146), so now's the time to use it! Why leave things up to guesswork when you can be precise with an instant-read thermometer? Just make sure to aim the probe carefully at the center of the steak to get the most accurate reading and to take the temperature at several spots to get a sense of what's going on in there. Remember that the steak will be ten to fifteen degrees cooler next to the bone, so plan accordingly.

The last thing to consider is the concept of carryover. When you pull a steak off the fire, it doesn't stop cooking immediately. All of the heat you've introduced remains in the meat, working its way to the center, and you must account for this residual heat when you estimate doneness. When you're cooking hot and fast, carryover will be more aggressive than when you're cooking low and slow. And then, the amount and forcefulness of the carryover also depends on the mass of meat that was heated and if there's a bone. A thin, wide skirt steak will not carry over too much as the heat will quickly dissipate, while a thick-cut ribeye will hold on to more heat. With the latter, it's good to pull the meat about five to ten degrees lower than the desired temperature and assume it will eventually get to where you want it to be. You probably want some concrete numbers—which is always risky with steak, but here it goes: To reach 132°F, the middle of medium-rare, aim to pull the steak off around 125°F to 128°F. But remember, every piece of meat is different, and feel always trumps temp! After that, let it rest for five minutes before slicing (we know that sounds like a short rest period, but trust us, we've tested; see page 161).

Worth Their Salt

Steak without salt is sacrilege. It just doesn't work. Salt isn't just salty. It enhances the flavor of whatever it's applied to. And when applied in the proper amount, salt should never cause you to say, "Oh, this tastes salty." Instead, you'll say, "Wow, this steak tastes damn good!"

But the question always comes up of *when* to salt. Often people don't think about it until the last minute, and then they rain a downpour of salt onto their steak while the pan is heating up. Unfortunately, this is the worst time to salt the steak.

It's good to salt the meat in advance of cooking it, just not immediately before you heat it. Because there is an electrical attraction between NaCL (sodium chloride) and H₂O molecules when you salt a steak, the first thing that happens is the salt draws moisture out of the meat. This extracted water then dissolves the salt, instantly creating a mini brine. After fifteen to twenty minutes, the meat starts to pull the salty moisture back into its cells. The salt penetrates into the fiber of the meat, traveling deeper into it the longer you wait. People worry that salt will dry out the meat (and over time it will, but meat will also dry out on its own over time), but in fact the opposite is true: it makes the meat juicier.

If you cook the meat only five minutes after you've salted it, you won't have given the steak enough time to pull the moisture back into its cells. There will be a wet slurry of salty water sitting atop the meat, which will slow down the browning of the exterior and speed up the cooking of the interior. Bad! If you start with wet meat and you're hoping to get a nice brown crust, you could end up with an overdone interior by the time you achieve it.

Because we can't help ourselves, and because we love this type of cooking experiment, we trial cooked a number of 1½-inch-thick ribeyes that had been salted at different intervals before cooking: 48 hours, 24 hours, 12 hours, 6 hours, 4 hours, 2 hours, 1 hour, 5 minutes, and just before going on the grill. We sprinkled each steak with a measure of kosher salt equivalent

to 1.5 percent of its original weight, which meant a four-hundred-gram steak got hit with six grams of salt. All of the ribeyes were cooked straight out of the 35°F refrigerator (again, if this runs counter to what you've been taught, take a look at page 160) on a *plancha* heated to 350°F until they reached an internal temperature of 127°F.

The results of the test were quite clear: the ones that had been salted longer not only cooked better—more evenly and faster—but tasted better, too. Our favorite was the steak salted 48 hours before we cooked it. On the grill, it quickly formed a deep and even crust (maybe because the exterior had dried a bit). When we looked at a cross section after slicing, there was a pretty dramatic shift between the crusted exterior and the pink interior. Most of the other steaks had a more gradual gradient. The flavor of the 48-hour steak was also the best. The salt had thoroughly penetrated and integrated with the meat, seasoning it inside and out.

The steaks salted between 24 and 48 hours all turned out equally well. The main difference from the 48-hour meat was that more gradual gradient between the well-done exterior and mid-rare interior. They all tasted good and had a good integration of salt and meat, but they were not transcendent like the 48-hour steak was.

The difficulties mounted for the steaks salted for 4 hours and under. Even on the 4-hour steak, there was a wet residue on the surface. When cooked, all of these steaks developed blotchy crusts. Most disappointing (when compared to the longer-salted steaks) was the flavor, which clearly tasted like salt on the outside and unseasoned meat on the inside. There was no integration.

Listen, if you don't have time to plan ahead and end up salting immediately before or during cooking, we're not going to tell you to throw your steaks away. They will still taste good, but you won't end up with that beautiful merging of meat and salt. But if you can remember to salt your meat four hours or more in advance, you'll be golden.

Generally, it's nice to keep at least a couple of different types of salt on hand. Coarsely grained kosher salt is easy to sprinkle with the fingers. A medium-grain sea salt has a great briny flavor and some slightly larger crystals, which are good for an aggressive salt flavor and the occasional crunchy bite.

Even if you've presalted—as long as it wasn't too heavy—a little finishing salt is an effective touch. To this end, every kitchen should have a big bowl handy of lovely, flaky finishing salt. Maldon sea salt, which comes from the southeast coast of England, is not too strongly flavored, is delicately scented with minerals, and either dissolves quickly on the surface of the food or offers a lovely little crunch when encountered by the teeth. Just sprinkle a bit of it or some other comparable salt on top of the steak before it hits the table.

Fats and Oils: Never Cease with the Grease

Another question that often comes up with steak is, do you need to use butter or oil in the pan or on the grill when cooking? The answer is largely a matter of preference and depends on the method of cooking.

On the grill: Many people spray the grates with oil before throwing on the meat. An easier solution is to rub a little cooking oil over the meat before putting it on the grill. You get more thorough coverage of the meat, and the oil acts as a conductor of heat to help the steaks cook more quickly and evenly. Just remember that when preparing the grill, always scrape down the grates with a grill brush before cooking and then put a little oil on a folded paper towel and, using tongs, wipe down the grates.

In the pan: For the same reasons just cited, it's a good idea either to coat the meat with oil or to put a little oil in the pan. An elegant solution is to use the meat's own natural fat. If you have a thick ribeye with a fat cap on one side, place it on its fatty side in a hot pan to render out some of the fat. When you have enough melted fat to cover the pan, turn the steak on its flat side and begin cooking.

What about finishing the steak? Should you use butter or oil at the end? That's a matter of preference, but it never hurts. Butter can be a strong flavor, but it goes well with salt and protein and certainly improves bland meat. For pan-cooked steaks, many chefs toss in a few pats of butter along with garlic and thyme and finish the steak by pan basting the seasoned, melted butter over the meat for a minute or two before plating and cutting. For his part, Jordan loves the Italian practice of dousing the cut meat with a generous drizzle of fine extra-virgin olive oil, which gives it wonderful richness and a hint of flavor. A good olive oil can be sweet, nutty, slightly bitter—all flavors that accent the steak beautifully. And as the juice from the steak runs into the platter and commingles with the oil, you get the most delicious little liquid for dipping meat, bread, whatever into as you mop up the scraps.

Sometimes it all boils down to family tradition (Aaron's father's cold butter baste, for example).

Does Steak Need to be at Room Temperature before Cooking?

For decades—generations, maybe—one of the primary instructions in any steak recipe was to let the meat come to room temperature before cooking. Recipes would usually call for the steaks to be removed from the refrigerator twenty to thirty minutes before cooking to ensure they cooked more evenly and quickly. But we're here to tell you this is baloney. There are *many* reasons why this is bad advice for steak.

Let's start with the obvious: twenty to thirty minutes is a joke. A half hour is not enough time to let the meat warm by two degrees, let alone thirty degrees (the difference between your fridge and room temperature). Actually, it will take several *hours* for a steak to get up to room temperature. Those hours sound great if you're a bacteria or a fly trying to get some of that juicy raw meat! Sorry, we don't mean to be alarmist, and your meat is probably fine if you do let it sit out. If we were talking about a large hunk of meat like a pork roast or a brisket, a few hours at room temperature isn't a bad idea (though the relentlessly cautious USDA would frown), considering how long it takes to cook and the risk of overcooking the outside by the time the inside comes to temperature. But this isn't really relevant when it comes to small cuts like steak.

We're going to go way against common wisdom here and say that *sometimes* you want the steak to be cold when you cook it. This is especially true for a very thin cut, where the trick is keeping the inside at medium-rare while producing a good crust. The colder the meat to begin with, the longer it will take to heat up, giving you the time to brown the exterior properly. Thick steaks (an inch and a half to two and a half inches) are another question. There, the challenge is getting the interior done enough in the relatively short time it takes to build a deep crust.

Basically, unless you want to leave your steak out for hours and hours, you're going to be cooking it with some chill on it from the fridge. Guess what? That's what almost all restaurants do. They can't have raw meat sitting around at room temperature all day, and the chill helps with thin steaks anyway. Whether or not you've tempered your steaks or are cooking them straight from the chill, the point is to be aware of the temperature of the meat when you put it on. As the exterior begins to sizzle, visualize what's happening with the cold meat internally. Understanding the temperature of the meat and cooking accordingly is much more important than having it at a certain temperature before your start.

The Tyranny of Grill Marks and the Myth of the One-Time Flip

In the past, in magazine photos, ads, and television shows, that crosshatched pattern of dark, charred grill marks was the hallmark of a perfectly juicy steak right off the grill. The thinking on that has changed, and nowadays we recoil with horror at the sight of conventional grill marks. Why? Grill marks indicate a delicious Maillardian crust, so why limit that tastiness to just a small portion of the steak's total surface? Go for the all-over crust—that's where the flavor is! Of course, the danger in going for the all-over crust is that the area where the bars of the grill touched the meat becomes not just crust but also bitter, blackened, burned char. So the grill marks can sometimes become a flaw, not a symbol of success.

Combatting this requires denying another steak myth, one that chefs continue to perpetuate today: the one-time flip. That's when you put a steak on the fire or in a pan, you don't turn it for a set number of minutes, and then you turn it only once. Although this is a good way to get dark grill marks, it is not a good way to create a crust. Science has even debunked it. As food-science writer Harold McGee told the *New York Times*, "It's true that frequent flipping cooks the meat more evenly, and also significantly faster: flip every minute instead of once or twice and the meat will be done in a third less time. This works because neither side has time to absorb a lot of heat when facing the fire or to lose heat when facing away. You don't get neat grill marks or the best char this way, but with high enough heat, the surface develops plenty of flavor."

To Rest or Not to Rest?

The advice to rest a piece of meat after it comes off the heat falls into the same category as advice about tempering the meat and flipping it only once: it's old-school, it's the way both of us were taught to do it, and its importance might be greatly exaggerated.

Now, we're not telling you to skip resting and just cut into the meat immediately. But we don't think we need to convince you that it's better to eat hot steak than lukewarm steak!

We tested the question of resting on five steaks, each weighed before and after cooking as well

FROZEN

A few years ago, the food magazine *Cook's Illustrated* published a piece that began, "Rather than follow the convention of thawing frozen steaks before grilling them, we discovered that we could get steaks that were just as juicy by cooking them straight from the freezer." Not surprisingly, given how catchy notions spread on the Internet, that content was seized and amplified by various webzines, producing articles with titles like "Want the Best Steak of Your Life? Don't Thaw the Steaks before Cooking Them" and "Why You Should Never Thaw Frozen Steaks before Cooking Them."

Even we, anti-tempering evangelists that we are, were dubious of this advice. But we tested it out (yay, science!), taking a frozen steak and throwing it on a hot grill to get a sear and then finishing it in the oven at 275°F, just as the magazine directed. And, yes, it worked. Eventually. The steak took quite a while in the oven to cook to medium-rare. Visually, it appeared okay. And the internal temperature signaled that it was cooked properly. But then, when we tasted the meat, we were not impressed. The texture was tough and chewy, the flavor muted and dull. In short, it tasted like a steak that had been frozen just moments before. Yes, you can cook a steak this way. But why would you do that to a good piece of meat?

as after resting and after cutting. The steaks were rested for 0, 5, 10, 15, and 20 minutes. The results were telling and clear. The steak that was unrested lost three times the amount (by percentage) of liquid than the rested steaks lost—no good. The steak that rested for 20 minutes lost the least amount of juice. But—and here's where we get sciency again—the amount lost wasn't statistically much more than the steak rested for 5 minutes. So our advice is, for normal steaks more than one inch thick, between 3 and 5 minutes should be sufficient. Thicker pieces of meat need more time to rest—closer to 15 minutes or even more. These you can keep warm by loosely covering with

a piece of aluminum foil. Steaks that have been reverse seared are cooked so gently that the temperature is quite uniform and the juices are well distributed, so 1 to 2 minutes off the heat is sufficient. If you can touch it, you should slice it.

Choose Your Own Adventure, Steak-Cook Edition

How you cook your steak obviously depends on what steak you are cooking, and we'll get into that, don't worry (see page 172). But for now, we're going to use thick-cut (one inch and above) steaks like ribeyes or strips as a control group to help you decide which method is right for you.

HOT AND FAST

This is the basic way to cook a steak—starting hot and just going for it. It's obvious, and you can do it on the stove top or on a grill.

On the stove top, you can set up only two zones: the high heat of a cast-iron or steel pan over the burner and a preheated oven at 250°F. On the grill, you can set up two or three zones, depending on your needs (sometimes that third zone is great for slow cooking a steak).

Pros

This is hands-down the easiest way to cook a steak. It requires almost no forethought or preparation to execute. This makes it effective when you've done no planning or preparation and just want a steak and want it now. Sometimes this happens.

Cons

You run the greatest risk of overcooking the meat. By searing and browning the outside first, you're introducing a lot of heat to the steak right off the bat, and it's hard to go back once the thing is heated.

How to Do It

1. Ideally at least 4 hours before the cook, season the steaks generously with salt and keep them, uncovered, in the fridge. If you're cooking on the stove top, preheat the oven to 250°F and heat a cast-iron or steel skillet over high heat. If you're grilling, build a nice, glowing-hot coal bed in your grill using one of the grill setups on pages 147 to 150. The target temperature is 400°F for the direct-heat zone and around 250°F for the indirect-heat zone. Thoroughly dry the surface of the meat with paper towels and lightly apply some neutral oil with a high smoke point (like grape seed oil).

2. When the pan reaches 350°F to 400°F (a few drops of water flicked onto the surface should evaporate in 2 to 3 seconds) or the grill fire reaches its target temperatures, add the meat to the skillet or grill (do *not* cover the grill). Move the meat regularly and flip every 30 to 60 seconds to develop a nice brown crust. The color you want is a nice dark brown with orange and red tones to it. Don't let it blacken. If it does, take it off immediately!

3. When the crust has been achieved, move the meat to the cooler zone. This will be after 3 to 5 minutes per side (depending on the temperature of both the beef and the fire), or if you're moving the meat and flipping often, a total of about 10 minutes. Indoors, this would mean transferring the steak to the oven (transfer the meat to a sheet pan if you don't want the exterior to keep cooking) to finish in the preheated oven.

On the grill, this would mean moving the steak onto the cool side of the two-zone setup.

4. Using a digital thermometer, keep track of the internal temperature of the meat and pull it when it is 10 degrees shy of your desired doneness temperature. Depending on the thickness of the steaks, this can take anywhere from 6 to 12 minutes.

5. Let the meat rest for a few minutes on the counter away from a breeze to allow the temperature to equalize throughout the interior. If you don't want the meat to cool too quickly or you're working in a cold room, cover it with aluminum foil. Slice (against the grain) and serve.

REVERSE SEAR

The term *reverse sear* was coined sometime in the last fifteen years, but in northern Spain they just call it "how we've always been cooking steak for as long as we can remember." And the grill cooks of northern Spain know what they're doing when it comes to steak (see page 131).

Pros

The reverse sear is the most foolproof and practical way to cook a thick steak perfectly, and is especially popular in restaurant kitchens. When you cook the interior slowly and methodically, it ends up consistent. You don't have the thick band of overcooked meat that conventional hot-and-fast cooking often leaves. By slow cooking the meat first, you dry off the surface, so the Maillard reactions will happen faster and more fully than with a steak with some moisture. What's more, you end up with seemingly impossible tenderness. That's because slow cooking allows native enzymes in the steak to go to work breaking down some of the muscle fiber, leaving a wonderfully silky texture.

Cons

There are two reasons why this isn't the most convenient method. The first is effort. It's not hard to preheat an oven and a pan in a kitchen. But getting your grill set up properly (if you're using a baffle) takes a little effort and fore-thought, and making sure the cool zone is holding a low temperature (200°F to 225°F is ideal) takes skill and experience.

The other major cost of the reverse sear is time. It just takes longer to cook your steak this way. A big piece of meat can take hours to get to doneness; then, you have to rest the meat for quite a while before searing. If you have plenty of time, though, you can cook your steak at a superlow temp (sometimes Aaron goes as low as 170°F), ensuring a beautifully precise cook. Your time is well served by the superiority of the meat, and patience and time become much easier if you have a cold beer in hand and some good company!

How to Do It

1. Ideally at least 4 hours before the cook, season the steaks generously with salt and keep them, uncovered, in the fridge. If you're cooking on the stovetop, preheat the oven to 200°F. If you're grilling, build a small- to moderate-size coal bed in your grill using one of the grill setups on pages 147 to 150. The target temperature is around 200°F for the indirect-heat zone. You'll build the fire back up to blazing hot for the sear later. Thoroughly dry the surface of the meat with paper towels.

Important Note • When doing the reverse sear on a grill, it's important to protect the meat from the high heat of the coal bed. Even given the rectangular shape of the PK Grill, one edge of the steaks will be closer to the coals than the other, and there's a risk of overcooking that side. Therefore, in order to truly protect the cooler side from the coals, there are a couple of solutions. You can put a piece of metal between the two sides of the grill as a baffle. This is where a small sheet pan or sizzle plate comes in handy. Or you can throw a small stainless-steel bowl on the grate over the steaks, protecting them from the direct radiative heat.

Another Important Note • To reverse sear on a closed grill, the heat must be kept low. It's very easy to overload the grill. Even one extra piping-hot briquette can make a huge differ-ence in temperature. For this, you have to know your cooker and how much fuel is required to take it to 200°F for what will be *at least* a 20-minute cook, sometimes much longer. For a well-insulated cooker like a PK, that might be, say, six or seven briquettes. For a Big Green Egg, it may be fewer. For a thin, steel Weber, it may take a few more. The point is, be careful. If it's too high, the steaks may dry out on the outside before reaching the desired internal temperature.

2. Remove the steaks from the refrigerator. If cooking in the oven, place the steaks on a rack set over a pan (this is so the meat isn't in con-tact with the metal of the pan). Alternatively, add the steaks to the indirect-heat side of the grill and *cover* the grill. Because you'll be grill-ing with the lid closed, it's important to keep track of the heat level, making sure it remains at the target temperature. If the coal bed proves too large and the temperature keeps creeping up, open the lid frequently to let heat escape. Do not move or flip the steaks.

3. Using a digital thermometer, keep track of the internal temperature of the meat and pull it when it is at least 10 degrees shy of your desired doneness temperature. Depending on the thickness of the steaks, this can take anywhere from 20 to 45 minutes—or hours for a giant, bone-in steak. But give it time, as the low temperature allows the meat to cook evenly all the way through. When the steaks are finished with this stage, they won't look appealing; they'll be in good shape for the final cooking in the next step, however. Incidentally, when they've reached that desired internal temperature, you can pull them from the fire and let them hang out for 30 to 60 minutes while you build up heat for the next step. (Actually, you could rest them up to 3 hours—it's important to rest before searing.)

4. If cooking on the stove top, preheat a cast-iron or steel skillet over high heat until it's blazing hot (400°F to 500°F, or when a drop of water will instantly vaporize). Make sure the meat is dry, then rub it with a little oil before adding it to the skillet. On a grill, you'll need to build up your fire in the direct-heat zone. After pulling the steaks, keep the lid open and rustle the coals to get them glowing hot again or add more lit coals if needed. Coat the steaks with a little neutral oil (like grape seed oil), then put them to the fire. Move the meat regularly and flip every 30 seconds or so to develop a nice brown crust. The color you want is a nice dark brown with ocher and red tones to it. This should take 1 to 2 minutes per side, regardless of the thickness of the steaks.

5. Let rest briefly—only a minute or two, as slow cooking allows for even temperature distribution throughout the meat, which is usually the goal of resting. Slice (against the grain) and serve.

STEAK ON THE COALS

If the reverse sear seems overly complicated to you, here's an approach that couldn't be simpler. Go caveman style and ditch the grill and the grates and forget about the two zones. Nothing could be more basic and primitive than this: just throw the steak on the coals. If that sounds crazy, it sort of is. But it's also a leap of faith—kind of like when Tony Robbins gets people to walk barefoot over hot coals as a self-confidence exercise. But with this, instead of having (ideally) perfectly unseared, uncooked feet, you get perfectly seared and cooked steak. And it can really boost your steak confidence!

Yes, there's sensible theory behind just throwing your steaks onto coals that are over 1000°F. When the steak is in direct contact with hot coals, it is indeed conducting that heat. However, meat, which is 75 percent water, and fat are not good heat conductors, so the steak cooks relatively slowly. In addition, because the meat sits right on the hot coals, there is no room for air and, therefore, no fire, as flames can't exist without oxygen. The result is that meat can be seared and cooked even when thrown into the fire.

Pros

There's an appeal in this most primal, basic, simple way to cook meat. Cavemen might have even had more sophisticated methods. So some people love this technique for its simplicity and for the smoky, charry way it makes the steaks taste. It's also impresses guests and saves on cleanup time—no scrubbing down the grill.

Cons

Often the taste of coal-cooked meat has a somewhat charred, earthy, ashy note that may even include a few bitter bites here and there. Nothing is wrong with this, and, like we said, some people enjoy it. But we happen not to love it. Also, the exterior doesn't cook terribly evenly, meaning it's downright difficult if not impossible to achieve that lovely all-over Maillardian crust.

How to Do It

1. Ideally at least 4 hours before the cook, season the steaks generously with salt. If working with steaks an inch thick, it's a good idea to temper them for at least an hour or so, to bring up the internal temperature, as they'll cook quickly on the coals. And if your steak is more than 1½ inches thick, before throwing it on the fire, you may want to reverse sear it (see steps 1 through 3, pages 166 to 167) in a 200°F oven to 15 degrees below your desired temperature. This step is optional.

2. Build a nice, glowing-hot coal bed using lump hardwood charcoal or real wood coals. Do not use briquettes because of their impurities. The coal bed must be large enough so that when you turn the steaks in step 4, you can turn them onto fresh coals. It's better than returning them to the same coals.

3. When the coals are at peak heat—glowing orange, not emitting flames, and covered lightly with ash—blow (or fan) all of the ash off of them. They will have reached anywhere from 900°F to 1100°F, so be careful and don't burn yourself!

4. When you're ready to cook, don't oil the steaks first, as that introduces a flammable substance. Dry them with paper towels and then, using tongs, nestle the steak into a flat bed of coals, trying not to leave any major air gaps. Cook without disturbing for 3 to 5 minutes on the first side (this depends, of course, on the thickness of the steak), then flip the steaks onto a fresh section of coals. If you smell burning meat (not searing but burning), you know it's time to flip. Cook the second side for another 3 to 5 minutes.

5. Using a digital thermometer, keep track of the internal temperature of the meat and pull it when it is about 15 degrees of your desired doneness temperature. There may be some small coals or a little ash clinging to the steak. This is not a problem. Simply brush them off with the tongs.

6. Let the meat rest for a few minutes on the counter away from a breeze to allow the temperature to equalize throughout the interior. If you don't want the meat to cool too quickly or you're working in a cold room, cover it with aluminum foil. Slice (against the grain) and serve.

BLAST FURNACE STEAK

Here's another technique that has surfaced in the last several years, bubbling up from the ranks of steak obsessives who are always trying to find new ways to blast their meat with ever-increasing amounts of heat. The tradition of cooking steaks with brutally, almost comically high heat is not a new one. In the Midwest and Mid-Atlantic, the old term *Pittsburgh rare* exists for a steak that has been heavily charred on the outside but remains rare or, more likely, raw on the inside. This comes from the fact that steel workers in Pittsburgh were known to throw steaks into the iron-smelting furnaces that operated at over 2000°F. The story goes that they rarely had much time for lunch and needed high-energy food for their grueling work. The steak would go into the furnace (sometimes slapped onto the side wall), would be turned after a number of seconds, cooked a little longer, and then removed. This is just a slightly more extreme version of Aaron cooking steaks on a shovel in the 700°F coals of his offset smoker's firebox, which he used to do occasionally for dinner when he'd be up all night on a long cook and the brisket wouldn't be coming off for twelve hours.

In the event that you don't keep a roaring blast furnace or lit firebox regularly going at home, the way that's become popular to blaze steaks with potent flames is to cook them directly over the charcoal chimney. It's true that the chimney works by insulating and concentrating the heat of a few coals to get a larger amount lit. As you know, when it comes to temperature, the chimney gives off wisps of powerful red and blue fire and brings coals to a brilliant, glowing orange state. Why not harness that heat for searing steak?

This technique works best with steaks less than an inch thick. Any thicker and there's simply not enough time to cook the interior before the exterior carbonizes. It's great with thin, tougher cuts that are better with rare interiors, such as flank and outside skirt.

Pros

Superheated coals concentrated in the chimney cook the outside of the steak in a jiffy before too much heat can work its way to the interior, making it perfect for a high-contrast sear along with rare meat in the center. Also, you don't have to set up the grill and cleanup is minimal.

Cons

Try this technique at your own risk. Some people love it, but in our experience, the risks of ending up with a bitter, overcharred steak is high.

THICKNESS VERSUS WEIGHT

Despite what you may have heard, when deciding how long to cook your steaks, thickness has a much greater impact on the cooking time than weight. A two-pound steak that's only one inch thick will cook considerably faster than a one-pound steak that is two inches thick.

- The intuitive sense would be to cook thinner cuts, like skirt steaks or even thinly cut T-bones or ribeyes, over lower heat because they are more delicate. And conversely, to cook thick cuts over massive high heat because they can take it. In fact, the opposite is true. It's better to cook thin cuts very quickly over high heat.

- With thin cuts, you don't have to be concerned about the level of doneness inside, as the heat used to cook the outside will quickly penetrate to the heart of the meat. Thick cuts do better with reverse sear, hot and fast on the stove top, and two- and three-zone setups. Thinner cuts do better with direct sear, direct on coals, and blast furnace.

How to Do It

1. Ideally at least 4 hours before the cook, season the steaks generously with salt and keep them, uncovered, in the fridge. If your steaks are more than ¾ inch thick, before throwing them on the fire, you may want to reverse sear them (see steps 1 through 3, pages 166 to 167) in a 200°F oven to 15 degrees below your desired doneness temperature.

2. Heat a charcoal chimney following the instructions on page 142. Thoroughly dry the surface of the meat with paper towels and lightly apply some neutral oil with a high smoke point (like grape seed oil).

3. When the charcoal is glowing hot and emitting tongues of orange flame, put a thick metal grate over the top of the chimney and put the steak on the grate. Make sure the whole setup thing is steady and not out of balance. The charcoal heat will instantly start sizzling the surface of the steak, and flames may leap up to lick the meat. Flip and move the steak often so no side starts to burn until you get a nice all-over deep brown crust. About 1½ minutes per side should do it.

4. Let the meat rest for only a minute or two or, for a thinner steak, slice immediately (against the grain) on a cutting board that captures the juices, then serve.

The Steak-Cut Decision Tree

You now know literally everything you could possibly know about every permutation of grill setups and cooking methods that will yield a perfect steak. But the one thing we have not discussed is which setups and methods are most appropriate for each cut and type of steak. You didn't think we'd forget that important variable, did you?

- **Grass-fed and other very lean steaks** • Despite the fact that the great grass-fed beef producers like Alderspring and First Light make wonderfully marbled meat, most grass-fed beef you'll find will be leaner than grain fed and will thus require a more attentive style of cooking. The extra fat and marbling in grain fed serves to insulate the leaner sections, as the fat conducts heat more slowly and absorbs the heat first, melting and extending the cooking process. With less fat, grass-fed meat cooks about 30 percent faster. Grass-fed cattle also move more over the course of their whole lives than grain-fed cattle do, so their muscles have worked more and thus can be tougher.

Tough grass-fed steaks come from too much high heat, which causes the muscle fibers to tense and squeeze out their moisture. And without much fat content to slow things down, the meat can turn tough in an instant. So sear the exteriors of the steaks hot, but then finish at temperatures up to fifty degrees lower than for grain-fed meat, and only to the rarer side of medium-rare or even to rare or bloody; carryover cooking after removal from the heat is more extreme in grass-fed steaks. This is how the French and Italians tend to eat their steaks, which are usually much leaner than American beef. Hot and fast and reverse sear work great, but avoid direct on the coals and blast furnace.

- **Fatty cuts** • Fat is forgiving when it comes to cooking steaks. It begins melting at a lower temperature than water boils, buffering and lubricating the flesh. In general, fatty steaks can be cooked faster and longer than lean ones, though you will still want to pay close attention to temperatures and doneness. For instance, a well-marbled ribeye can take longer and more extreme heat than a typically lean tenderloin, which needs to be cooked more gently. All methods will work well, so use the thickness of the steak to determine which one. Thicker steaks will demand reverse sear or hot and fast with oven finishing, while thinner steaks can't take on-the-coals or blast-furnace heat.

- **Dry-aged meat** • There is no special method for cooking dry-aged steaks. The process is pretty much in line with standard steak cooking. However, there are a couple of factors you may want to consider. One is flavor. Dry-aged meat has a particular funky flavor, which can be powerful or mild depending on the length and intensity of the aging process. To preserve and highlight the flavor of age, many people who dry age meat prefer to cook it in as neutral a way as possible—in a pan with a little neutral oil or butter. The thinking is that the smoke and charcoal seasoning from the grill can overpower the flavor of an already estimable piece of meat.

As far as cooking dry-aged meat, just remember that a well-aged steak (forty-five days or more) may have lost 20 to 30 percent of its water volume. That doesn't mean it will dry out in the pan or on the grill (that extra water in an unaged steak typically evaporates during cooking). But it does mean that it's a denser piece, with only protein and fat to conduct the heat, which means a slower process. Our recommendation is to be patient and cook rather slowly to let the heat move evenly through the interior. The meat will also be more tender thanks to the enzymatic action during aging, so don't go above rare to medium-rare, as the steak already is at its textural peak. Try cast iron on the stove top for the full-on unadulterated flavor of dry aging. But if you're interested in the pairing of smoke and dry-age funk, try Aaron's Franklin Formation (see page 148).

For more specific guidance on how to cook various cuts and styles of steak, refer to the How to Cook Steak flow chart on pages 214 and 215.

CHAPTER 9

Sides, Sauces, and Drinks

As a kid, Aaron's favorite meals were definitely when his dad would cook steaks at home. But for some reason, the things that really stick out in his mind about those meals was eating iceberg lettuce drenched in ranch dressing and a baked potato with the insides saturated with butter and salt. The steaks were always good, but he remembers loving the sides just as much.

It's a weird thing that way. No one would ever dispute the idea that the most important part of a steak dinner is the steak. Yet many of us carry a surprising fondness and longing for the nonmeat dishes we ate alongside the steak. And if some of us dig deeply enough into our memories, we may even have a revelation that the sides were our favorite part of the meal.

To this day, Jordan doesn't want to eat steak if he can't have a simple green salad with vinaigrette beside it (or at least a crunchy, tangy Caesar salad before it). Something about the interplay between the rich, fatty steak and the cutting acidity and crunch of the salad makes the combination nonnegotiable. Potatoes are a fixture in his memory, too, though he doesn't so much remember baked ones as he does the classic French pairing of crispy, golden fries and steak at such Parisian bistros as Le Severo (see facing page), where Jordan also recalls ordering a second side of sautéed chanterelle mushrooms (see page 180) because the first one was so good.

Steak is a wonderful canvas for fresh produce at its peak. Jordan wistfully recalls the childhood pleasures of charcoal-grilled steaks beside butter-slathered summer corn on the cob, with the sweet corn the perfect foil for the salty, savory steak. Aaron thinks about all the times he's had a fresh tomato salad with succulent bavette, their juices commingling on the plate.

Why, when you have all of this great, expensive meat, are sides so important—so desirable? Maybe the meat is more intense than we realize and our perceived appetites for it exceed our actual physical needs. Maybe the sides stand as buffers, foils, and interveners to keep us from eating more meat than we need.

One thing Jordan and Aaron agree on is that at home they *always* prefer a steak-centric meal with the simplest of side dishes. After all, a steak is delicious on its own, and much of the appeal of cooking steaks is that they don't require much prep or work. This isn't Thanksgiving, where we have to burden the table with elaborate sides to compensate for, ahem, innate deficiencies (we're looking at you, roast turkey).

We desire clean, punchy flavors and textures that both complement and contrast with the steak. A simple salad, potatoes, grilled vegetables—that is how a good meal comes together!

When it comes to sauces, the steak you're serving is hopefully so flavorful that no condiment is needed. (Same goes for barbecue, folks.) But sometimes, even if the steak is good, a little lubrication or complementary flavor is welcome. It might be a drizzle of soy sauce, a pat of garlic butter, or a spoonful of a classic béarnaise. But the one sauce Aaron turns to again and again is a salsa verde that can be an ongoing part of your pantry with little effort.

The following recipes for sides might seem comically simple to you. That's because they are! But they're also the things we never get tired of, so please don't be insulted by their inclusion here. They're almost like condiments themselves, the very basic things we eat with steak.

8 rue des Plantes
75014 Paris, France
tel: (+33) 01-45-40-40-91 • lesevero.fr

If you are in Paris and in the mood for a quintessential *steak-frites* experience, make the short trek out to the sleepy, residential 14th arrondissement to the diminutive bistro Le Severo. Actually, the steak at this quaint, old-school room is not quintessential, as that would suggest a shabby cut of meat. Rather, the steak at Le Severo, run by former butcher William Bernet, is superb: well-selected *côte de boeuf* (thick-cut bone-in ribeye for two) aged between three and five weeks (or shell out for the more-expensive one-hundred-day aged cuts). Other offerings are usually the *faux-filet* (strip steak) and the *onglet* (our hanger).

There is only one cook in the kitchen, yet he turns out immaculate steaks. The French tend to take their steaks *bleu*, which is seared on the outside but raw on the inside. If you prefer a rare medium-rare (as cooked as you'll be able to get), order it *saignant*. The steaks come with reliably crispy, golden *frites*. And don't skip the punchy *salade verte* and a plate of sautéed *girolles* (chanterelle mushrooms). Much of the lengthy wine list is written on chalkboards across one wall, and the wines are usually excellent—pithy, soulful bottles from small, hardworking producers. And this small, hardworking restaurant has only ten tables, so be sure to reserve yours several days in advance.

SIDES, SAUCES, AND DRINKS

Green Salad with Garlic Vinaigrette

Jordan is a salad fanatic. He goes almost as crazy about finding perfect little heads of crisp baby lettuces—Little Gem, butter, oak leaf—as he does for well-marbled meat. The simple, unadorned green salad—*salade verte*, as the French say—is a remarkable creation unto itself and a brilliant accompaniment to steak. You've probably had the two together countless times, even if you didn't bother to appreciate the brilliance of the pairing. It's all about contrast: the lightness and crispness of the lettuce is a counterpoint to the rich density of the meat, while the tang of vinegar, garlic, and oil keeps the mouth fresh after a heavy bite.

The salad should be both crunchy and silky and be lightly coated with some sort of vinegar-based dressing. Whole leaves from a butter lettuce, their spherical shape intact, or the crunchy interior leaves of a romaine work especially well, but anything fresh and crisp does the trick. A mix of greens is wonderful, too: combine a head each of butter and romaine with the bitter notes of frisée or other chicory. You can serve a few handfuls of the mix and keep the rest in a plastic bag in the refrigerator for the next couple of nights. Adding whole herb leaves—parsley, basil, lovage, mint—is also never a bad idea.

Feel free to embellish your vinaigrette. Finely minced shallot adds a little sweetness and complexity, while herbs such as dried dill contribute a bright, verdant flavor.

SERVES 4 TO 6

1 head butter lettuce, leaves separated

2 cups frisée or chicory leaves (optional)

1 cup mixed fresh herbs (such as parsley, basil, lovage, and mint; optional)

1 tablespoon fresh lemon juice

1 tablespoon champagne vinegar

2 cloves garlic, minced or pressed

1 tablespoon minced shallot (optional)

¼ cup extra-virgin olive oil

1 tablespoon Dijon mustard (not whole grain)

Generous pinch of kosher salt

Small pinch of sugar

Rinse all of the greens carefully and spin them dry in a salad spinner. Chill the leaves in the fridge until ready to serve.

In a small Mason jar with a lid, combine the lemon juice, vinegar, garlic, and shallot and let sit for 10 minutes. Add the oil, mustard, salt, and sugar, cap tightly, and shake vigorously until the vinaigrette emulsifies and is thick and creamy.

Transfer the greens to a large bowl, drizzle with a couple tablespoons of the vinaigrette, and toss until the leaves are lightly and evenly coated, adding more vinaigrette if needed. (Start with a small amount of vinaigrette, as you can always add more. If dressing has pooled in the bottom of the bowl, you've overdressed the salad.) Serve right away.

Garlicky Sautéed Mushrooms

Jordan grew up eating mushrooms alongside steak because that's what his mother always cooked. Scents are powerful agents of memory, so for him the smell of sautéing mushrooms with garlic, butter, salt, and a generous dusting of cracked black pepper is almost inseparable from that of steak. Where did this great pairing come from? His mother says that she does it because her mother did. So where did Grandma get this technique? "It's probably from France," Jordan's mom says. "She took a lot from French cooking." Indeed, Julia Child has a recipe in *Mastering the Art of French Cooking* for *sauté de boeuf à la parisienne* that pairs steak and mushrooms. It calls for whipping cream, Madeira, and beef stock. This dish is infinitely more simple.

Mushrooms are almost a meat substitute. Just like a steak, they brown when they are cooked, lose some water, and develop a dense, savory texture. They're also chock-full of umami, which make them an excellent complement to steak. The mushrooms' function is the opposite of the role of an acidic salad. Instead of acting as a counterpoint, they enhance the steak by doubling down on richness and umami while also adding an earthy flavor.

— **SERVES 4** —

2 cups sliced brown cremini mushrooms (5 to 6 ounces), see Note

1 tablespoon unsalted butter

2 cloves garlic, minced or pressed

1 tablespoon extra-virgin olive oil

3 or 4 thyme sprigs

Flaky sea salt and freshly ground black pepper

1 tablespoon chopped fresh flat-leaf parsley

Note • Always buy whole mushrooms and cut them yourself. Baskets of chopped or sliced mushrooms have often been sitting around dehydrating for days in store produce departments. The easiest way to slice a mushroom is to cut a narrow sliver off the bulb to create a flat surface and then lay the mushroom on that flat surface and cut it into as many slices as you please.

Put the butter and the garlic in a cold sauté pan and turn on the heat to medium. Starting off this way allows the garlic to relax and steam a little as the butter releases moisture, keeping the garlic from browning too quickly. As the butter melts, drizzle in the oil. When the butter has melted and mixed with the oil and the garlic is beginning to crackle, add the mushrooms and toss or stir to coat them with the fat. Add the thyme sprigs, turn down the heat to medium-low, and gently sauté the mushrooms until they've reduced by one-third to one-half, about 10 minutes.

Season to taste with salt and with several generous twists of the pepper mill, then remove the long thyme stems and sprinkle with the parsley. Serve a spoonful of mushrooms on top of or just alongside each steak.

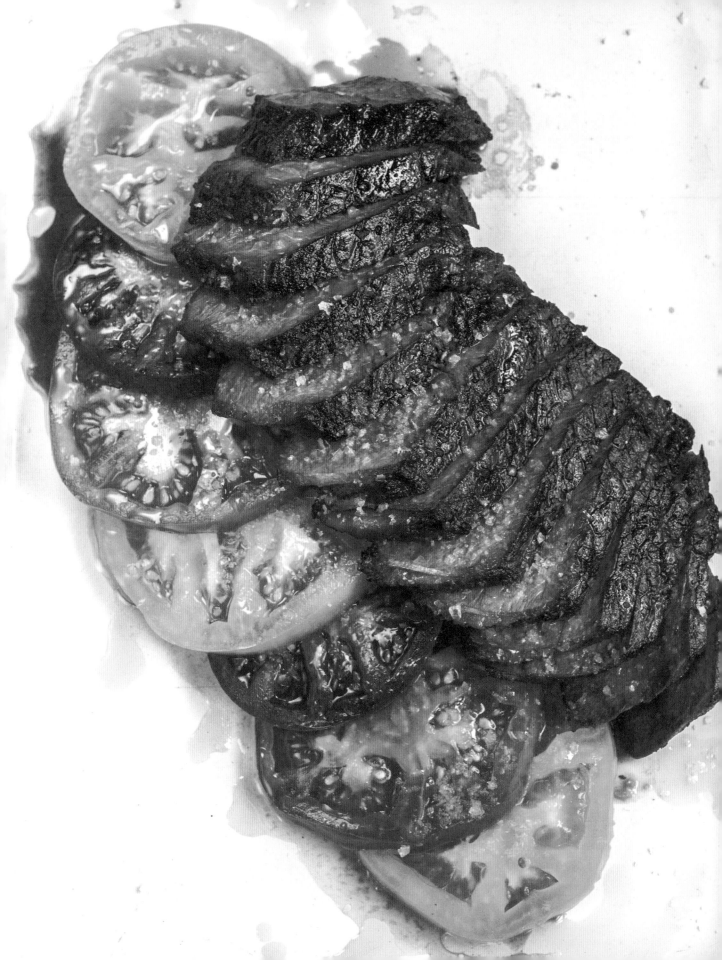

Raw Tomatoes

This is not a joke! Nothing, you say, is sillier than offering a recipe for raw tomatoes, just the way nature made 'em. True. Instead, consider the inclusion of this concept as a recipe to remind you that nothing—nothing!—is more delicious with a juicy, well-seared steak than a few thick slices of sweet in-season tomatoes.

Served underneath a steak, the tomatoes add sweetness, succulence, acidity, and flavor. If the meat you're cooking is exceptional, the tomatoes will only heighten the experience. And if the meat you're cooking is meh, well, they'll supply some of the flavor and succulence missing from the experience. On the plate, steak and tomato juices mix together, forming a delicious sauce for anything that touches it. Do this only in summer when tomatoes are at their peak!

SERVES 4 TO 6

2 or 3 large tomatoes, in different colors (red, orange, and yellow make for a nice look)

Flaky sea salt and freshly ground black pepper

Extra-virgin olive oil, for drizzling

Rice wine vinegar, for drizzling

Cut the tomatoes into ¼- or ½-inch-thick slices and arrange them on the individual plates or the platter (if serving family style) on which you'll be serving the meat. Just before serving, sprinkle with a little salt and a few grinds of black pepper. Place the steak, sliced or whole, on top of the tomatoes and drizzle generously with the oil and vinegar.

Twice-Baked Potato

Even though the Home Frites recipe on page 187 managed to avoid double cooking the potatoes, they can't escape it here. If you're not up for making fries, but still desire that sacred combination of meat and potatoes, the only answer is the classic twice-baked potato. The double-baking process provides great versatility—one bake to cook it, the other to bring it together.

SERVES 4

4 large russet potatoes

Sea salt

4 tablespoons unsalted butter, at room temperature

½ cup sour cream

1 cup grated white Cheddar cheese

6 slices bacon, cooked, cooled, and coarsely chopped

½ cup finely chopped fresh chives

Preheat the oven to 375°F. Rinse and dry the potatoes, then lightly coat them with salt (this is to give their skin a little extra flavor). Place the potatoes on a sheet pan and bake until they are tender to the touch, about 1 hour. Remove from the oven and let cool for a bit.

Meanwhile, in a bowl, combine the butter, sour cream, and Cheddar (or any cheese you prefer; Gruyère and Havarti also work well). Set aside.

When the potatoes have cooled somewhat but are still warm to the touch, cut off the top one-fourth of each. One at a time, scrape the warm flesh from the small top slices into the bowl with the butter mixture and discard the skins. Using a small knife, carefully slice between the flesh and the skin of the remaining large portion of each potato, gently

loosening the flesh and being careful not to slice through the skin. Scoop out the warm flesh into the bowl holding the butter mixture; the heat of the potato flesh will begin to melt the other ingredients. Reserve the empty skins.

Now, grab an old-school potato masher. Aaron prefers the kind with a flat mashing plate with square cutouts rather than the type with a rounded wire base. (In the 1950s and 1960s, Flint manufactured hands down the best potato mashers, but these gems are getting really hard to find, perhaps because Aaron bought them all off of eBay.) Mash the potato mixture until all of the ingredients are fully integrated. Add the bacon and chives and stir with a spoon until thoroughly mixed. Season with salt.

Scoop the potato mixture back into the empty potato skins, piling it well above the tops, and place the stuffed potatoes on the same sheet pan. Set the stuffed potatoes aside at room temperature for up to 1 hour.

Preheat the oven to 350°F. Bake the potatoes until heated through, about 20 minutes. Then, turn on the broiler and broil the potatoes until the tops are browned, shifting them around as needed to brown them evenly. Serve hot.

Home Frites

Whether you like French food or not, the French really got one thing right. The ubiquitous French bistro dish *steak-frites* is an all-timer, an iconic pairing of two foods that never gets old. What makes it work? Again, contrast and complement. The crunch of well-cooked fries provides a counterpoint to dense but chewy steak. The sweetness of the oil and the starchy potato complement the beefiness of the meat. Salt is the liaison. Most of us would love to be able to replicate this at home, but the fries are the stumbling block.

Have you ever looked into the preparation of French fries? For such a seemingly simple food, most fries are the result of a multiday and labor-intensive process. The procedure (or some variation of it) that many people claim makes the best fries involves several steps: The potatoes are cut and soaked in water for from a couple of hours up to a day, drained and dried, cooked in oil at a fairly low temperature, drained well, and frozen. Then, when the order comes in, the frozen fries are dropped into hot oil and fried at a high temperature until brown. This lengthy process is one reason why so few people bother to make them at home. Well, that and the fact that most people avoid the hassle of deep-frying. Thus, fries are a treat when you go out to restaurants.

However, it doesn't have to be this way. That lengthy process is common in a restaurant kitchen where fries have to be on the table—or handed through a drive-through window—within minutes of an order being placed. If you have a little more time, which home cooks do, you can make absolutely delicious, crunchy, satisfying French fries at home with little effort.

Some people call this method "cold oil" fries. The other remarkable thing about this technique is that the fries reputedly absorb one-third less oil than the standard twice-cooked ones do. You can choose whatever oil or fat you want to cook the fries in with little guilt. That's not just because the fries absorb less but also because the relatively low cooking temperature of 300°F doesn't damage the oil in the same way that high-temperature frying does. Peanut, vegetable, and coconut oil all work. Animal fats like lard, duck fat, tallow, and ghee (clarified butter) also work well. They're full of healthy fats, have a high smoke point, and leave a nice flavor.

It takes about forty-five minutes to cook these fries. Prep time is only what it takes to slice the potatoes. You can cook them as well-done as you like, and fries, unlike steak, are best when cooked to well-done. They should be crunchy and stiff. Flaccid fries are a farce.

— **SERVES 2 TO 4** —

continued

Home Frites, continued

2 to 4 russet potatoes (depending on how many fries you desire)

Cooking oil or rendered fat (such as canola oil, coconut oil, vegetable oil, peanut oil, duck fat, lard, tallow, or ghee), for deep-frying

Kosher salt

Have ready a large bowl filled with cold water. Peeling the potatoes is optional. Slice the potatoes into batons ¼ thick and 2 to 3 inches long. As they are cut, submerge them in the water. Let the potatoes soak for at least 15 minutes or up to 4 hours.

Line a bowl with paper towels and set it near the stove top. Drain the potato batons and pat them dry, then put them in a heavy pot and pour in enough oil or rendered fat just to cover them. Turn on the heat to medium-low. A few minutes into the cook, as the oil starts to heat up, use a heat-resistant spatula or a wooden utensil to move the potatoes gently around in the pot, dislodging any that might be trying to stick to the bottom. Do this again a few minutes later. As the potatoes begin to cook more deeply, they begin to soften, and, if you move them around too much, they will break, leaving little half fries that are still delicious but less impressive.

Eventually the pot will come to a boil. Adjust the heat to maintain a medium boil—not too fast and not too slow. Every 5 minutes, check on the fries. When they start floating, after 30 to 40 minutes total, they can be scooped out of the pot. Look at their color to gauge doneness, too. We prefer a nice tawny brown.

Turn off the heat and, using a slotted spoon, transfer the fries to the paper towel–lined bowl to drain briefly. Toss the fries a bit and then remove the paper towel. Sprinkle with salt, toss some more, and serve immediately.

Grilled Vegetables

The art of grilling vegetables can take two paths. One, you can do them gently over slow-fading coals. This is a good way to tenderize thick, stemmy vegetables like broccoli, cauliflower, or asparagus that need a little more time. The other path is the opposite: cook them superhot and fast. This is how Aaron likes to do them—over the superheated chimney with the blast furnace method (see page 169). His method takes very little time and offers a bit of char and some toothsome, semicrunchy bites. It almost mimics the Japanese binchōtan method if you don't have any of that expensive charcoal on hand.

To go the low-and-slow method, use the coal bed after you've cooked the steaks and they are resting. All you need to do is turn the vegetables until they are tender.

To do the blast-furnace method, use a cheap metal cooling rack like the ones you can buy at restaurant supply stores and put it on top of a charcoal-filled chimney at peak heat.

We've included specific vegetables here, but feel free to choose other market-fresh options, such as cauliflower florets, whole green or spring onions, quartered red or yellow onions, whole asparagus spears, whole ramps, halved Belgian endive, halved escarole, quartered radicchio, halved carrots, and more.

— **SERVES 4** —

12 broccolini stalks, tough ends removed

20 green beans, stems trimmed

16 sugar snap peas

2 tablespoons extra-virgin olive oil, plus more for tossing

Kosher salt and freshly ground black pepper

Few dashes of fresh lemon juice

In separate bowls, toss the broccolini, green beans, and snap peas with the oil and a little salt, coating evenly.

If using the low-and-slow method, when the grill is hot, arrange the vegetables on the grates (or in a grill basket) over the fire. Depending on the intensity of the heat, either let them go for a while or stand by and move them around and flip them so no side gets burned. They are ready when they are just tender and lightly charred in a few spots.

If using the blast-furnace method, pile on about 4 broccolini at a time and cook for no more than 30 seconds on one side, then turn them all over and do the other side. Cook the stems directly over the hottest coals and leave the crowns just beyond the flames to protect them from the searing heat. Next, cook the green beans briefly before they blister too much and then follow with the snap peas, moving them both around with the tongs so they don't burn. After you remove the vegetables, they'll continue to cook a little, thanks to the carryover heat.

Before serving, toss the vegetables with a little more oil, if needed, and with the lemon juice and salt and pepper to taste.

Salsa Verde

Steak has made the career of many a sauce. A.1., *chimichurri*, béarnaise, au poivre—where would any of these be without having been given a star turn next to steak? But the greatest of them all is salsa verde. Back in the day, its friends and family just called it "green sauce," but then it got famous and went upscale, changing its name to something a little more elegant, much as Archibald Leach became Cary Grant.

Three qualities make salsa verde the champion sauce. One, it is versatile. Yes, its intense flavor, tanginess, and umami richness mean it can go toe-to-toe with steak, and we're convinced it's better with a smoky grilled steak than with one cooked in a pan. But it is equally awesome with fish, grilled birds, even pasta. Two, it's improvisational. We'll give you a recipe here, but consider it just a starting point. Salsa verde can be adapted to fit your taste, so long as you don't leave out the two foundational ingredients (and the source of its umami and punch): anchovy and garlic. Three, it lasts and can evolve. Aaron keeps a running jar of it in his fridge, refreshing it every time he has some extra of a new green. Whatever you've got—mint, rosemary, radish tops—can be thrown into the mix. Salsa verde will just evolve over time and will always be there for you when you need it.

MAKES ABOUT 2 CUPS

2 bunches flat-leaf parsley

4 cloves garlic

3 olive oil–packed anchovy fillets

1 teaspoon fine sea salt

¼ cup well-drained small capers

1 cup extra-virgin olive oil

1 teaspoon honey

1 teaspoon rice vinegar

1 lemon

Pick the leaves from the parsley stems and discard the stems. You should have about 2 cups. Using a chef's knife and a cutting board, finely mince the parsley, then transfer to a bowl.

Using the flat side of the chef's knife, smash the garlic on the cutting board and sprinkle

with the salt. Chop and flatten the garlic and salt together until a paste forms. Next, chop the anchovies into the paste, then smear and scrape the mixture back and forth on the cutting board until the ingredients are evenly distributed and you have a fine paste. Scoop the paste into the bowl with the parsley. Finely chop the capers and transfer them to the bowl.

Add the oil, honey, and vinegar to the bowl and stir to mix well. Finally, using a fine-rasp grater, grate the zest from the lemon directly into the bowl, then stir to mix.

Make the sauce several hours, but preferably a full day, ahead of serving to allow the flavors to blend. To store, transfer to a jar, cap tightly, and refrigerate for up to 2 months. Bring the sauce to room temperature before serving.

Charred Jalapeño–Anchovy Compound Butter

Tried-and-true companions for steak, compound butters never get old. They're nothing more than a highly effective way to add a lovely jolt of additional flavor and a little silky fat to the meat. The concept is simple: take room-temperature butter and mix in some punchy flavors. Popular compound butter additions include anchovies, mushrooms, or herbs, but really anything goes.

Here, we found that the umami-rich combo of anchovy and garlic provides a perfect base for the jalapeño. Blackening the chile adds nuance and brings out its flavor. Don't worry about too much chile heat, as jalapeños today tend to be pretty tame. If you want real heat, sub in a serrano or habanero chile.

This recipe is geared to make two good-size dollops of compound butter, but it scales easily for larger amounts, and it's not a bad idea to make more if you like it. Wrapped tightly, the butter will keep in the fridge for a few weeks or in the freezer for up to three months. And while it's tasty on steaks, it's also delicious melted on corn on the cob, grilled chicken, and roasted fish.

— MAKES ENOUGH FOR 2 STEAKS —

2 tablespoons unsalted butter

1 large jalapeño chile

½ teaspoon minced garlic

1 teaspoon anchovy paste

Allow the butter to come to room temperature on the countertop while preparing the other ingredients. To char the jalapeño, if you've got a hot grill going, simply grill the jalapeño on all sides until blackened all over. If cooking indoors, hold and turn the chile with insulated tongs or a skewer over a medium stove-top gas flame until blackened all over. Allow the charred jalapeño to cool.

When the chile has cooled, cut it in half lengthwise, remove and discard the stem and seeds, and mince finely. By now, the butter should be easily spreadable. If not, let it continue to warm until it is soft enough. In a small bowl, combine the butter, jalapeño, garlic, and anchovy paste and mix well.

Lay a square of plastic wrap or aluminum foil on a work surface (plastic wrap is easier to use). Use a rubber spatula to get all of the seasoned butter onto the square, shaping it into a rough log, and then use the plastic wrap or foil to roll and shape the butter into a uniform log. Wrap the butter in the plastic wrap or foil and refrigerate until firm and chilled.

To use, cut the desired amount off the log and leave it to melt on top of a steak hot off the grill.

Perky Red Wine Sauce

Just as any baseball pitcher has to have a fastball, any steak cook worth his or her beans should have a classic red wine sauce in the repertoire. It's very "French bistro," and who doesn't love a little taste of Paris? Recipes for a rich, complex Gallic red wine sauce—aka *sauce bordelaise*—tend to get slightly wonky, requiring lots of prep and ingredients like demi-glace and bone marrow. There's no need to go to all that trouble when you can craft a simpler, yet scrumptious red wine sauce in just a few minutes. This version is especially delicious because the unusual addition of lemon juice gives it an acid perkiness that contrasts beautifully with rich meat.

As for the red wine, it doesn't matter what you use as long as it's dry. And smooth (not whole grain) Dijon mustard makes for the most appealing texture.

This recipe is a framework that you can adapt to your circumstances. If you're grilling steaks over coals and want a red wine sauce, then follow the directions here. If you're cooking a steak in a pan on the stove, make the sauce in the same pan (after tossing out all of the fat) and start by sautéing the onions so you can stir up any delicious browned bits stuck to the pan bottom. Also, there's room to add other ingredients. Chopped mushrooms would be a natural in this; just cook them while simmering the wine. Want it to be richer? Throw in a splash of heavy cream. Want even more savory flavor? Toss in a rosemary branch with the thyme.

All those variations will help any pitcher succeed, but mastering the fastball is nonnegotiable.

— MAKES ENOUGH FOR 2 STEAKS —

2 cups red wine

1 yellow onion, chopped

2 cloves garlic, minced

8 thyme sprigs

2 tablespoons fresh lemon juice

2 tablespoons Dijon mustard (not whole grain)

2 tablespoons cold unsalted butter, cut into a few pieces

Kosher salt and freshly ground black pepper

1 tablespoon chopped fresh flat-leaf parsley (optional)

In a small saucepan, combine the wine, onion, garlic, and thyme and bring to a low boil over medium heat. Simmer until the wine has reduced by half. Turn off the heat, and when the wine has stopped bubbling, pull out and discard the thyme sprigs. Add the lemon juice and mustard and whisk until blended. Whisk in the butter until it melts and the sauce thickens slightly, then season to taste with salt and pepper.

Plate the steaks and spoon the sauce over the top, or spoon the sauce onto individual plates and lay the steaks on top. Sprinkle with the parsley and serve.

Drinking Steak

What to drink with a steak is as important a question as what sides to serve with it or who to eat it with or even which college to send your kids to. That is to say, it's important. Why? Because can you imagine only drinking a glass of water with a steak? If you're going to put steak on the menu, it needs to be matched in level and intensity on the beverage front. The balance and harmony of the meal demand it.

Aaron physically can't grill anything without a beer in his hand (or it waiting impatiently for him on the table nearby), and he often carries the style of beer he's drinking into dinner with the steaks. At his house, it's almost guaranteed to be an Austin beer like Live Oak Pilz in a can. Jordan has had many memorable bottles of wine with steak and seemingly none of them was bad. But there was that one frigid winter night a couple years ago, where the heat in the house wasn't working and he, his wife, Christie, and a couple of friends were staying up late huddled around the fireplace for any shred of warmth. Around midnight, hunger returned, and Jordan threw a steak over a little grate in the fire and opened up one of his favorite Italian reds, a Barolo Monvigliero from Fratelli Alessandria in Verduno. When the sizzling, slightly smoky steak came out of the fire, it was perfect with the heady dark cherry flavors of the wine. Talk about staying warm. . . .

The good news is that steak is versatile with beverages. It doesn't work with everything—put away the margaritas and daiquiris, for example, or the Sauvignon Blanc—but it does open its big, steaky arms wide in embrace of a vast number of possibilities. And to be clear, we're talking *adult* beverages here. Let's look at the major categories.

BEER

To quote Homer Simpson, "Ah, good ol' trustworthy beer. My love for you will never die." According to Aaron, beer is what to drink with steak. Remember that old restaurant chain Steak and Ale? They got at least one thing correct! And all styles work pretty darn well. If you're doing it right, you've been drinking beers through the entire steak-cooking process, so it just makes sense to continue on into the meal. Aaron prefers light, crisp beers in general, about the same ones that go with barbecue, unless it's wintertime. That's a different scene.

Not a big fan of superhoppy beers like huge IPAs or really bitter pale ales, he stays away from them in general, which works here because they're not that good with steak. They don't actually go with many foods, but sharp and tart hops particularly grate against the flavor of beef. If you like extreme hoppiness, consider adding a sauce or condiment to the steak. A pungent, herbal salsa verde or *chimichurri* sauce will help bridge the gap.

Steak calls for beers that show the flavor of the grain, whether it's a creamy, sweet, oaty flavor or a roasty, toasty malt. Provided they're well made, some lighter beer styles will work with steak. A nice, malty Kölsch, for instance, could be good with a leaner, thinner steak. A pilsner with substance is always good no matter what, but it's also great with steak, especially on a hot summer night. A classic brown ale works in fall or winter.

Dark beers are classic with steak, as they've got all this creamy richness that plays right into the silky texture of the meat, as well as that roasty, toasty quality that picks up the char. Look for porters, stouts, and bocks that aren't too extreme in alcohol or hops.

Live Oak Pilz • One of the best beers around, this is a go-to pilsner that's also great with steak. Live Oak is an Austin, Texas, brewery that makes clean, perfectly balanced beers in largely classic styles. This one has a nice grainy feel and a modest hoppiness that give it a little edge.

Double Mountain Kölsch • A great Oregon brewery, Double Mountain makes this crispy ale all year long. It's unfiltered, so there's a nice creaminess to it, and it has a bit more hoppy character than you'd find in a straight-up German Kölsch. It's great with a steak, especially when you want the meat to really take center stage.

Anchor Steam Beer • From Anchor Brewing Company in San Francisco, this is just one of the great all-around beers that never gets old. It's right down the middle—not too light, not too heavy, not too sweet, not too bitter. The body is perfect to put with beef, but it's still crisp and refreshing, too.

WINE

Red wine was seemingly invented for steak. Indeed, it's not hard to imagine the ancient Romans or the Celts tucking into their rich hunks of fire-roasted aurochs while quaffing some lustrous red tapped straight from the barrel. For Jordan, steak can almost be an excuse to crack some lusty bottle of red wine, as few other foods have the chutzpah to go with some of today's richer reds. He's been writing about wine for years, and his wife is a former sommelier who now is a wine professor at the Culinary Institute of America in Napa Valley, so he's constantly surrounded by wine, except when he's with Aaron, when he's constantly surrounded by beer. But beef and red wine is one of the greatest matches on Earth, and he never gets tired of putting the two together.

The affinity between red wine and beef is no accident, and chemistry explains why they work so well. When you eat a bite of steak, it laces the mouth with molecules of fat and protein that cling to receptor cells on the sides and the roof as well as the tongue. This is how we taste steak and why, as its flavor lingers on the mouth, it bestows our minds and bodies with a sense of well-being and nourishment at the intake of nutrients like protein and fat.

Let's take one second to look into red wine. Wine contains compounds called tannins, which are organic, antioxidative substances that occur in tree bark and wood as well as in the skins, seeds, and stems of grapes (and also in tea leaves). The reason red wines—and not many whites—contain tannin is that the color and substance of the reds come from steeping the juices of the grapes with their skins (and occasionally stems) during fermentation. During this process, tannins are extracted from the skins, much in the same way the color and flavor of tea comes from steeping a tea bag in hot water. And like tea, if you steep wine too long, it becomes bitter and astringent. But if the winemaker does the job well, the level of tannins in the wine will be just right, and the wine will be robust, substantial, and structured rather than bitter or astringent. Tannins contribute mightily to the sense of body in a red wine.

Chemically, tannins also bind to protein and fat molecules, like the ones that are clinging to the inside of our mouths after a particularly succulent bite of steak. So when you have that sip of red wine, it's literally coursing through the mouth, grabbing ahold of the loitering steak molecules and stripping them off of your tongue. The result of this theft is not an immediate sense of loss, as the delicious flavor of a fruity and savory red wine replaces the flavor of meat. Rather, the result is a sense of revitalization. Wine has cleansed the palate and refreshed it, prepping it for the next bite of delicious steak. In this way, for better or worse, red wine helps us consume more steak and makes it more pleasurable, so that instead of the buildup of proteins and fat become boring and ponderous, our mouths are continually revived, allowing the pleasure of eating steak to be experienced again and again. The binding of tannins also makes the wine taste silkier.

Pretty much any red wine fulfills this function. Cabernet Sauvignon, the world's most popular wine grape, also happens to be one of the most tannic of all reds, which only supports the popularity of beef. California Cabernet is even more tannic than Cabernet from Bordeaux, France, the most famous region for the production of the wine. But in most California Cabs, you might not sense the tannin as acutely as you do in Bordeaux wines (which historically have been known for astringency in their youth, a prime reason these wines were aged, as tannins fall out of the wine over time, making it smoother and softer) because the warmth and brightness of sun-drenched California vineyards ripen the tannins to a greater degree, making the wines thick and chewy. Plus, the wooden barrels in which these wines are aged contribute a toasty, charred flavor that echoes the Maillardian

sear on the exterior of the meat. This is why California Cabs have become a classic accompaniment to a good, American-style charcoal-grilled ribeye. The more sumptuous the steak is, the greater its affinity for big, tannin-rich reds.

Of course, reds other than Cabernet Sauvignon work well, too. Syrah, Merlot, Cabernet Franc, Tempranillo, and Sangiovese are all fairly tannic wines that will be just as good. Lighter, less tannic wines like Pinot Noir and Gamay also make great partners.

Red wine is not wine's only answer to steak, though. In many cases, white wine can also be a match. White wine lacks the tannin of red, but it still has great acidity. The acids in wine also cut through fat and refresh the mouth. (Red wines have acid too, just not usually as much as whites.) The reasons whites are less popular than reds with steak are body and flavor. Much as lighter, hoppier beers like pilsners aren't classic steak pairings, white wines lack the body and substance to stand up to steaks and their flavors tend toward herbaceousness and green fruits. One exception to this is Chardonnay, especially in its greatest incarnation in the white wine of Burgundy. Dallas steak chef John Tesar of Knife (see page 84) has shown how the pairing of white Burgundy and well-aged steak is the most remarkable combination. What makes this match so magically delicious? We have no idea, but it's amazing.

SAKE

The idea of pairing sake and steak might seem unexpected to Americans, but after visiting Japan in early 2018, Jordan was converted to the joys of *izakaya* beef paired with light, transparent sake. It wasn't an easy conversion, and to get it, you have to try to let your mind get into a particularly Japanese sensibility, paying attention to smaller, subtler details referencing texture, art, and nature.

Japan is, of course, the land of Wagyu cattle—the world's most outrageously decadent and marbled beef—and is where steak is consumed in bite-size cubes that are as rich as entire ribeyes in the United States. Drinking sake with those steak cubes is a common activity in Japanese steak houses and *izakayas,* which are essentially mellow drinking spots with short menus of simple dishes. Classic Japanese steak from rich, fatty Wagyu cattle might seem the perfect candidate to pair with Cabernet Sauvignon. And it does work well. But sake is pretty much the opposite of Cabernet

WINE AND STEAK, MATING FOR LIFE

Here is a rundown of some great steak and wine pairings from the wine regions of the world.

France • Several of the world's greatest steak wines—Bordeaux, Loire Valley (Cabernet Franc), Burgundy (Pinot Noir), and northern Rhône (Syrah)—are French. But to choose one, it would have to be northern Rhône Syrah. Just can't escape that pithy dark red and purple fruit, wild gamy notes, and moderate tannins are perfect with a juicy cut of steak. Almost any Syrah would do, but a moderately priced, easily sourced one like Saint Joseph Rouge from Domaine Faury is nearly ideal.

Italy • Many Italian wines are remarkable, but because the heart of Italian steak culture is in Tuscany, the compulsion is strong to go with a Sangiovese-based wine, native to the area. Something strong but not too heavy or oaky will do the trick, showing bright cherry fruit and lots of juicy acid to counter the fat in the steak. Try the Rosso di Montalcino from Le Ragnaie.

Spain • The greatest steak country in the world also has, unsurprisingly, tons of fantastic red wine, lots of it big and burly to go with the flavor bomb that is Spanish beef. But you don't want the wine to overpower the meat, which is possible, so something with a little grace and restraint is in order. With a great steak from an older cow, try a wine from great steak lovers, Olivier and Katia Rivière, whose Gabaxo, from Rioja, is made from Tempranillo and Garnacha.

California • In some ways a fusion of Spain, Italy, and France, California brings together a longstanding red wine tradition, a climate where it's almost always possible to grill steaks outside, and a great local meat scene. The variety of reds and of vineyards in California makes choosing difficult. But Napa Valley is king for a reason. There's a young guy making killer wines up on Diamond Mountain who also happens to be passionate about steak. His name is Ketan Mody and his wine projects, Beta and Jasud, are focused on handmade and hand-grown Cabernet Sauvignon from rocky, wild sites on Diamond Mountain and Mount Veeder. You can't find better steak wines than these, and it helps that Mody himself is a steak fanatic.

Sauvignon. Made from water and white rice, it has no tannin, no color, and its flavor is much subtler than that of a big red wine. Great sake is usually appreciated as much for its delicacy and grace as we respect wines and beers for their robustness and power.

So it's easy to see why people pair sake with the delicate tastes of fish and vegetables. But steak? Well, sake comes in many styles, some of which are not as delicate and finessed as the styles we usually see here in the States. Also, we have to remember that while the flavor of Japanese steak is reliably and intensely beefy, the texture can be quite different from American beef because of the amount and qualities of the fat. Wagyu steak offers that melt-in-the-mouth feeling thanks to a higher concentration of oleic acid. The graceful explosion of juicy, lithe fat in a bite of Wagyu is the real entry point for a sake pairing, as sake has a parallel silkiness.

A typical sake can be fine with steak, but a couple of styles really stand out. The first category—which is one really growing in popularity among sake aficionados—has two variations, *kimoto* and *yamahai*. These styles use native, wild bacteria in the fermentation. They bring an unpredictable and slightly earthy, wild, and umami note—it's subtle, but noticeable—that makes a wonderful pairing with the savoriness of meat.

Another category with great affinity for beef is *nama-zake*. The Japanese word *nama* means "fresh" or "raw," and that's exactly what a *nama-zake* is—unpasteurized, unadulterated sake. As with milk, beer, eggs, and so many other products, pasteurization is a process that neutralizes some enzymes and kills unwanted bacteria, ensuring a long and stable shelf life. But because many of these bacteria and enzymes influence the overall character of the brew, there are

trade-offs. Most sakes in Japan are pasteurized twice, which means they have been literally stripped of these defining elements. A great *nama-zake* will have a robust, vibrant, and complex flavor and mouthfeel. It may lack some of the delicacy and finesse of other styles, but that's simply because it remains in possession of all of its parts. Alongside a juicy, well-crusted steak, it will hold its own, providing umami-rich flavors and creamy texture to clean the palate.

Seeking out individual bottles of sake can be a tough task. It's better to know a few good importers whose products can be trusted, because they select great breweries and then take care of the (inevitably fragile bottles) throughout the importation process. Look for the names of these importers on the backs of the bottles: MTC, the sake division of mega Japanese product importer Mutual Trading Company, based in Los Angeles; Vine Connections, based in Sausalito, an unusual company specializing in South American wine and artful, high-end sakes; JFC, another big importer of Japanese products with a huge and rich sake book; World Sake Imports, based in Honolulu, which has a small but brilliantly chosen selection; and New York's Joto Sake, a reliable importer of fascinating and high-quality product.

SPIRITS

Sorry, gin, but without question, the best spirits to pair with steak are whiskey and mezcal. Yes, we celebrate and revel in the venerable tradition of martinis and steaks. However, the association of the two isn't exactly a pairing. Martini consumption ought to come before and leading up to the steak. A martini is cold, clean, and crisp, a seemingly sensible way to transition out of the prescribed rationality of the workday into the carnal pleasures of dinner and beyond. But

16 West 22nd Street
New York, New York
tel: (212) 401-7986 • cotenyc.com

New York has a venerable and well-documented steak house culture, so to write another tribute to Peter Luger or Keens or Sparks seems unnecessary. It's more fun to talk about a new shrine to beef that has emerged in recent years: Cote. We've all had Korean barbecue, but Cote fashions itself as a Korean steak house, a detail emphasizing the focus on high-quality, dry-aged meat.

That focus is instantly apparent on looking at the menu, which features large, color images of the best cuts, from marinated short rib to hanger to ribeye to "Cote steak" (chuck flap). All beef is Prime or higher and dry aged in the basement aging room a minimum of a week, with cuts aged from 45 to over 100 days available on request (we even tasted some at 220 days). As in Korean barbecue, Cote's steak is cooked by staff on a little glowing grill set into the tabletop and is accessorized with all manner of tangy, fermented Korean goodness, such as soy stew (anchovy broth with zucchini, tofu, and potato), kimchi stew, and *banchan* (a collection of umami-rich side dishes). All of the accompaniments make for deliciously zesty contrast with the unctuous beef that's coming right off the grill to your plate. Although the sexy vibe of this Flatiron District hot spot is both modern and Western, the flavors don't hold back on Korean funk. It's a wonderfully satisfying experience.

Another thing Cote gets right is the beverage program. The inclusion of slurpy frosé tells you that the place doesn't take itself too seriously, but the creative cocktails are complex and well balanced. And the lengthy, well selected wine list—dedicated to small, rarefied producers—balances perfectly with the Korean elements. Cote is a unique and delicious experience that should be on the radar of any true steak lover.

the two should remain separate because the martini (and we're talking gin here; vodka is just flavorless booze, so don't bother with it) is the opposite of a steak. It's cool and bright, slick and herbal, almost giving the feeling of disinfecting the mouth. Steak is dark and warm and juicy and chewy and bloody. If you're a spirits drinker first and foremost, have the martini(s) in advance and change gears with the steak.

Whiskey is the classic pairing for a reason. Sweet woodiness from barrel aging echoes the toasty savoriness of the steak's grilled crust and smoky overtones. The sweetness from the grain of whiskey connects to the subtly caramelized sweetness of the Maillardian crust. And whiskey's rounded, soft texture plays to the juicy explosion of well-marbled meat on the tongue. When it comes to choosing whiskeys to pair with steak, anything goes. But the sweeter-tasting profiles of American whiskeys do seem to make the best matches, whether it's the corn-based softness of bourbon or the spicy savor of rye. (And let's not forget that most American cattle are fed grain in their last months, making the pairing even more intuitive.)

Other whiskeys work well, too, but warrant some discernment. For instance, single-malt Scotch whisky can be great with a steak, but not all styles. Heavily peated single malts, such as the famous ones from the islands of Islay or Skye, are often so powerfully briny and flavored with iodine or seaweed that they can overwhelm the inherent sweetness in a good piece of beef. The more approachable Speyside styles work better. Scotch has a drier and more austere character than the typical American whiskey, highlighting the grain over the wood. Because single-malt scotch has such a fiercely unique expression of character, the old classic blended scotches (Johnny Walker,

Chivas, and the like) are good compromises for steak. These whiskeys blend dozens of different scotches together to form some sort of a composite expression of Scotland as a whole. The best of them will balance subtle smoky notes against a range of grain and oak flavors to come up with something tasty, if not fervently expressive of any particular place or intention.

Japanese whisky can also be very good with steak. Like sake, most Japanese whisky prizes finesse and balance over other qualities. Although their cues come from Scotland, Japanese malts are gentle brushes with silk compared with the cudgel of many single-malt scotches. They tend to ride the line between savory and sweet and powerful and subtle. This deft balancing act they perform make them good for, let's say, ordinary steaks. If you're going for a big-impact steak—starting with a superthick cut, heavy smoke and seasoning, and a big, dense crust—a Japanese whisky might be overwhelmed. However, thinner cuts seasoned simply and carefully can be perfect with a Japanese malt.

When it comes to agave-based spirits, mezcal, because of its smokiness, makes a more interesting steak match than tequila. And we're just talking straight up here, not in a margarita or any other cocktail that diffuses the flavor of the spirit. Tequila can work adequately with a steak, but its general notes of pear and herbs tend not to complement beef. When you age tequila—when it becomes *reposado* or *añejo* style—it takes on more of the character of whiskey and will match with steak a little better. In contrast, premium mezcal, which is made with agave cooked in an underground pit, possesses a native smokiness that harmonizes beautifully with grilled steak. If you throw in a side of grilled Padrón peppers and onions, the pairing will be perfect.

Resources

The Best Mail-Order Meat

Here are a few reliable places to order some of the best steaks in the country.

Alderspring Ranch • alderspring.com

Betsy Ross • Best to message on Facebook

Carter Country • cartercountrymeats.com

Creekstone Farms • creekstonefarms.com

Crowd Cow • crowdcow.com

Flannery Beef • flannerybeef.com

Heritage Foods • heritagefoods.com

Holy Grail Steak Co. • holygrailsteak.com

Joyce Farms • joyce-farms.com

Snake River Farms • snakeriverfarms.com

Great Grills

Korin Konro Hibachi • korin.com

Lodge Sportsman Grill Hibachi • lodgemfg.com

PK • pkgrills.com

Santa Maria Grill • santamariagrills.com

Weber Original Kettle • weber.com

Sweet Steak Knives

Laguiole on Aubrac • laguiole-en-aubrac.fr

New West Knifeworks • newwestknifeworks.com

Opinel • opinel-usa.com

Acknowledgments

Together, we'd like to thank a number of people without whom this book would not have been possible. On the book-team side, it starts with our dear literary agent, David Hale Smith, who will never turn down even an average steak and is as good in the boardroom as he is at the table. Next, we want to thank Aaron Wehner and Ten Speed Press for making this book happen. We were gifted with unbelievable support and effort from a team of massively talented people, beginning with our editor and good friend Emily Timberlake, who got us over the finish line with her energy, creativity, and humor. Having Elizabeth "Betsy" Stromberg, book designer and part-time art director extraordinaire, on the job ensured the book would look wonderful. Sharon Silva proved way more than a copy editor: her meticulousness, knowledge of food and cooking, and good taste greatly improved the final product.

Thanks also to Emma Campion, Serena Sigona, Karen Levy, and Ken Della Penta for making this book better.

Of course, we bow down to the great Wyatt McSpadden, who besides being at the very top of the photography game, gracing our work with his brilliant eye and camera technique, also knows so much about everything that he truly impacts the content of the text as well. He's always on hand for a good pep talk, a good laugh, and a good hug, too. Thanks, Wyatt, you're the best. You know who's also the best? Jeff Stockton, Wyatt's photo assistant, who was at most of the shoots, and Jeff's moustache, which was also at most of the shoots.

We are indebted to Bryan Butler and Ben Runkle of Salt & Time in Austin, Texas. Their generosity with their knowledge and time was a huge asset to this book. We are also grateful to a couple of real—and really great—chefs, Adam Perry Lang and John Tesar, who shared their insights on beef aging and on cutting and cooking steaks and who have been so supportive in general. Another real chef, Matthew Van Orden, was instrumental at photo shoots, helping prepare all of the dishes from the book, keeping things clean, and teaching us some stuff along the way.

We considered ourselves lucky to have one Bryan Butler (the butcher) in the book. But in the end were we blessed with an unexpected boon: another Bryan Butler, this one the remarkable illustrator whose images brought clarity and artistic variety to these pages. Thanks, BBs!

Thanks to Joey Machado of B&B Charcoal, for keeping us well fueled throughout the year as we test cooked. And thanks to Scott Moody of PK, our favorite grill maker, for all of his support on this book and over the years.

And last but not least, as large a thank-you as we can muster to Alfonso Terrazas and his team at Creekstone Farms, which supplied most of our beef during test cooks and aging experiments. The quality of the beef we had to work with was simply astounding, and the generosity Alfonso and everyone at Creekstone showed us was, well, also simply astounding.

From Aaron

Man, there are so many people to thank for helping make this book possible, I could write a book just about that! First and foremost, I say a crazy big thank-you to my wife, Stacy, who has been there every step of the way. She does what's needed, from making sure the house is presentable to finding me a fresh pair of jeans to take to an event, checking my underwear, and all the time giving me crap for everything. But seriously, because I get all the attention, no one has any idea of how essential Stacy is to everything we do. She works so hard, and there would be no *Franklin Steak*, *Franklin Barbecue*, or even Aaron Franklin as you know him without her. Thank you so much, Stacy.

Thanks to my coauthor, Jordan Mackay, who is not only a great writer, and a great friend, but also insanely passionate about food and the craft of cooking with fire. His excitement and talent have proven to be the perfect counterbalance for these projects. Thank you, Jordan! I'm looking forward to the next. . . .

Then, I've got to thank all of the people involved with Franklin BBQ and related enterprises. They keep the ship sailing smoothly while I run around doing things like this book. There are a few people I lean on most. Andy Risner, my right-hand guy at the restaurant, is just so reliable, so good to work with, and such a supertalented cook. Alex Gantos, my left-hand guy, keeps all other ships sailing smoothly. I'm fortunate to have found two highly skilled and reliable people I can really trust. Big thanks also to Miki and Julie at the restaurant for working so hard, keeping things organized, making guests happy, lending a helping hand when I need it, and always having smiling faces.

Last, much thanks to my mom and dad, who, in the process of feeding me and keeping me alive, introduced me to steaks at an early age. My dad has been grilling T-bones my entire life, and working on this book showed me how much that's meant to me.

From Jordan

First and foremost, thanks to Aaron Franklin, great friend and compadre in meat books, whose endless reservoirs of humor and goodwill—not to mention his extraordinary expertise in so many areas—make him an absolute joy to work with, and yes, even when his schedule is almost impossibly busy.

I must offer infinite gratitude to (and for) my wife, Christie Dufault, who doesn't love steak nearly as much as I do and prefers to eat plants, but nevertheless tolerated years of endless steak talk as well as a great deal of beef cooking and grilling. It's over now, Honu. Perhaps.

I've got to offer a similar note to Aaron's wife, Stacy, who has become a great friend over the years, but who also allowed me to be a constant presence in her house and in her social and family life for long stretches while I was in town working on the book.

Beyond those crucial people, I want to acknowledge many of the experts we consulted and who offered outstanding ideas, explanations, and often beautiful meat to try: Clifford Pollard and Kevin Cimino of Cream Co., who are going to change the meat world; Bryan and Katie Flannery of Flannery Beef, who shared lots of honest information and, more important, were such a pleasure to hang out with; John McLaughlin of McLaughlin Farm, who not only was a wonderful source for everything Highland cattle but also remained a warm and encouraging voice in my inbox throughout the writing; Jason Ross of First Light Farm sent amazing meat, as did Joe Heitzeberg of Crowd Cow and Cameron Hughes of Holy Grail.

Others joined me on or facilitated my research into all things steak. Toshio Ueno guided me around Japan's beefy side and taught me a lot about sake along the way. Sancho Rodriguez went above and beyond in helping schedule and coordinate a week of steak eating in Basque Country, which proved a revelation. Thanks, too, to José Gordón of El Capricho, who floored me as much with his incredible passion and dedication as he did with his beef and cooking. My dear friend David Feldstein has been a frequent presence on the steak trail with me and shares the passion of exemplary beef and wine. Alyson Careaga, another dear friend, has been a constant source of encouragement and help, generously lending her immense talents and energy whenever I needed them. Ted and Andrea Vance were with me on some of the steak tour and survived far more beef than they're used to eating. A shout-out as well to serious steakthusiast and great friend Ashley Santoro, who traveled far to eat steak with me. And a most profound and humble thanks to steak (and tartare) seeker numero uno Talitha Whidbee, with whom I have eaten more steaks than anyone over the years and who has given me so much along the way.

Last, I want to acknowledge the great writer Mark Schatzker, whose original book *Steak* was an inspiration and a guide and is an absolute must-read if you want to understand beef and steak at much greater depths than what you'll find here (it's also a brilliantly fun read). Connecting with Mark was an important moment for me in the writing of this book, as he shared his thoughts and opinions and helped me make some invaluable associations. Also, please read his life-changing book about nutrition and flavor, *The Dorito Effect*.

Index

Omaha Steaks, 30
Oregon Country Beef, 36
The Organic Butcher, 50
organic meat, 44
oven, finishing with, 102

P

Parker, Robert, 33
pasture-raised beef, 44, 46
pecan wood, 133, 134, 135
pepper steak, 57
PK Grill, 111–13, 207
Pollard, Cliff, 25
Porter, Valerie, 9
porterhouse, 65–66, 76
Porter Road, 50
potatoes
    Home Frites, 187–88
    Twice-Baked Potato, 184
primal cuts, 57
Prime beef, 38, 39, 41, 54
Prime Foods Distributor, 82, 85
prime rib, 59
"Product of the USA," 46
Publix, 35
Purely Meat Co., 50

R

Rancher's Reserve, 36, 38
resting, 161–62
reverse sear, 165–67
ribeye, 59–60, 68, 76
rib roast, 59
Rivière, Olivier and Katia, 202
Ross, Betsy, 20–21, 207
Runkle, Ben, 31, 50, 52–55, 69, 75

S

safety, 38
Safeway, 36, 38
sake, 201–3
Salad, Green, with Garlic
    Vinaigrette, 179
Salsa Verde, 193
salt, 156, 158–59
Salt & Time, 29, 31, 50, 52–53,
    72, 75
Santa Maria grills, 108, 109, 110, 207

Sappington, Adam, 123
Schatzker, Mark, 42
Scotch, 205
seam butchery, 75
Select beef, 38, 39, 41
sheet pans, 145–46
shovels, 145
Singer, Nate, 26–27
sizzle platters, 146
skirt, 72–73, 77
Smith, Steve, 13
Smith & Wollensky, 82
Snake River Farms, 12, 207
sous vide, 104–5, 107
spinalis dorsi, 59, 60, 63, 68,
    91, 93
Stafford, Orin, 125
standing rib roast, 59
Steak Cookoff Association, 113
steaks
    bone-in vs. boneless, 60
    with butter, 159–60
    buying, 25, 29–31, 45, 207
    color of, 45
    crust of, 154–55
    cuts, 56–57, 59–60, 65–74,
      76–77
    doneness of, 155–56
    flipping, 160–61
    frozen, 161
    labeling of, 42, 44, 46
    marbling in, 41–42, 45
    with oil, 159–60
    resting, 161–62
    salting, 156, 158–59
    temperature of, before
      cooking, 160
    thickness of, 170
    See also beef; cooking
      methods; *individual cuts*
strip, 65, 67–68, 76
subprimals, 57

T

tannins, 200–201
Taylor's Market, 50
T-bone, 65–66, 76
tenderloin, 65, 66–67, 69, 76
tequila, 205
Tesar, John, 82, 84, 96, 201
thermometers, 146
Thornhill, Taylor, 34

three-zone setup, 147–48, 151
tomahawk steak, 57, 60
Tomatoes, Raw, 183
tongs, 144
towels, 146
tri-tip, 73–74
trowels, 145
two-zone setup, 147, 151
Tyson, 22, 35

U

USDA grades, 38–39, 41

V

Vegetables, Grilled, 190
Vine Connections, 203

W

Wagyu beef, 11–13, 16, 23–24, 36,
    37, 202–3
wet aging, 38, 86
whiskey, 203, 205
Williams, Allen, 16, 18
wine
    pairing steak and, 200–201, 202
    Perky Red Wine Sauce, 197
wood
    advantages and disadvantages
      of, 129–30, 151
    choosing, 130
    cutting, 136
    fire, starting, 150
    seasoning, 132
    setup for grilling with, 149–50
    sourcing, 135–36
    types of, 132–35
World Butchery Challenge, 52
World Sake Imports, 203

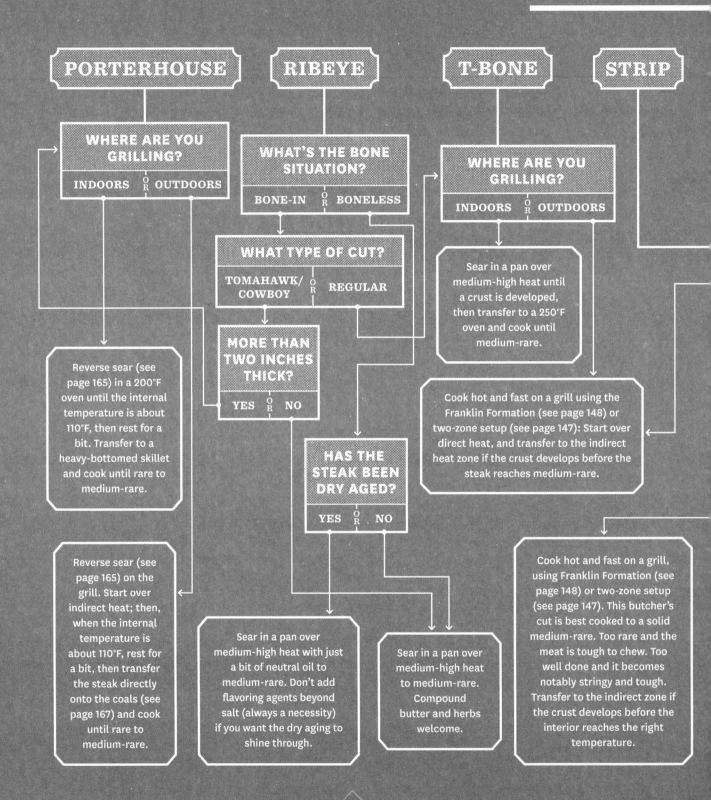

PORTERHOUSE

WHERE ARE YOU GRILLING?

INDOORS O R OUTDOORS

Reverse sear (see page 165) in a 200°F oven until the internal temperature is about 110°F, then rest for a bit. Transfer to a heavy-bottomed skillet and cook until rare to medium-rare.

Reverse sear (see page 165) on the grill. Start over indirect heat; then, when the internal temperature is about 110°F, rest for a bit, then transfer the steak directly onto the coals (see page 167) and cook until rare to medium-rare.

RIBEYE

WHAT'S THE BONE SITUATION?

BONE-IN O R BONELESS

WHAT TYPE OF CUT?

TOMAHAWK/ COWBOY O R REGULAR

MORE THAN TWO INCHES THICK?

YES O R NO

HAS THE STEAK BEEN DRY AGED?

YES O R NO

Sear in a pan over medium-high heat with just a bit of neutral oil to medium-rare. Don't add flavoring agents beyond salt (always a necessity) if you want the dry aging to shine through.

Sear in a pan over medium-high heat to medium-rare. Compound butter and herbs welcome.

T-BONE

WHERE ARE YOU GRILLING?

INDOORS O R OUTDOORS

Sear in a pan over medium-high heat until a crust is developed, then transfer to a 250°F oven and cook until medium-rare.

Cook hot and fast on a grill using the Franklin Formation (see page 148) or two-zone setup (see page 147): Start over direct heat, and transfer to the indirect heat zone if the crust develops before the steak reaches medium-rare.

STRIP

Cook hot and fast on a grill, using Franklin Formation (see page 148) or two-zone setup (see page 147). This butcher's cut is best cooked to a solid medium-rare. Too rare and the meat is tough to chew. Too well done and it becomes notably stringy and tough. Transfer to the indirect zone if the crust develops before the interior reaches the right temperature.

Cook Steak

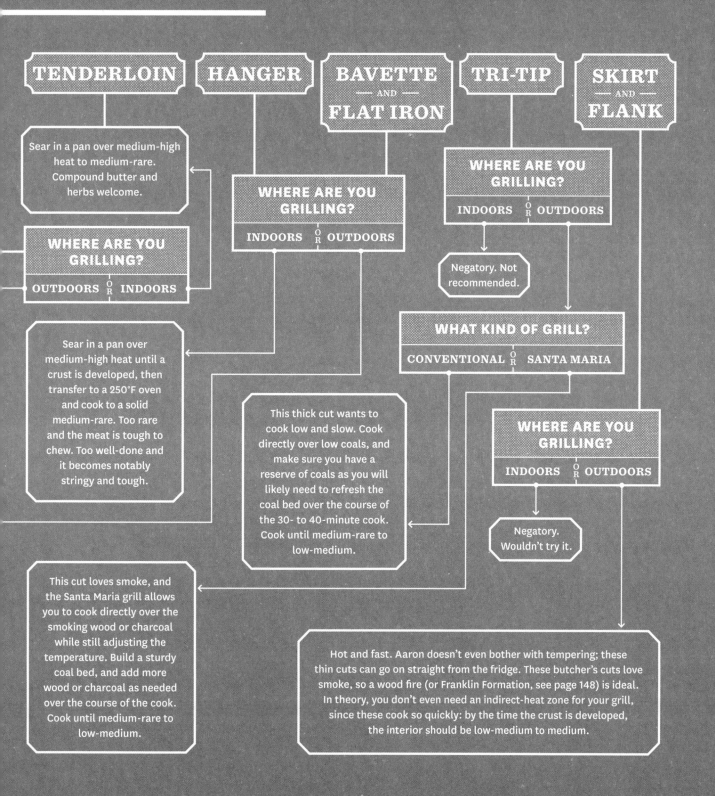

TENDERLOIN

Sear in a pan over medium-high heat to medium-rare. Compound butter and herbs welcome.

WHERE ARE YOU GRILLING?

OUTDOORS _{OR} INDOORS

Sear in a pan over medium-high heat until a crust is developed, then transfer to a 250°F oven and cook to a solid medium-rare. Too rare and the meat is tough to chew. Too well-done and it becomes notably stringy and tough.

HANGER

WHERE ARE YOU GRILLING?

INDOORS _{OR} OUTDOORS

BAVETTE — AND — **FLAT IRON**

This thick cut wants to cook low and slow. Cook directly over low coals, and make sure you have a reserve of coals as you will likely need to refresh the coal bed over the course of the 30- to 40-minute cook. Cook until medium-rare to low-medium.

TRI-TIP

WHERE ARE YOU GRILLING?

INDOORS _{OR} OUTDOORS

Negatory. Not recommended.

WHAT KIND OF GRILL?

CONVENTIONAL _{OR} SANTA MARIA

WHERE ARE YOU GRILLING?

INDOORS _{OR} OUTDOORS

Negatory. Wouldn't try it.

SKIRT — AND — **FLANK**

This cut loves smoke, and the Santa Maria grill allows you to cook directly over the smoking wood or charcoal while still adjusting the temperature. Build a sturdy coal bed, and add more wood or charcoal as needed over the course of the cook. Cook until medium-rare to low-medium.

Hot and fast. Aaron doesn't even bother with tempering; these thin cuts can go on straight from the fridge. These butcher's cuts love smoke, so a wood fire (or Franklin Formation, see page 148) is ideal. In theory, you don't even need an indirect-heat zone for your grill, since these cook so quickly: by the time the crust is developed, the interior should be low-medium to medium.

Text copyright © 2019 by Hasenpfeffer LLC
Photographs copyright © 2019 by Wyatt McSpadden
Illustrations copyright © 2019 by Bryan B. Butler

All rights reserved.
Published in the United States by Ten Speed Press, an imprint of the Crown Publishing Group,
a division of Penguin Random House LLC, New York.
www.crownpublishing.com
www.tenspeed.com

Originally published in the United States in hardcover by Ten Speed Press, an imprint of Random House,
a division of Penguin Random House LLC, New York, in 2019.

Ten Speed Press and the Ten Speed Press colophon are registered trademarks of
Penguin Random House LLC.

The photo on page 53 appears courtesy of Bryan Butler and Ben Runkle
Illustration on page 8 by iStock.com/clu

Design by Betsy Stromberg

10 9 8 7 6 5 4 3 2 1

2020 Trade Paperback Box Edition